2

The Devil is a Part-
High Schoo

ART
KURON
MISHIM

ORIGINAL STO
SATOSHI WAGAHARA

CHARACTER DESIGN
029 (ONIKU)

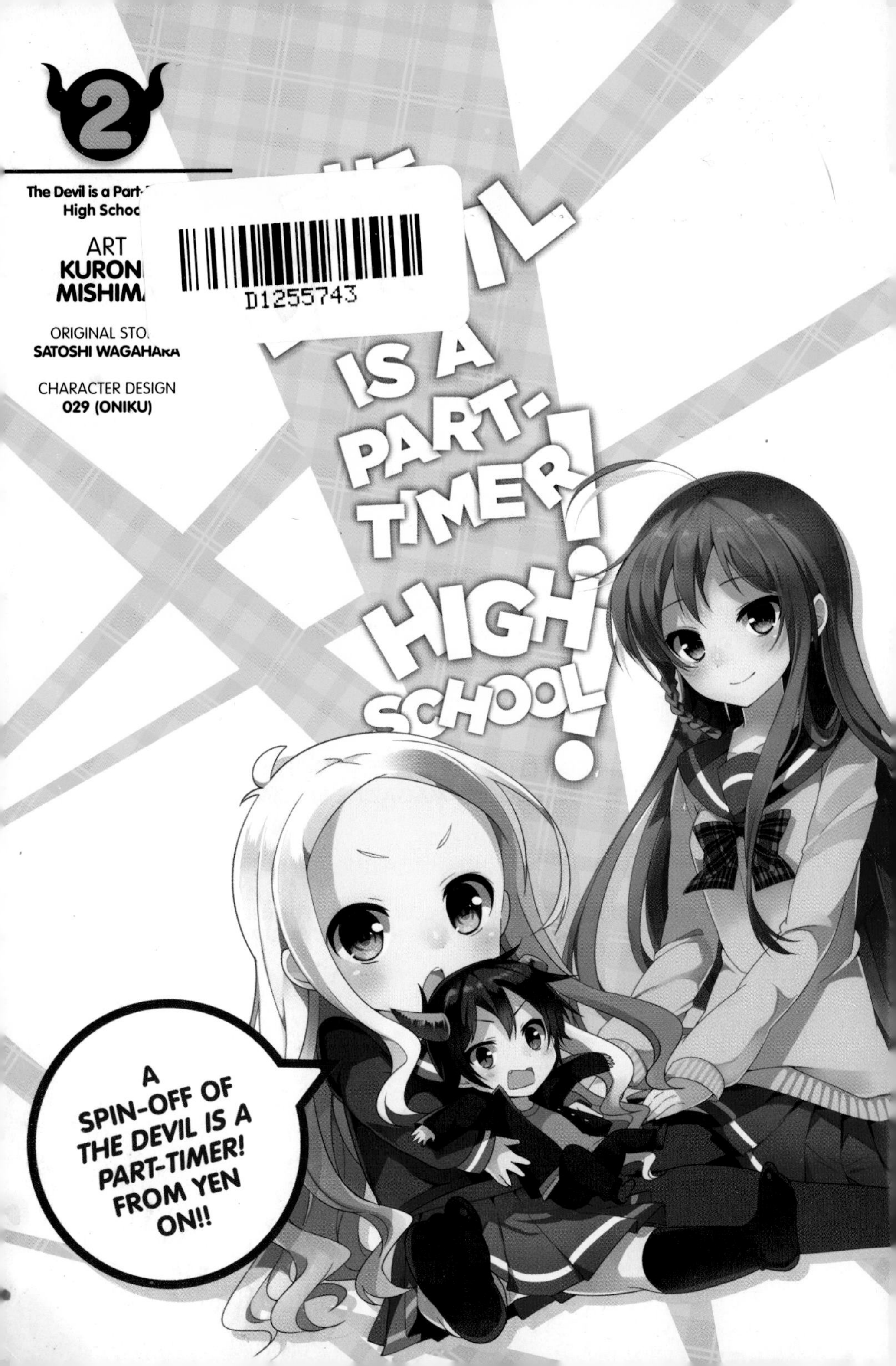

IS A PART-TIMER! HIGH SCHOOL!
A SPIN-OFF OF THE DEVIL IS A PART-TIMER! FROM YEN ON!!

The Devil is a Part-Timer! High School! 2

CONTENTS

8TH PERIOD THE FAIR MAIDENS MAKE SPARKS FLY 5

9TH PERIOD THE SCHOOLMASTER MAKES A WISE DECISION 25

10TH PERIOD THE HAPLESS DEMON SEEKS AID 41

11TH PERIOD THE UDON-SELLING GIRL RELIES 57
ON THE DEVIL KING

12TH PERIOD A NAMELESS SUPPORTER 73
MAKES A CONTRIBUTION

EXTRA CREDIT SPECIAL CHAPTER ① 89
DENGEKI BOOKS MAGAZINE SPECIAL #1

EXTRA CREDIT SPECIAL CHAPTER ② 97
DENGEKI BOOKS MAGAZINE SPECIAL #2

EXTRA CREDIT SPECIAL CHAPTER ③ SPECIAL EDITION FOR ASCII 106
MEDIA WORKS 20TH ANNIVERSARY PREMIUM BOOKLET

EXTRA CREDIT *THE DEVIL IS A PART-TIMER!* ANIME VOICE 108
RECORDING REPORT

CLOSING BELL AFTERWORD 112

THE DEVIL IS A PART-TIMER! HIGH SCHOOL!

CHARACTERS & RELATIONSHIPS

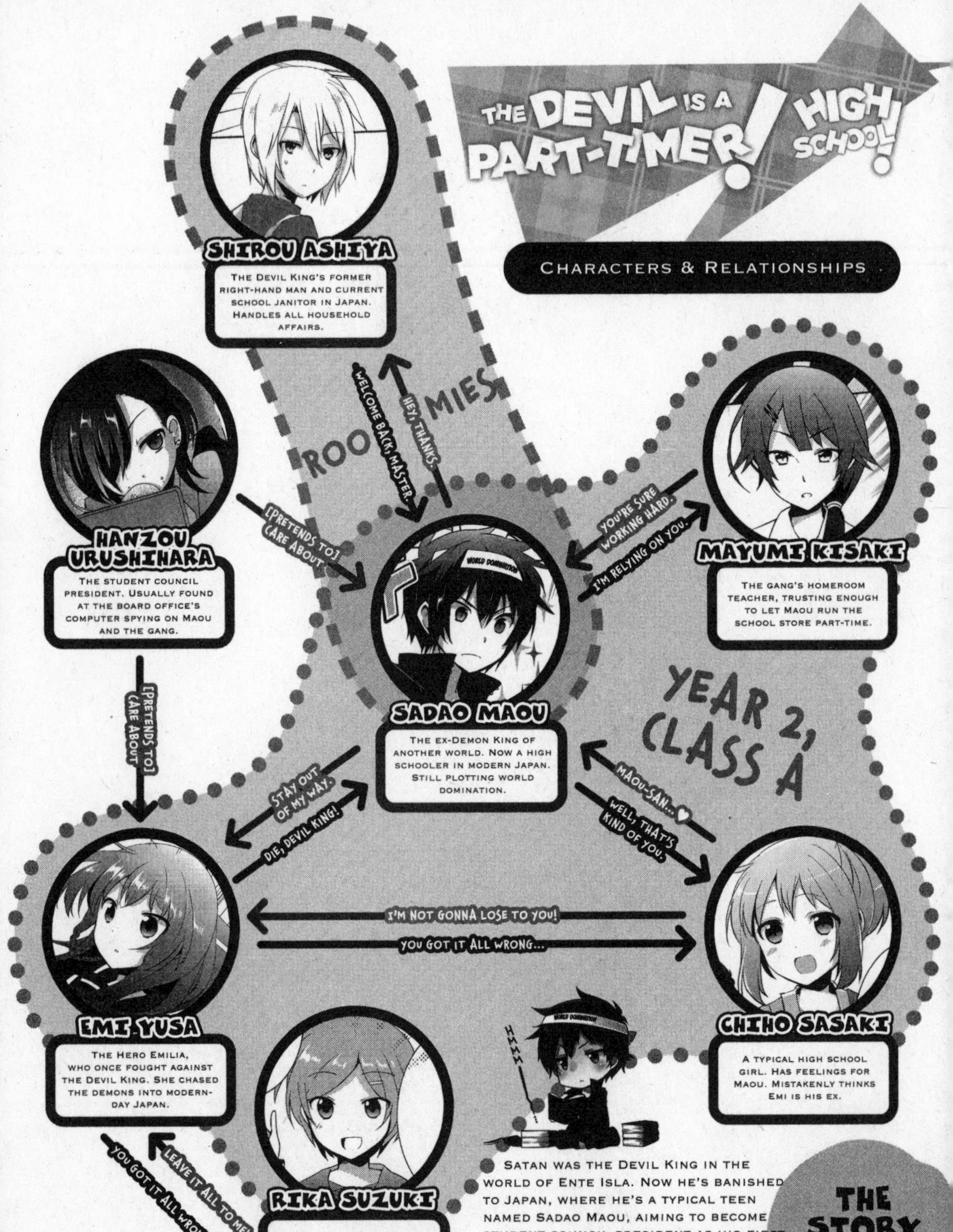

SHIROU ASHIYA
THE DEVIL KING'S FORMER RIGHT-HAND MAN AND CURRENT SCHOOL JANITOR IN JAPAN. HANDLES ALL HOUSEHOLD AFFAIRS.
ROOMIES
WELCOME BACK, MASTER.
HEY, THANKS.
HANZOU URUSHIHARA
THE STUDENT COUNCIL PRESIDENT. USUALLY FOUND AT THE BOARD OFFICE'S COMPUTER SPYING ON MAOU AND THE GANG.
[PRETENDS TO] CARE ABOUT
[PRETENDS TO] CARE ABOUT
MAYUMI KISAKI
THE GANG'S HOMEROOM TEACHER, TRUSTING ENOUGH TO LET MAOU RUN THE SCHOOL STORE PART-TIME.
YOU'RE SURE WORKING HARD.
I'M RELYING ON YOU.
WORLD DOMINATION
SADAO MAOU
THE EX-DEMON KING OF ANOTHER WORLD. NOW A HIGH SCHOOLER IN MODERN JAPAN. STILL PLOTTING WORLD DOMINATION.
YEAR 2, CLASS A
STAY OUT OF MY WAY.
DIE, DEVIL KING!
MAOU-SAN...♥
WELL, THAT'S KIND OF YOU.
I'M NOT GONNA LOSE TO YOU!
YOU GOT IT ALL WRONG...
EMI YUSA
THE HERO EMILIA, WHO ONCE FOUGHT AGAINST THE DEVIL KING. SHE CHASED THE DEMONS INTO MODERN-DAY JAPAN.
CHIHO SASAKI
A TYPICAL HIGH SCHOOL GIRL. HAS FEELINGS FOR MAOU. MISTAKENLY THINKS EMI IS HIS EX.
WORLD DOMINATION
HMM
LEAVE IT ALL TO ME!
YOU GOT IT ALL WRONG...
RIKA SUZUKI
THE GANG'S CLASSMATE, STILL DOGGEDLY ATTEMPTING TO PAIR MAOU AND EMI TOGETHER.

THE STORY SO FAR

Satan was the Devil King in the world of Ente Isla. Now he's banished to Japan, where he's a typical teen named Sadao Maou, aiming to become student council president as his first step toward world conquest. But the Hero Emilia—aka Emi Yusa—isn't about to let that happen, and the two remain rivals (and classmates) in this world. Meanwhile, Chiho, a classmate with more than a few feelings for Maou, has made the egregious mistake of thinking Emi is the ex-Devil King's ex-girlfriend.

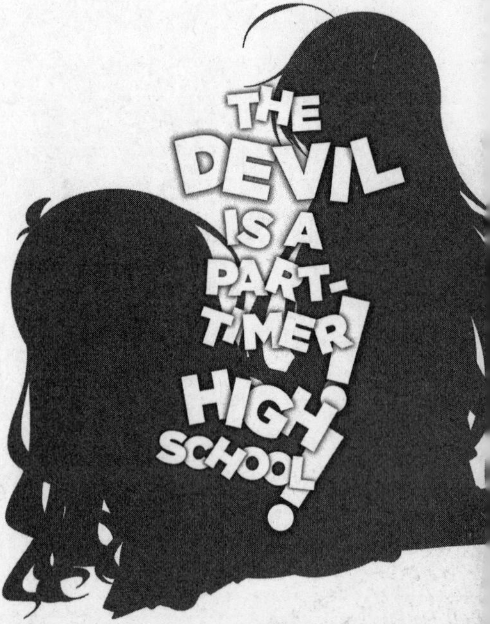
THE DEVIL IS A PART-TIMER! HIGH SCHOOL!

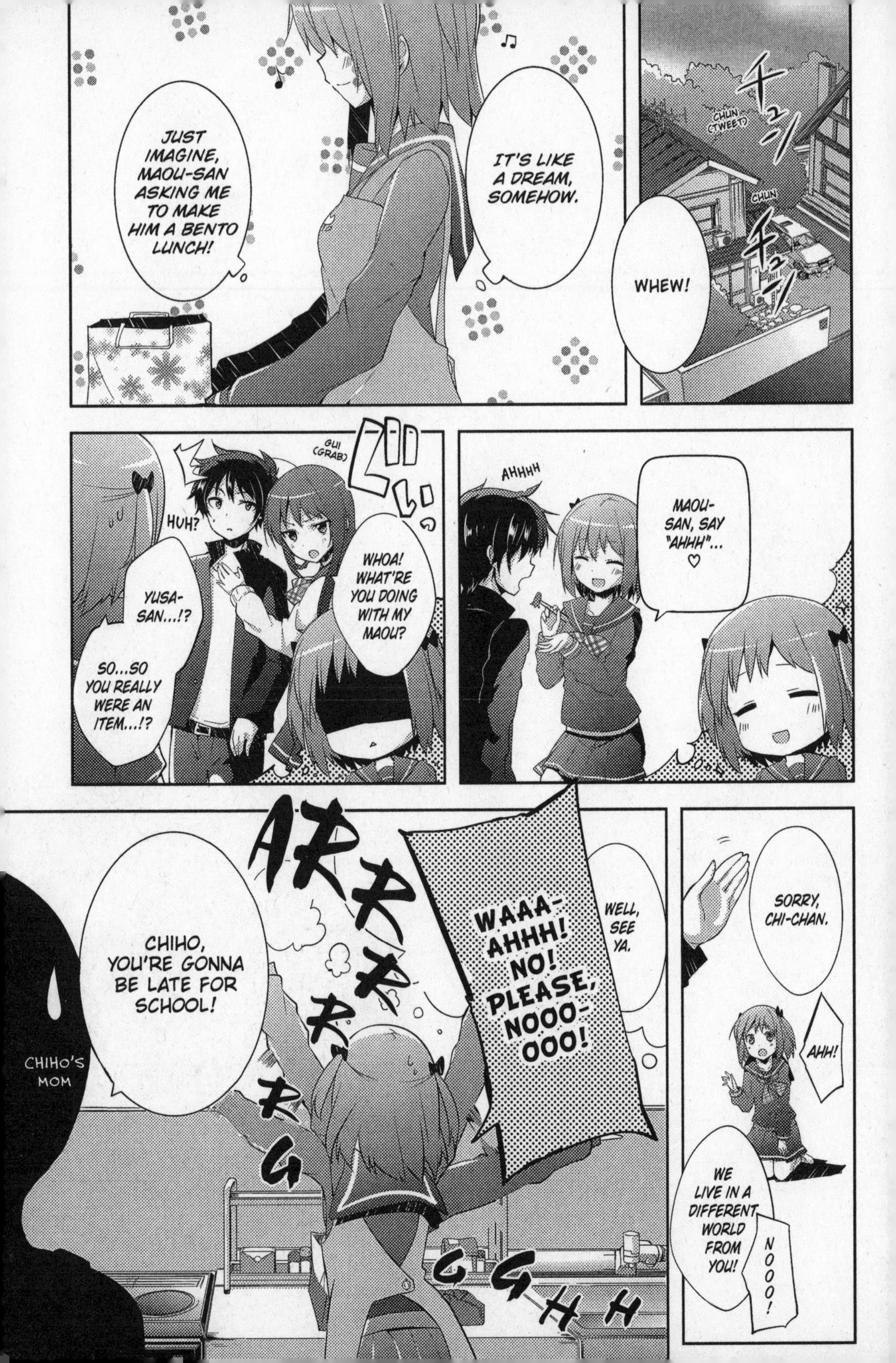
CHUN (TWEET)
CHUN
WHEW!
IT'S LIKE A DREAM, SOMEHOW.
JUST IMAGINE, MAOU-SAN ASKING ME TO MAKE HIM A BENTO LUNCH!
AHHHH
MAOU-SAN, SAY "AHHH"... ♡
GUI (GRAB)
WHOA! WHAT'RE YOU DOING WITH MY MAOU?
HUH?
YUSA-SAN...!?
SO...SO YOU REALLY WERE AN ITEM...!?
SORRY, CHI-CHAN.
AHH!
WE LIVE IN A DIFFERENT WORLD FROM YOU!
NOOOO!
WELL, SEE YA.
WAAA-AHHH! NO! PLEASE, NOOO-OOO!
ARRRRRRGGGHH
CHIHO, YOU'RE GONNA BE LATE FOR SCHOOL!
CHIHO'S MOM

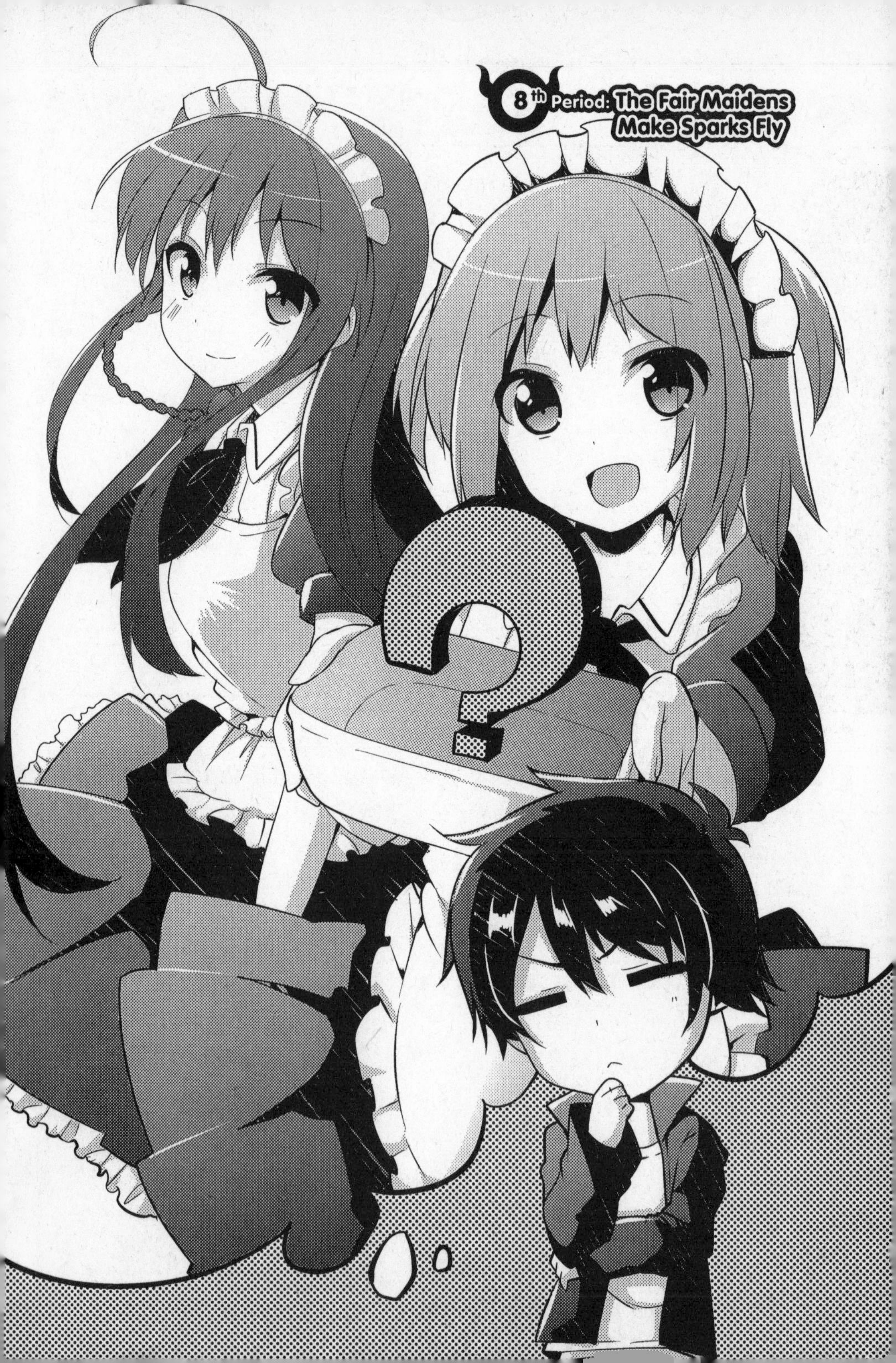
8th Period: The Fair Maidens Make Sparks Fly

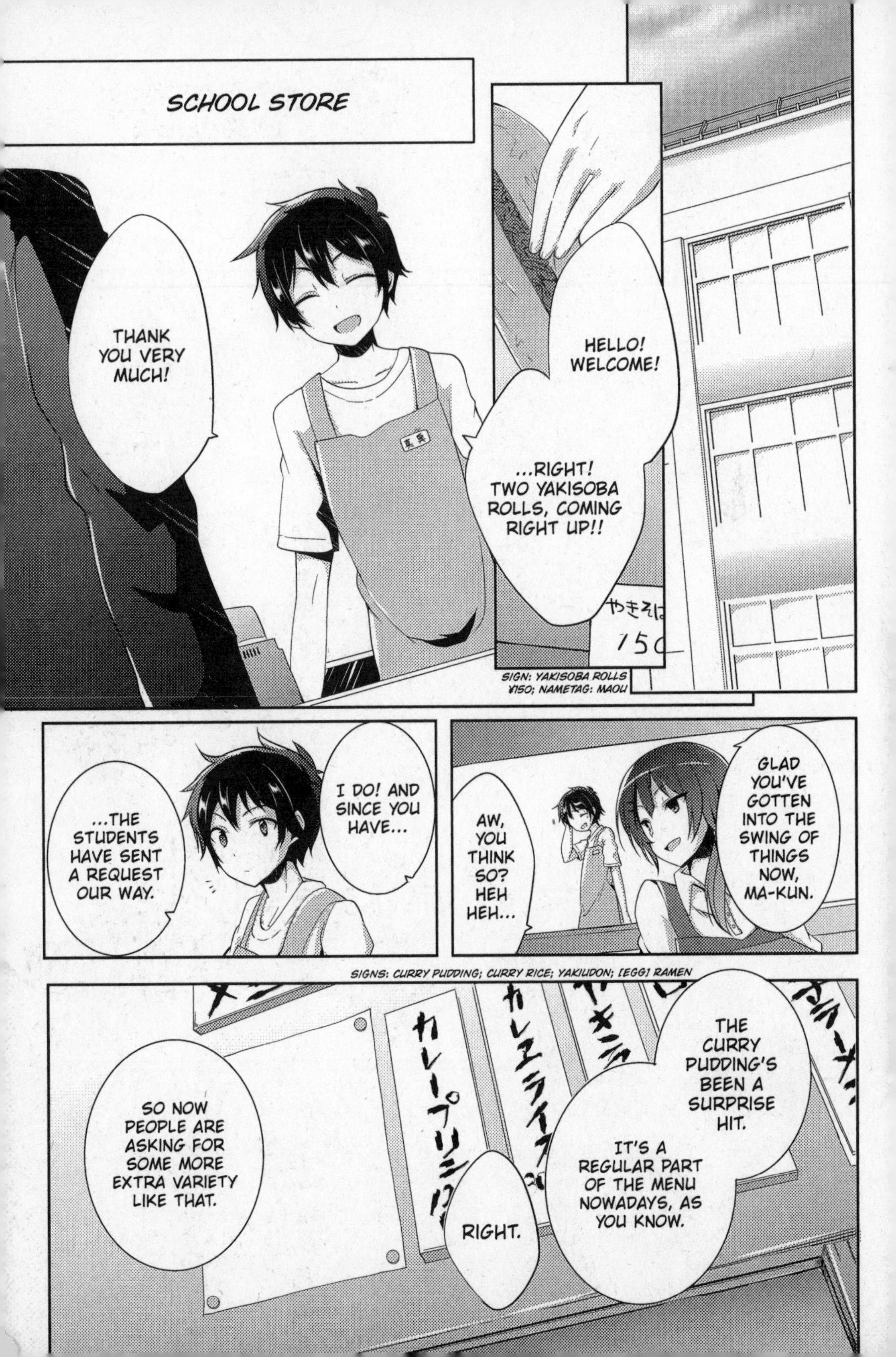

SCHOOL STORE
HELLO! WELCOME!
...RIGHT! TWO YAKISOBA ROLLS, COMING RIGHT UP!!
SIGN: YAKISOBA ROLLS ¥150; NAMETAG: MAOU
THANK YOU VERY MUCH!
GLAD YOU'VE GOTTEN INTO THE SWING OF THINGS NOW, MA-KUN.
AW, YOU THINK SO? HEH HEH...
I DO! AND SINCE YOU HAVE...
...THE STUDENTS HAVE SENT A REQUEST OUR WAY.
SIGNS: CURRY PUDDING; CURRY RICE; YAKIUDON; [EGG] RAMEN
THE CURRY PUDDING'S BEEN A SURPRISE HIT.
IT'S A REGULAR PART OF THE MENU NOWADAYS, AS YOU KNOW.
RIGHT.
SO NOW PEOPLE ARE ASKING FOR SOME MORE EXTRA VARIETY LIKE THAT.

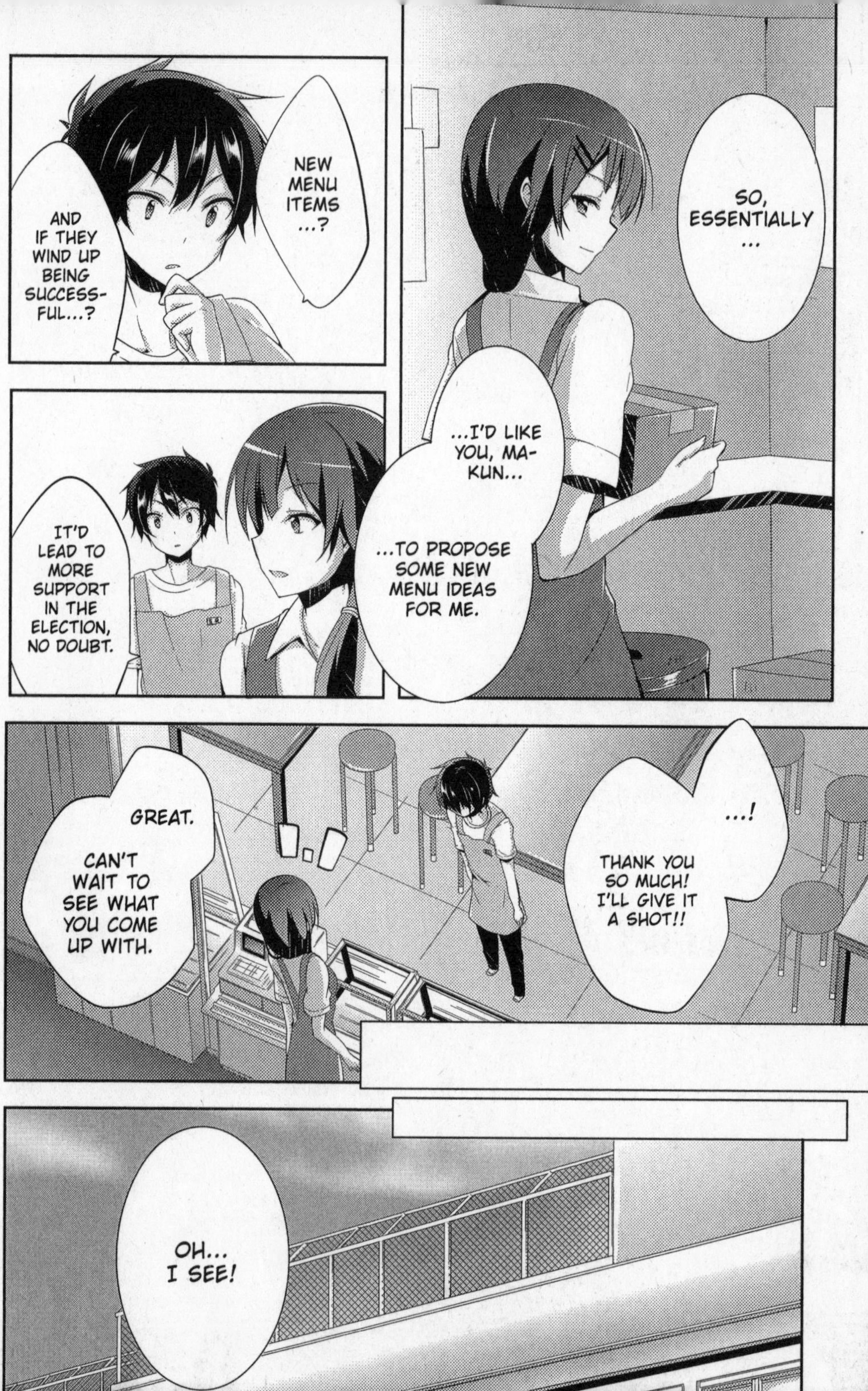
SO, ESSENTIALLY ...
...I'D LIKE YOU, MA-KUN...
...TO PROPOSE SOME NEW MENU IDEAS FOR ME.
NEW MENU ITEMS ...?
AND IF THEY WIND UP BEING SUCCESS-FUL...?
IT'D LEAD TO MORE SUPPORT IN THE ELECTION, NO DOUBT.
...!
THANK YOU SO MUCH! I'LL GIVE IT A SHOT!!
GREAT.
CAN'T WAIT TO SEE WHAT YOU COME UP WITH.
OH... I SEE!

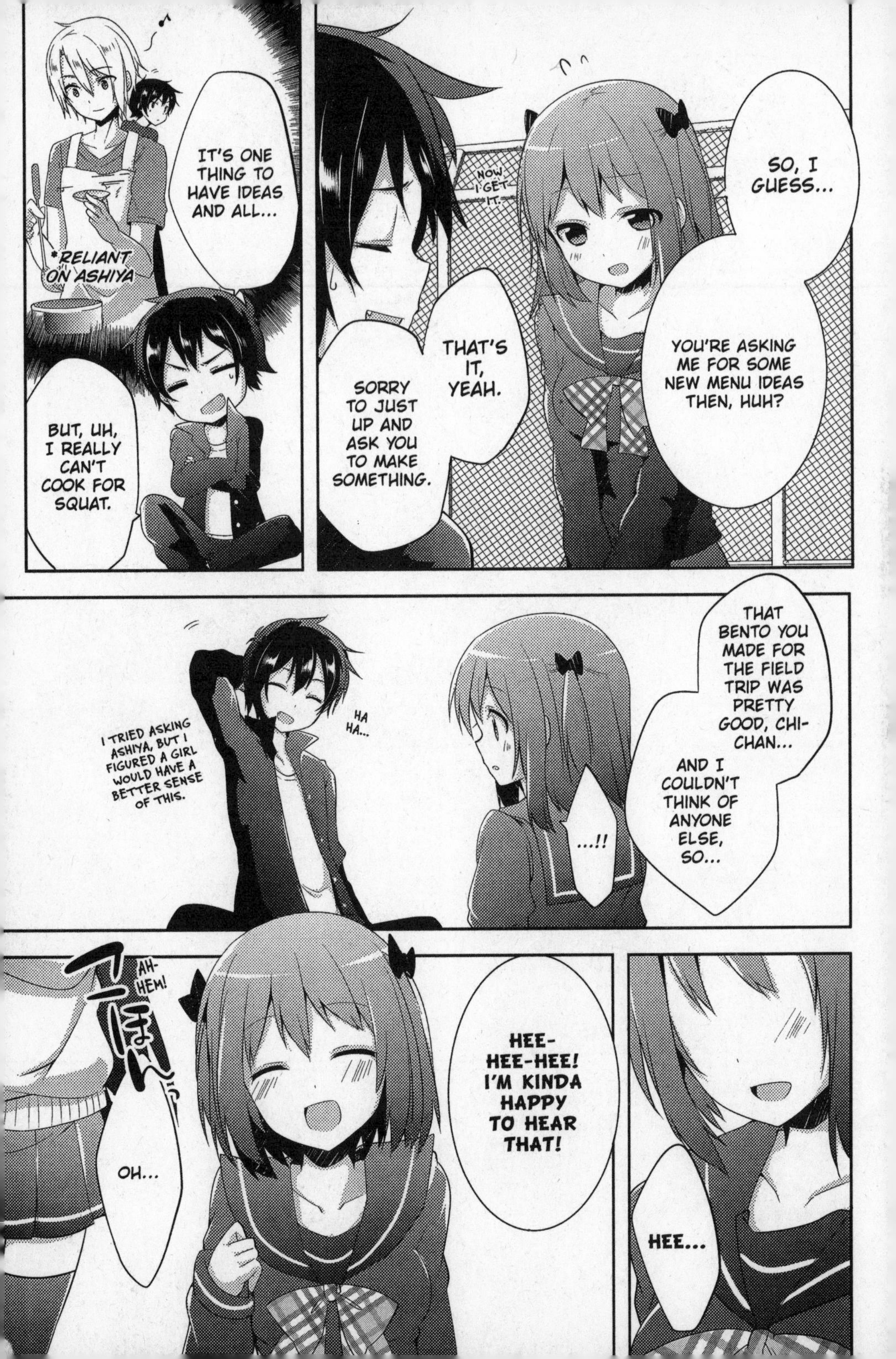

SO, I GUESS...
YOU'RE ASKING ME FOR SOME NEW MENU IDEAS THEN, HUH?
NOW I GET IT.
THAT'S IT, YEAH.
SORRY TO JUST UP AND ASK YOU TO MAKE SOMETHING.
IT'S ONE THING TO HAVE IDEAS AND ALL...
*RELIANT ON ASHIYA
BUT, UH, I REALLY CAN'T COOK FOR SQUAT.
THAT BENTO YOU MADE FOR THE FIELD TRIP WAS PRETTY GOOD, CHI-CHAN...
AND I COULDN'T THINK OF ANYONE ELSE, SO...
...!!
HA HA...
I TRIED ASKING ASHIYA, BUT I FIGURED A GIRL WOULD HAVE A BETTER SENSE OF THIS.
HEE...
HEE-HEE-HEE! I'M KINDA HAPPY TO HEAR THAT!
AH-HEM!
OH...

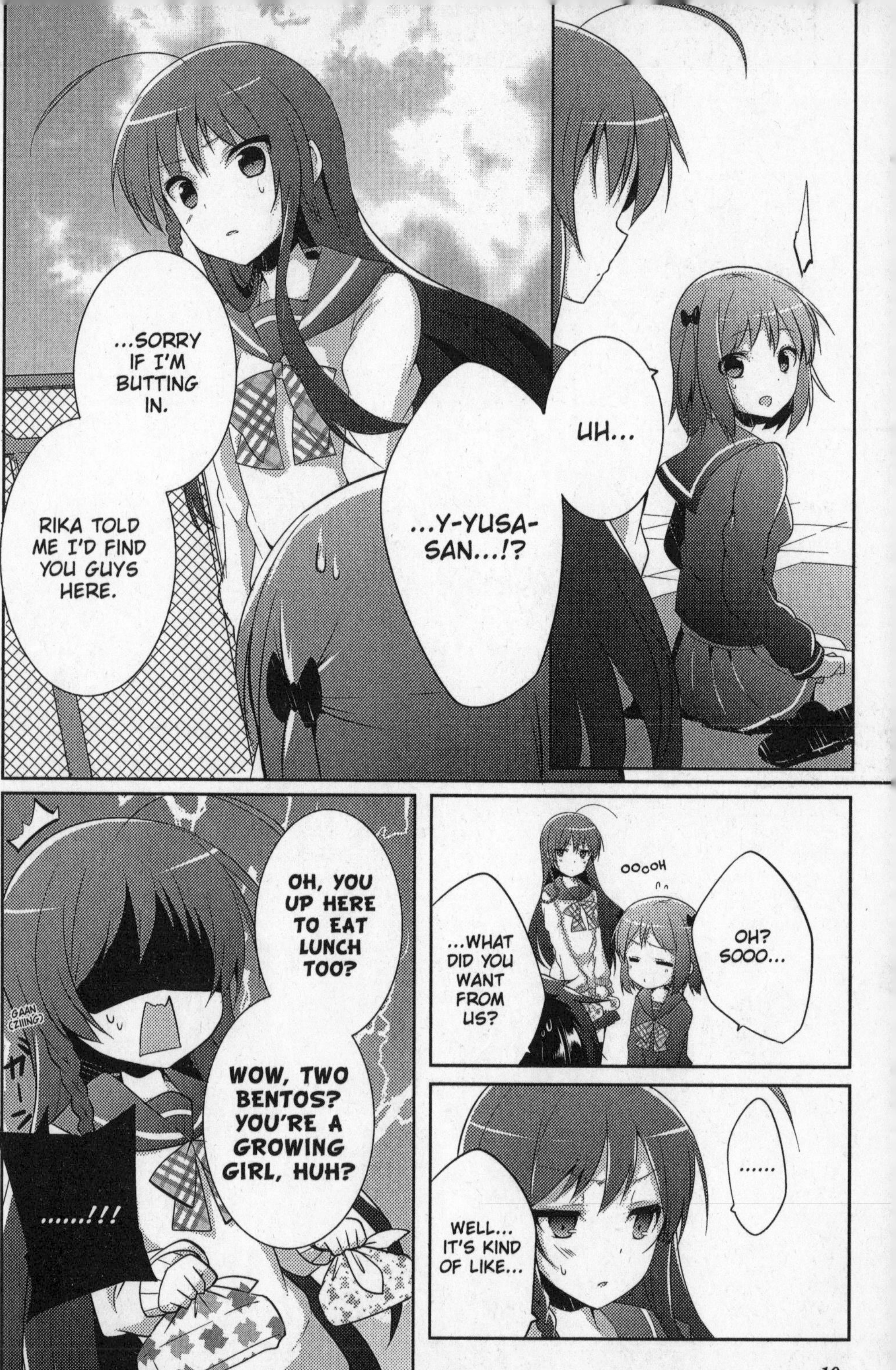
UH...
...Y-YUSA-SAN...!?
...SORRY IF I'M BUTTING IN.
RIKA TOLD ME I'D FIND YOU GUYS HERE.
OH? SOOO...
OOOOH
...WHAT DID YOU WANT FROM US?
......
WELL... IT'S KIND OF LIKE...
OH, YOU UP HERE TO EAT LUNCH TOO?
WOW, TWO BENTOS? YOU'RE A GROWING GIRL, HUH?
GAAN (ZIIING)
......!!!

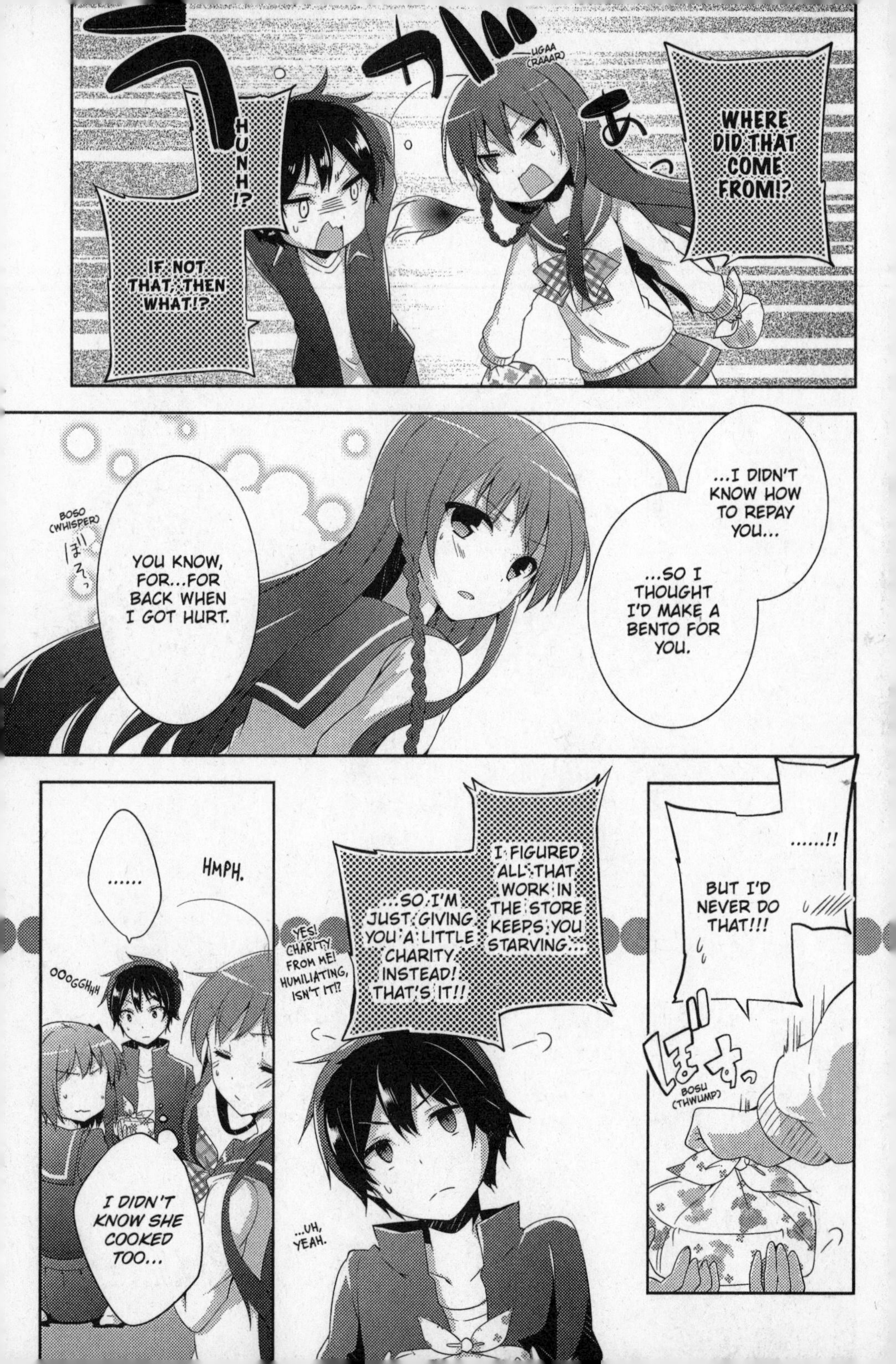
WHERE DID THAT COME FROM!?
UGAA (RAAAR)
HUNH!?
IF NOT THAT THEN WHAT!?
...I DIDN'T KNOW HOW TO REPAY YOU...
...SO I THOUGHT I'D MAKE A BENTO FOR YOU.
BOSO (WHISPER)
YOU KNOW, FOR...FOR BACK WHEN I GOT HURT.
......!!
BUT I'D NEVER DO THAT!!!
BOSU (THWUMP)
I FIGURED ALL THAT WORK IN THE STORE KEEPS YOU STARVING...
...SO I'M JUST GIVING YOU A LITTLE CHARITY INSTEAD! THAT'S IT!!
YES! CHARITY FROM ME! HUMILIATING, ISN'T IT!?
...UH, YEAH.
......
HMPH.
OOOGGHHH
I DIDN'T KNOW SHE COOKED TOO...

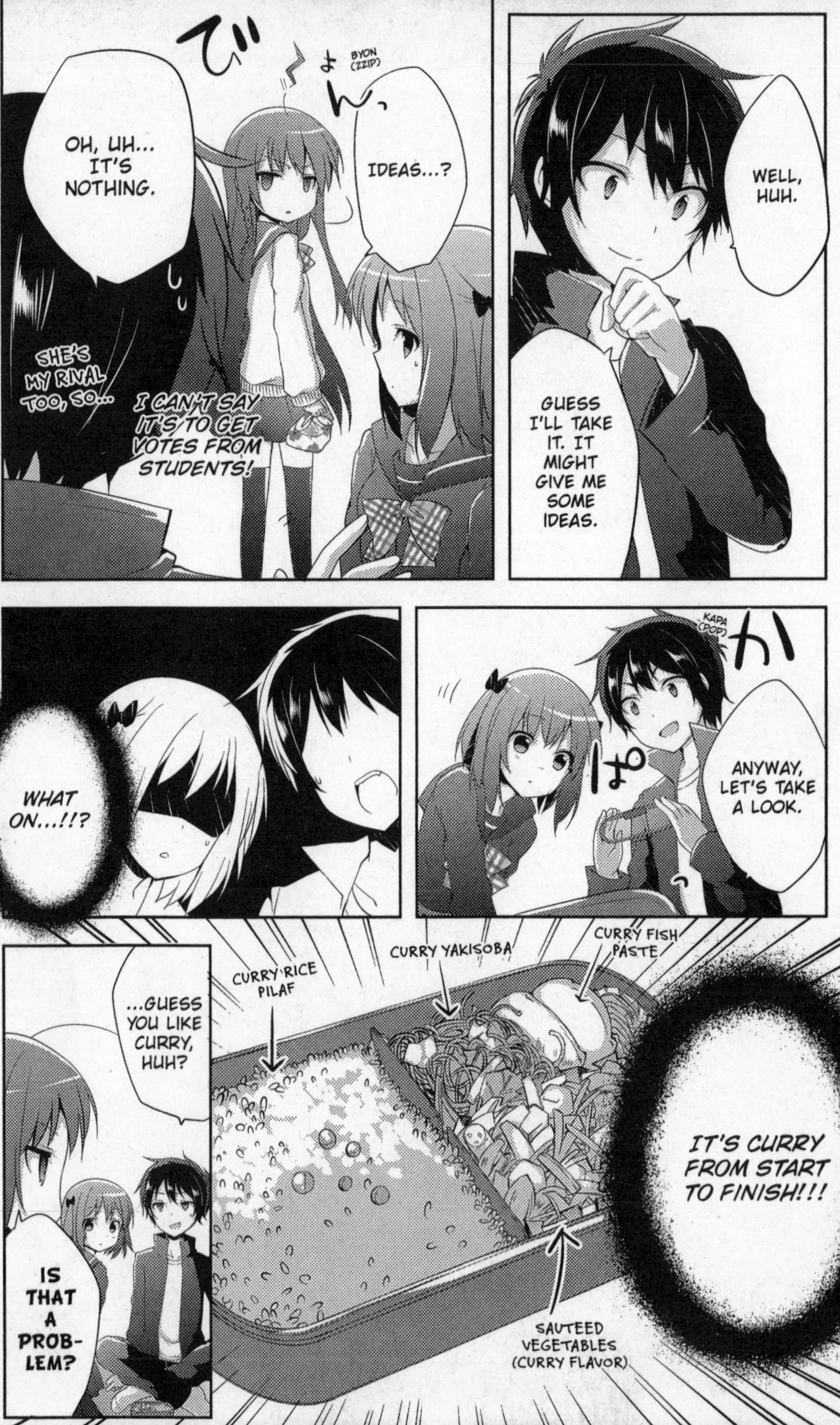
WELL, HUH.
GUESS I'LL TAKE IT. IT MIGHT GIVE ME SOME IDEAS.
BYON (ZZIP)
IDEAS...?
OH, UH... IT'S NOTHING.
SHE'S MY RIVAL TOO, SO...
I CAN'T SAY IT'S TO GET VOTES FROM STUDENTS!
KAPA (POP)
ANYWAY, LET'S TAKE A LOOK.
WHAT ON...!!?
IT'S CURRY FROM START TO FINISH!!!
CURRY FISH PASTE
CURRY YAKISOBA
CURRY RICE PILAF
SAUTEED VEGETABLES (CURRY FLAVOR)
...GUESS YOU LIKE CURRY, HUH?
IS THAT A PROB-LEM?

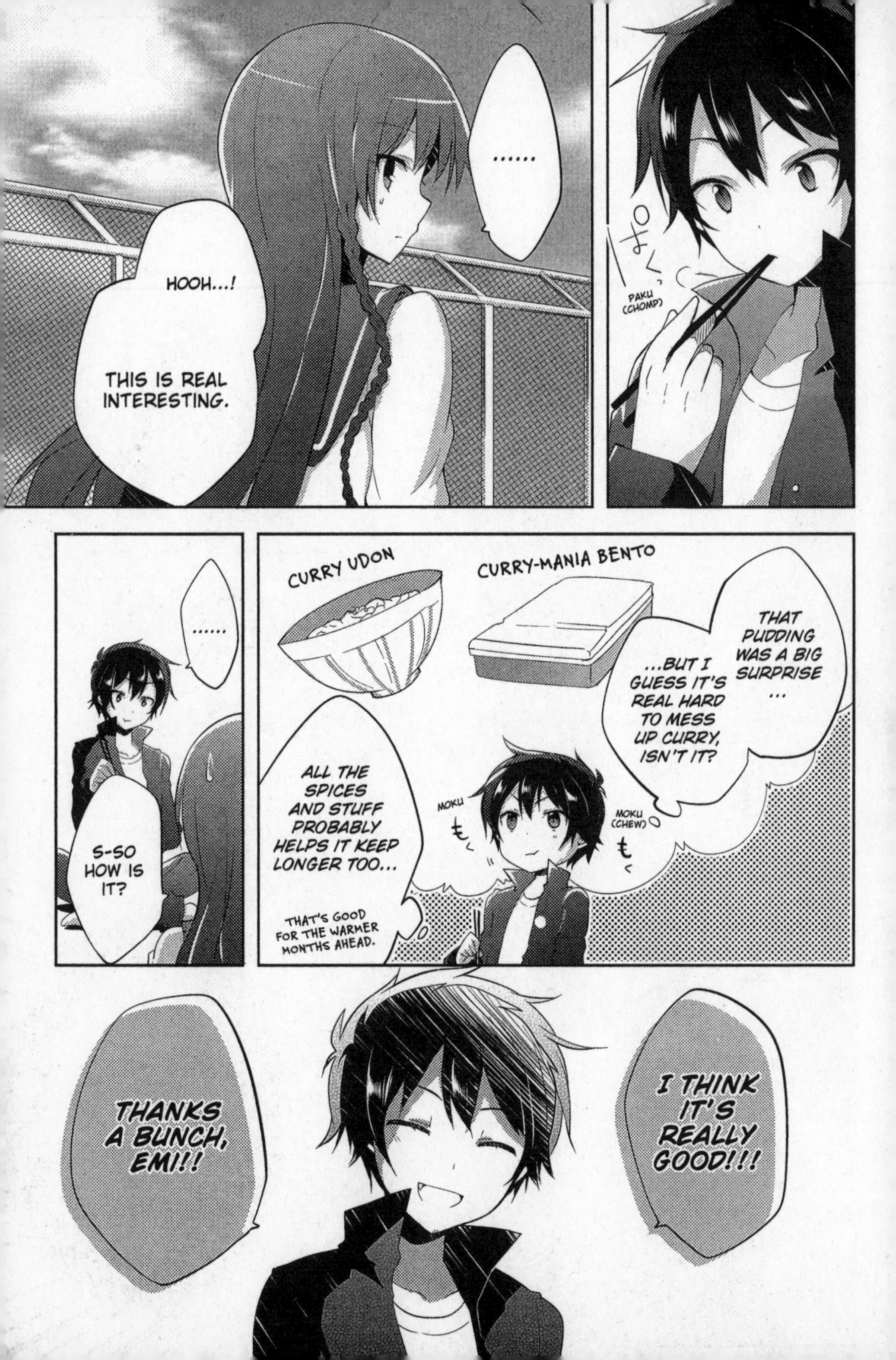
PAKU (CHOMP)
......
HOOH...!
THIS IS REAL INTERESTING.
CURRY-MANIA BENTO
CURRY UDON
THAT PUDDING WAS A BIG SURPRISE ...
...BUT I GUESS IT'S REAL HARD TO MESS UP CURRY, ISN'T IT?
MOKU (CHEW)
MOKU
ALL THE SPICES AND STUFF PROBABLY HELPS IT KEEP LONGER TOO...
THAT'S GOOD FOR THE WARMER MONTHS AHEAD.
......
S-SO HOW IS IT?
I THINK IT'S REALLY GOOD!!!
THANKS A BUNCH, EMI!!

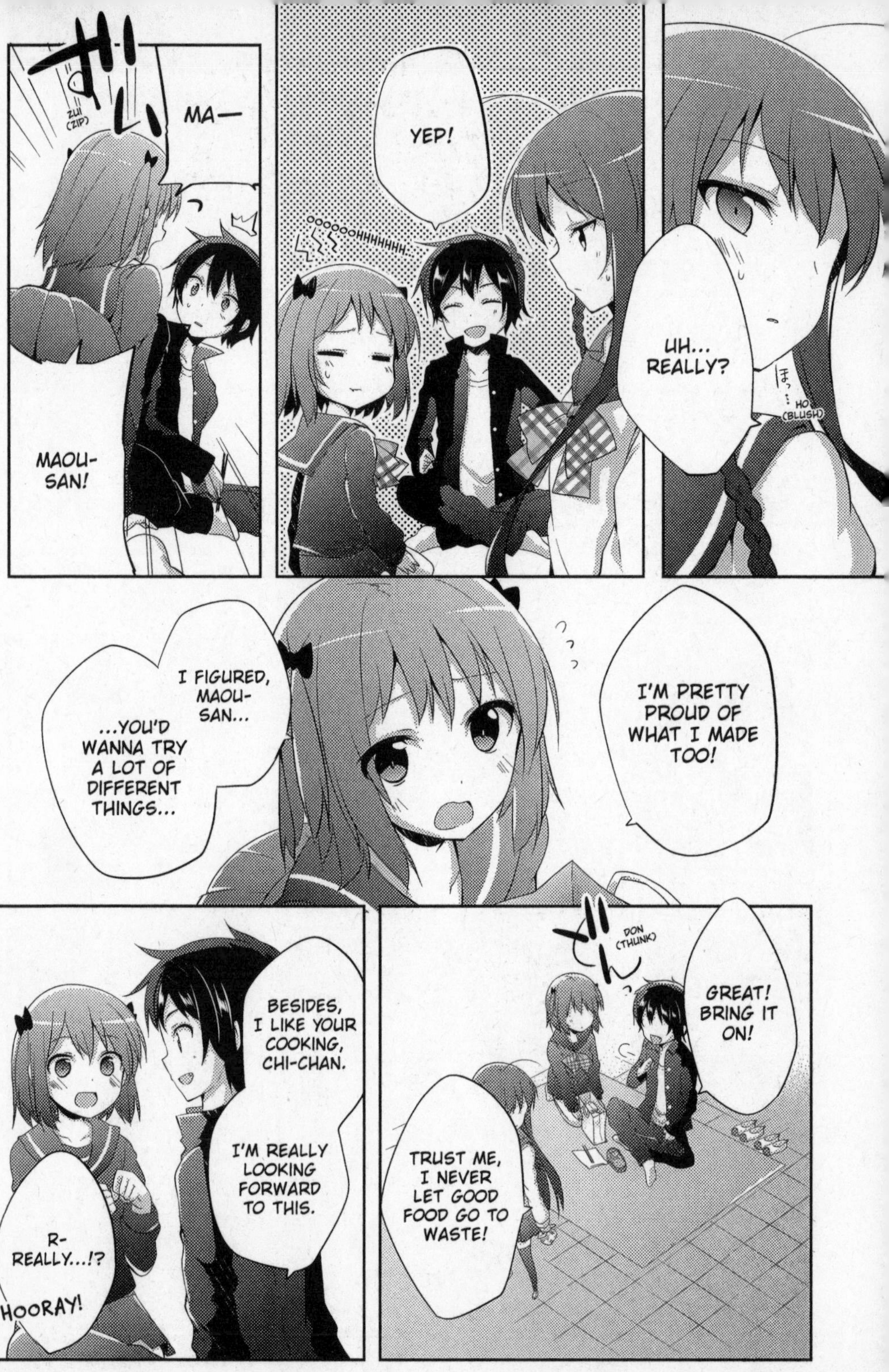
UH... REALLY?
ほっ
HO (BLUSH)
OOOOOOHHHHHHH...
YEP!
ZUI (ZIP)
MA—
MAOU-SAN!
I'M PRETTY PROUD OF WHAT I MADE TOO!
I FIGURED, MAOU-SAN...
...YOU'D WANNA TRY A LOT OF DIFFERENT THINGS...
DON (THUNK)
GREAT! BRING IT ON!
TRUST ME, I NEVER LET GOOD FOOD GO TO WASTE!
BESIDES, I LIKE YOUR COOKING, CHI-CHAN.
I'M REALLY LOOKING FORWARD TO THIS.
R-REALLY...!?
HOORAY!

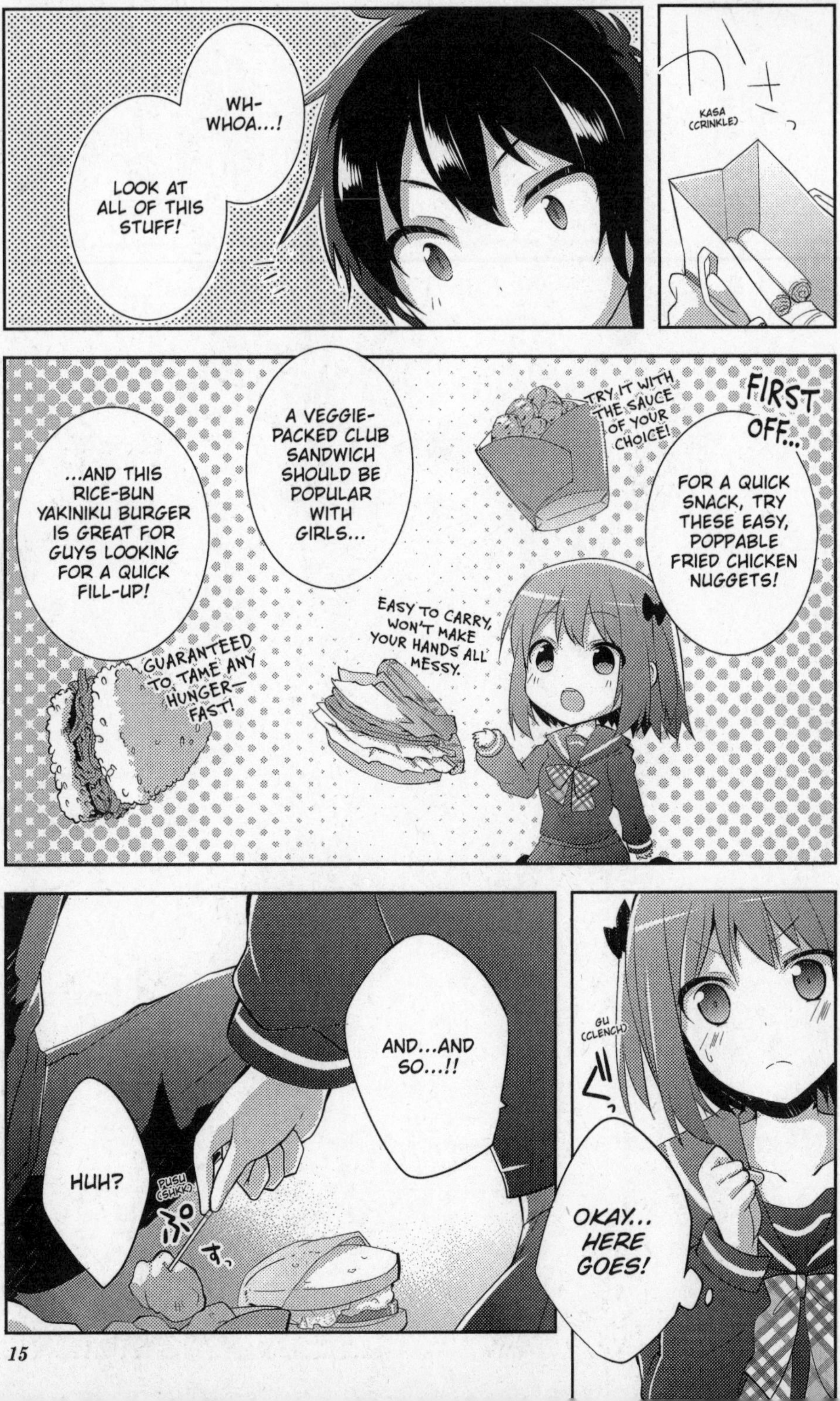
KASA (CRINKLE)
WH-WHOA...!
LOOK AT ALL OF THIS STUFF!
FIRST OFF...
FOR A QUICK SNACK, TRY THESE EASY, POPPABLE FRIED CHICKEN NUGGETS!
TRY IT WITH THE SAUCE OF YOUR CHOICE!
A VEGGIE-PACKED CLUB SANDWICH SHOULD BE POPULAR WITH GIRLS...
EASY TO CARRY, WON'T MAKE YOUR HANDS ALL MESSY.
...AND THIS RICE-BUN YAKINIKU BURGER IS GREAT FOR GUYS LOOKING FOR A QUICK FILL-UP!
GUARANTEED TO TAME ANY HUNGER—FAST!
GU (CLENCH)
OKAY... HERE GOES!
AND...AND SO...!!
PUSU (SHKK)
HUH?

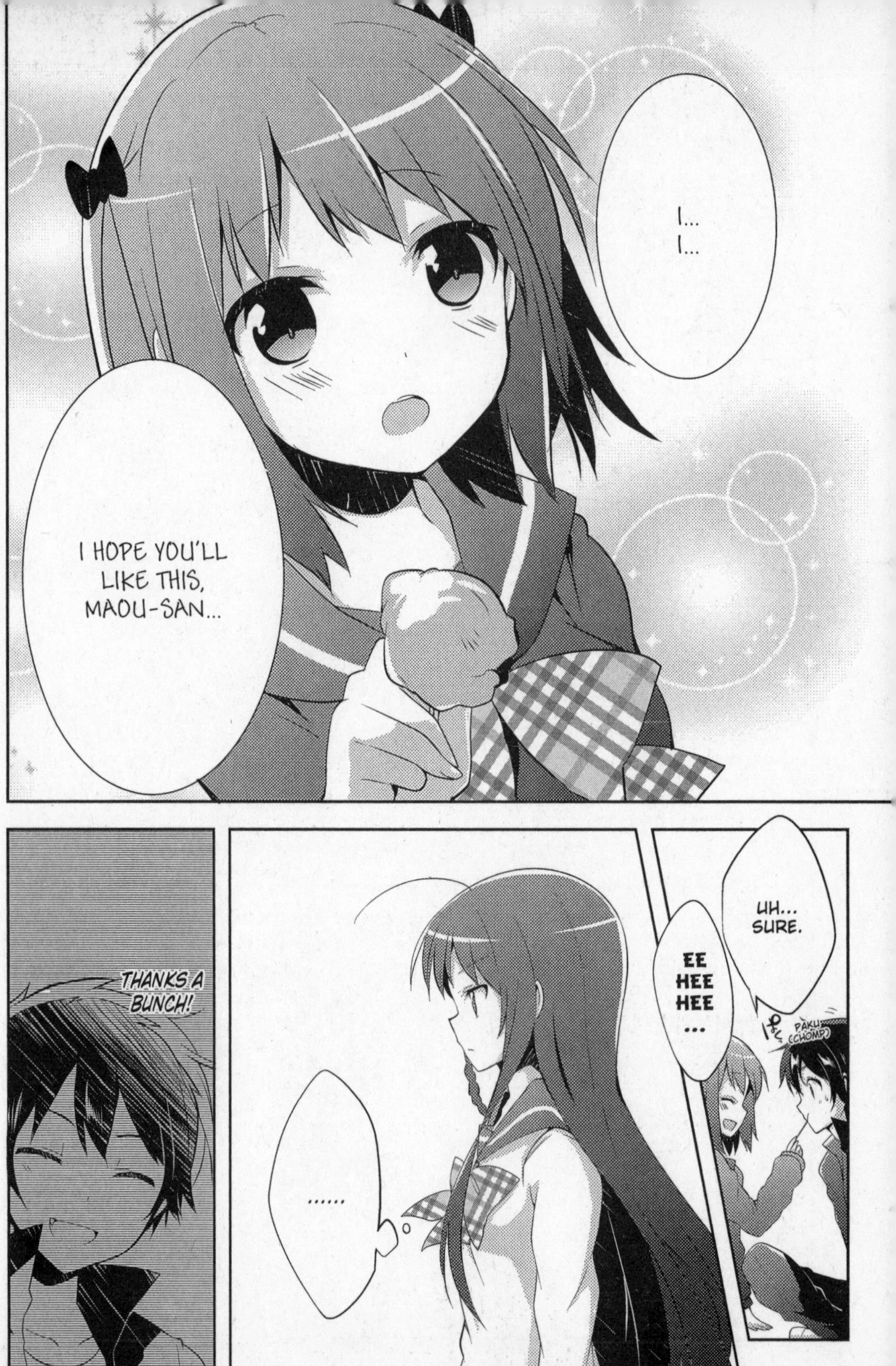
I...
I...
I HOPE YOU'LL LIKE THIS, MAOU-SAN...
UH... SURE.
EE HEE HEE...
PAKU (CHOMP)
......
THANKS A BUNCH!

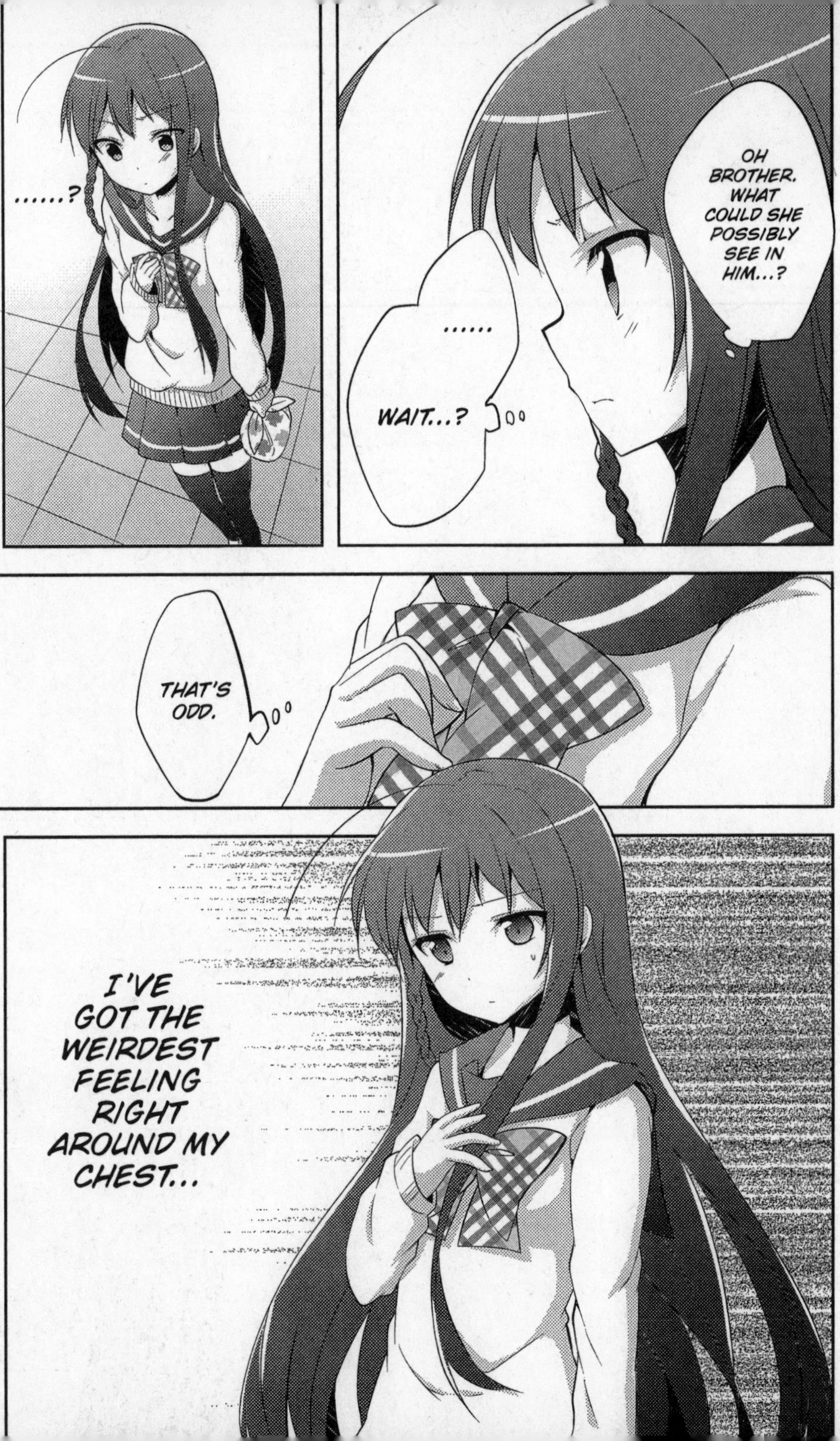
OH BROTHER. WHAT COULD SHE POSSIBLY SEE IN HIM...?
......
WAIT...?
......?
THAT'S ODD.
I'VE GOT THE WEIRDEST FEELING RIGHT AROUND MY CHEST...

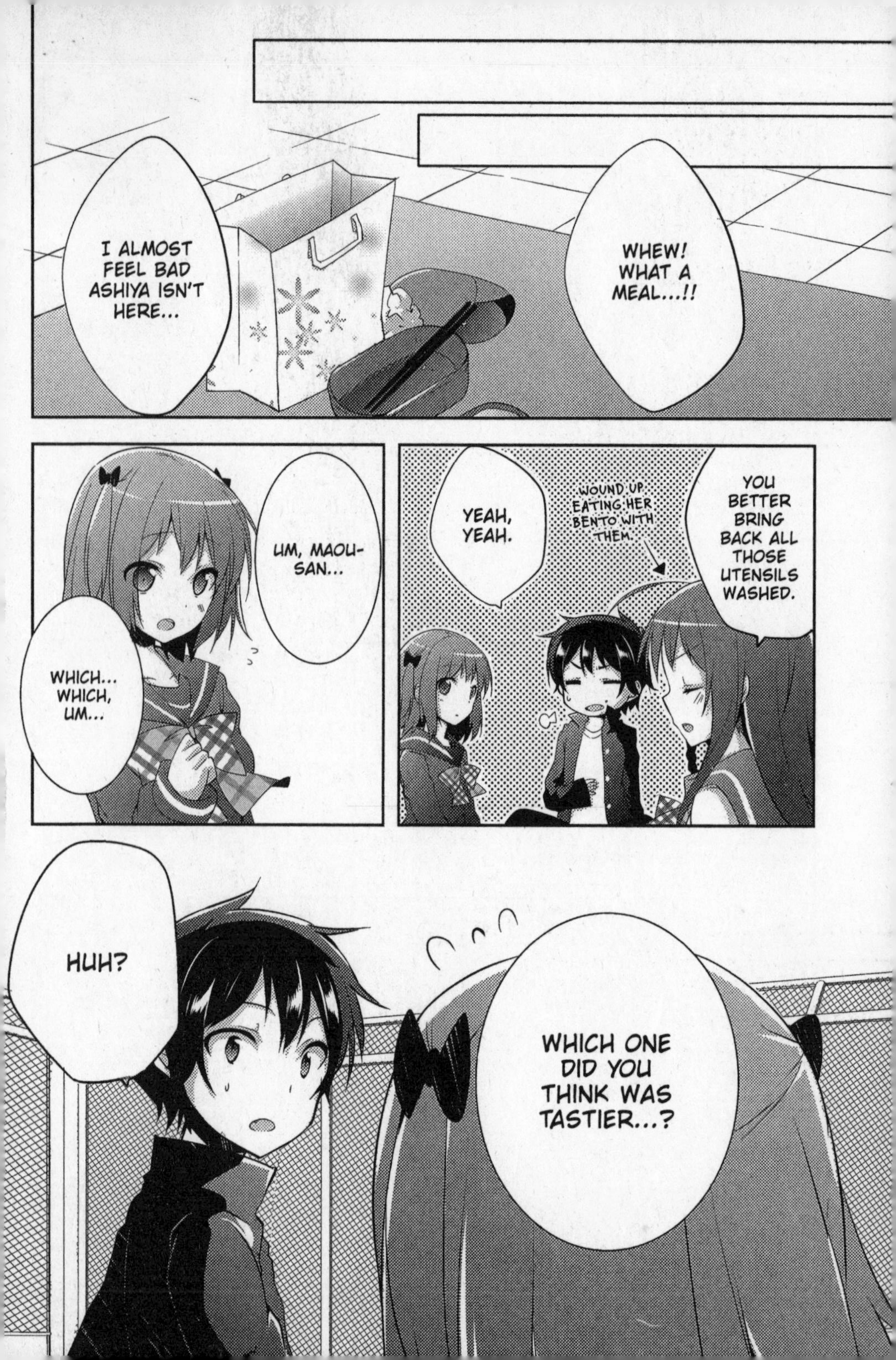
WHEW! WHAT A MEAL...!!
I ALMOST FEEL BAD ASHIYA ISN'T HERE...
YOU BETTER BRING BACK ALL THOSE UTENSILS WASHED.
YEAH, YEAH.
WOUND UP EATING HER BENTO WITH THEM.
UM, MAOU-SAN...
WHICH... WHICH, UM...
WHICH ONE DID YOU THINK WAS TASTIER...?
HUH?

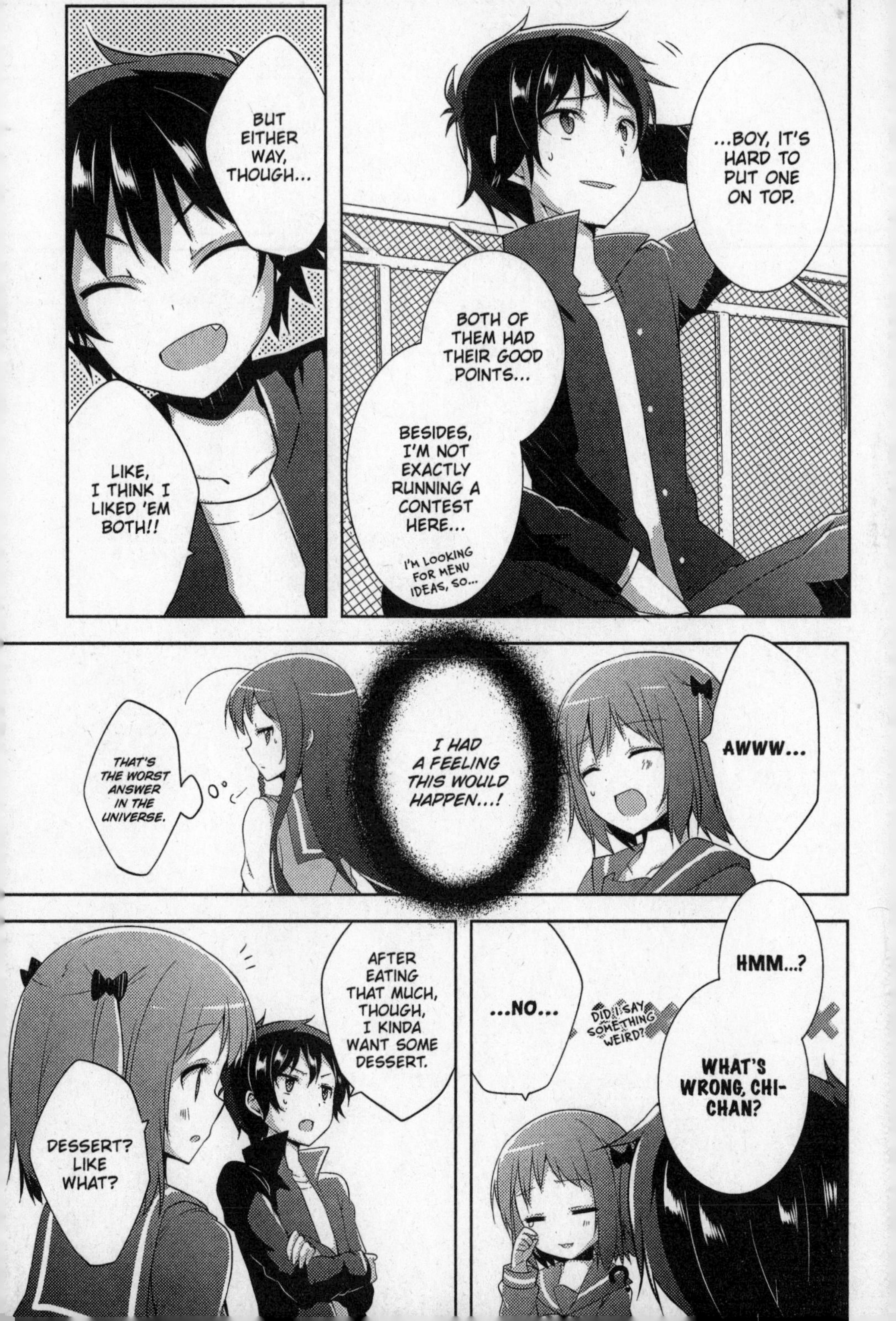
...BOY, IT'S HARD TO PUT ONE ON TOP.
BOTH OF THEM HAD THEIR GOOD POINTS...
BESIDES, I'M NOT EXACTLY RUNNING A CONTEST HERE...
I'M LOOKING FOR MENU IDEAS, SO...
BUT EITHER WAY, THOUGH...
LIKE, I THINK I LIKED 'EM BOTH!!
AWWW...
I HAD A FEELING THIS WOULD HAPPEN...!
THAT'S THE WORST ANSWER IN THE UNIVERSE.
HMM...?
WHAT'S WRONG, CHI-CHAN?
DID I SAY SOMETHING WEIRD?
...NO...
AFTER EATING THAT MUCH, THOUGH, I KINDA WANT SOME DESSERT.
DESSERT? LIKE WHAT?

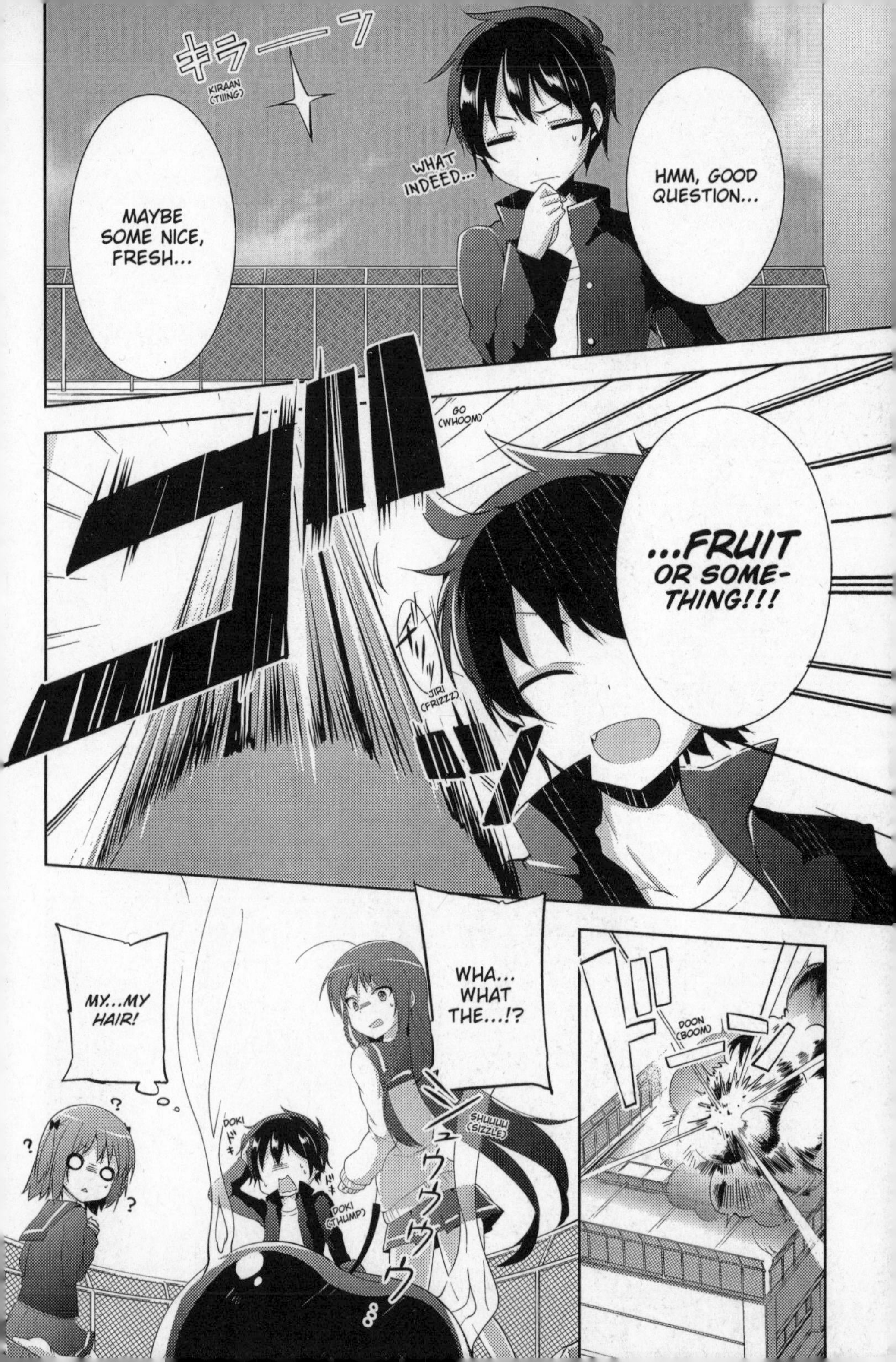
HMM, GOOD QUESTION...
WHAT INDEED...
キラーン
KIRAAN (TIIING)
MAYBE SOME NICE, FRESH...
GO (WHOOM)
...FRUIT OR SOME-THING!!!
JIRI (FRIZZZ)
DOON (BOOM)
WHA... WHAT THE...!?
SHUUUU (SIZZLE)
DOKI
DOKI (THUMP)
MY...MY HAIR!

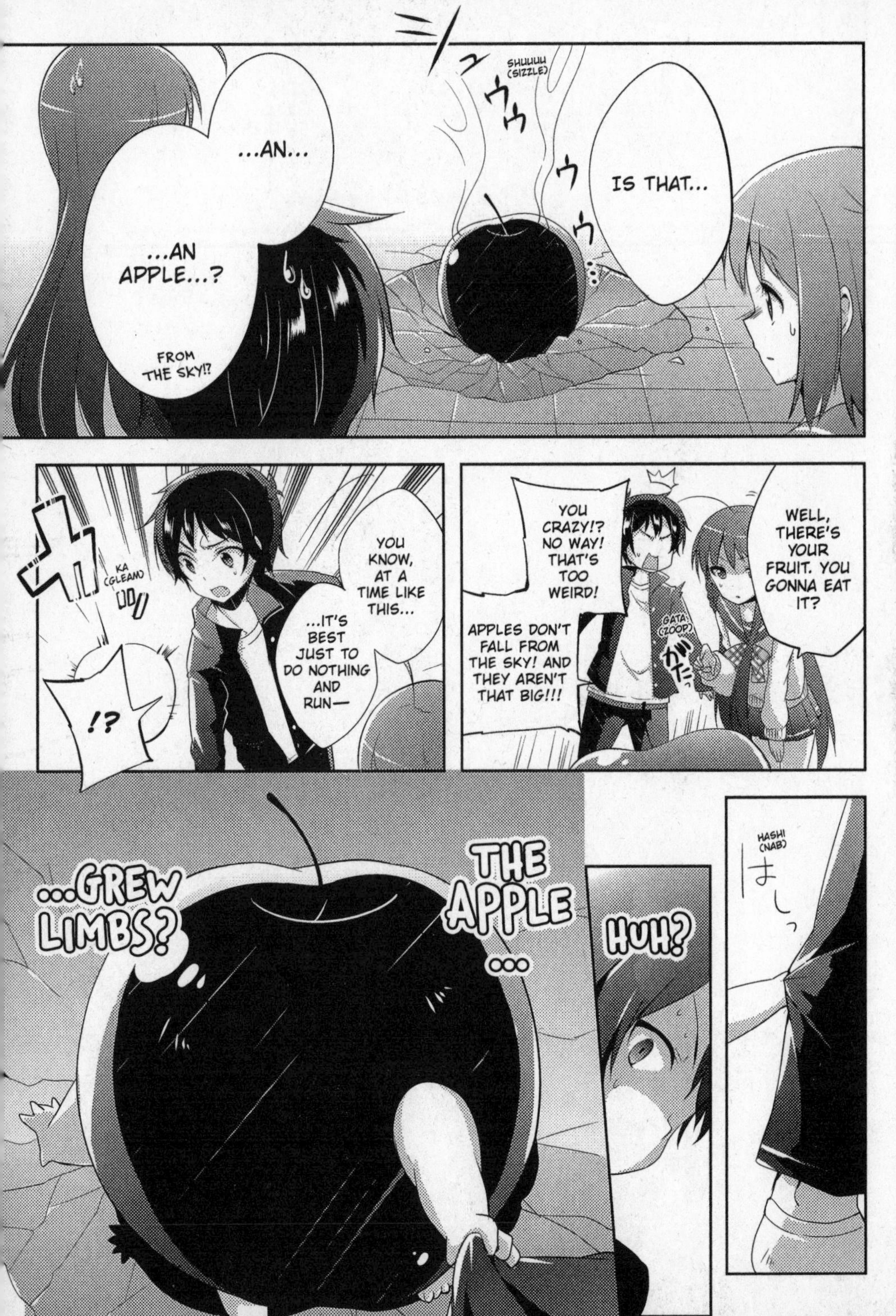
SHUUUU (SIZZLE)
IS THAT...
...AN...
...AN APPLE...?
FROM THE SKY!?
WELL, THERE'S YOUR FRUIT. YOU GONNA EAT IT?
YOU CRAZY!? NO WAY! THAT'S TOO WEIRD!
GATA (ZOOP)
APPLES DON'T FALL FROM THE SKY! AND THEY AREN'T THAT BIG!!!
YOU KNOW, AT A TIME LIKE THIS...
...IT'S BEST JUST TO DO NOTHING AND RUN—
KA (GLEAM)
!?
HASHI (NAB)
HUH?
THE APPLE...
...GREW LIMBS?

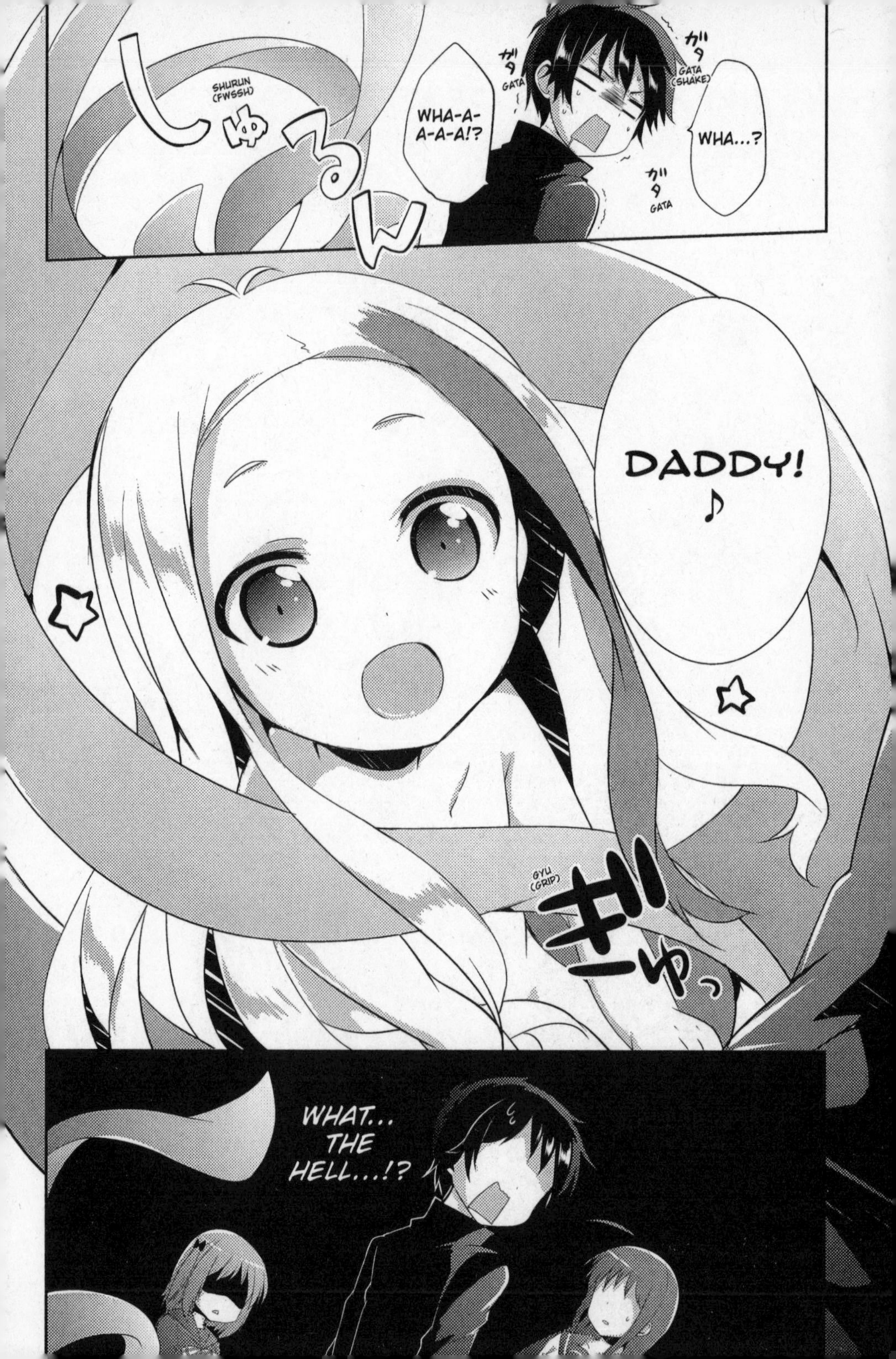
WHA...?
ガタ
GATA (SHAKE)
ガタ
GATA
ガタ
GATA
WHA-A-A-A-A!?
しゅるん
SHURUN (FWSSH)
DADDY! ♪
ぎゅっ
GYU (GRIP)
WHAT... THE HELL...!?

THE DEVIL IS A PART-TIMER! HIGH SCHOOL!

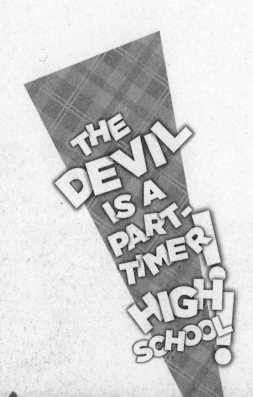

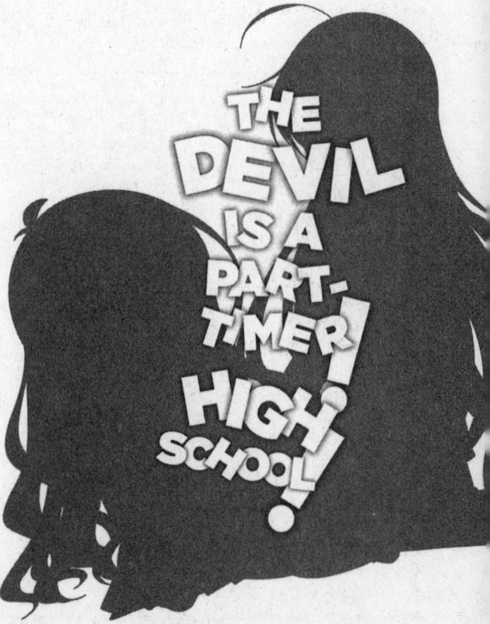
THE DEVIL IS A PART-TIMER!
HIGH SCHOOL!

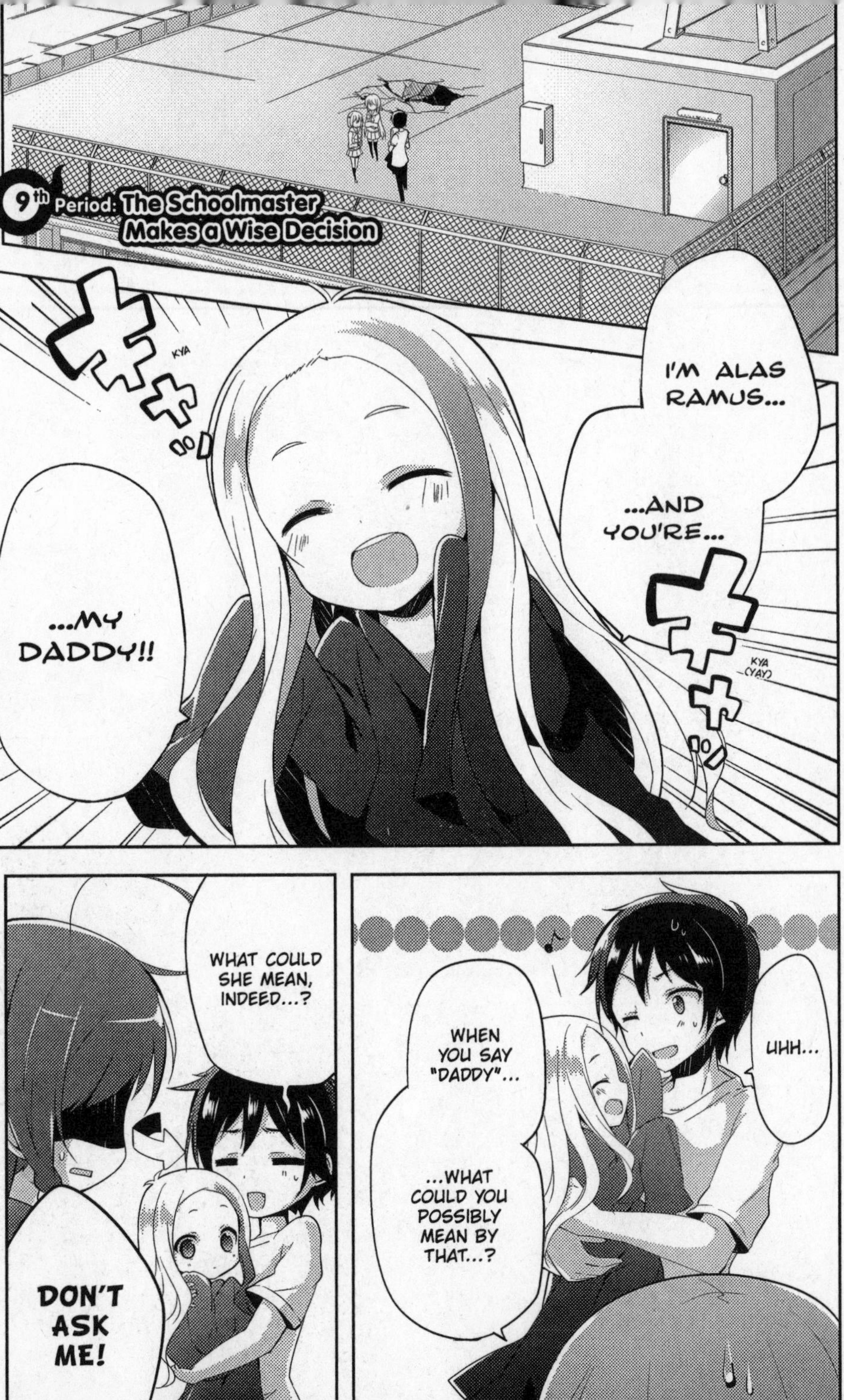
9th Period: The Schoolmaster Makes a Wise Decision
I'M ALAS RAMUS...
...AND YOU'RE...
KYA (YAY)
KYA
...MY DADDY!!
UHH...
WHEN YOU SAY "DADDY"...
...WHAT COULD YOU POSSIBLY MEAN BY THAT...?
WHAT COULD SHE MEAN, INDEED...?
DON'T ASK ME!

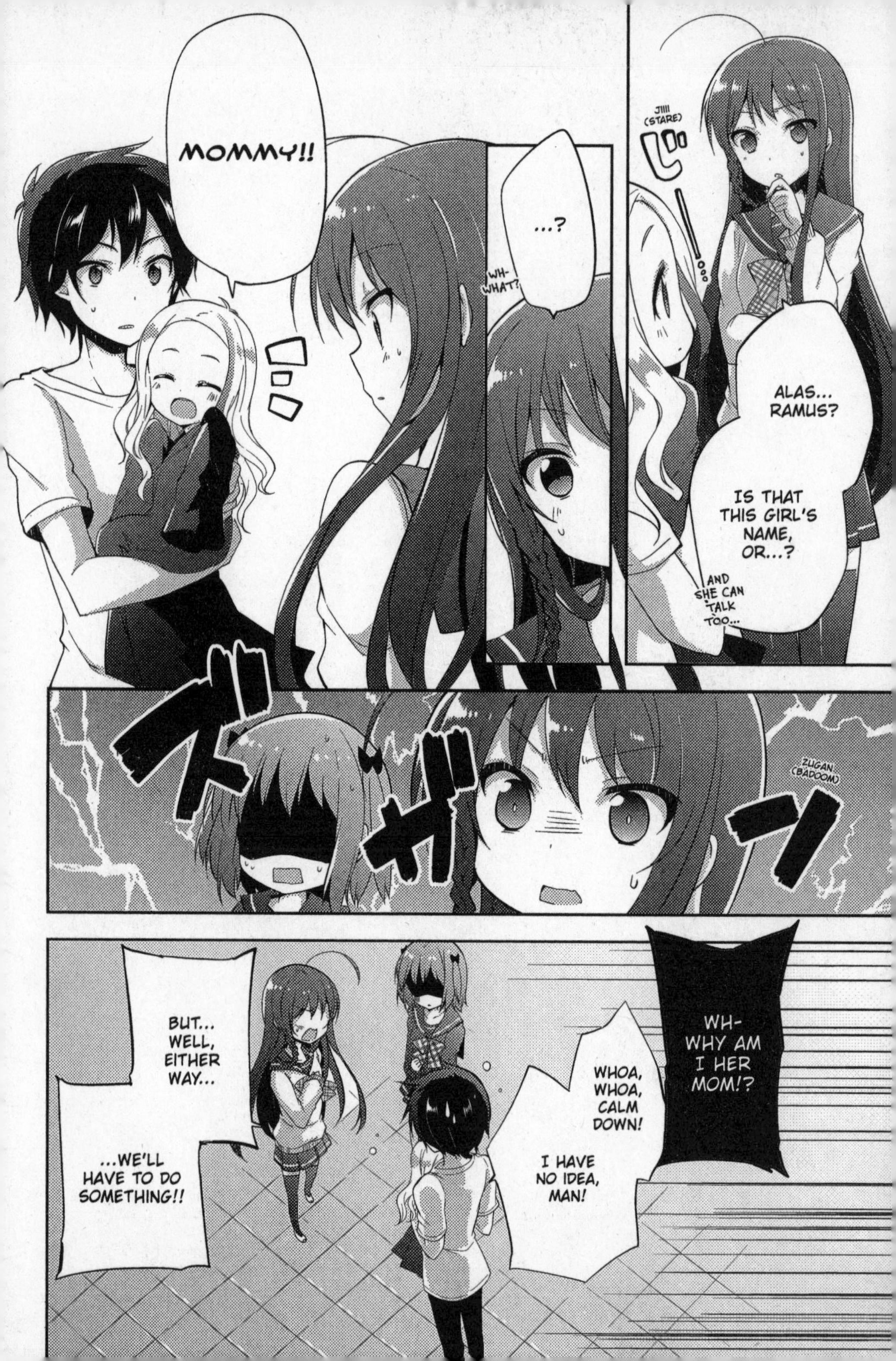
JIIII (STARE)
ALAS... RAMUS?
IS THAT THIS GIRL'S NAME, OR...?
AND SHE CAN TALK TOO...
...?
WH-WHAT?
MOMMY!!
ZUGAN (BADOOM)
WH-WHY AM I HER MOM!?
WHOA, WHOA, CALM DOWN!
I HAVE NO IDEA, MAN!
BUT... WELL, EITHER WAY...
...WE'LL HAVE TO DO SOMETHING!!

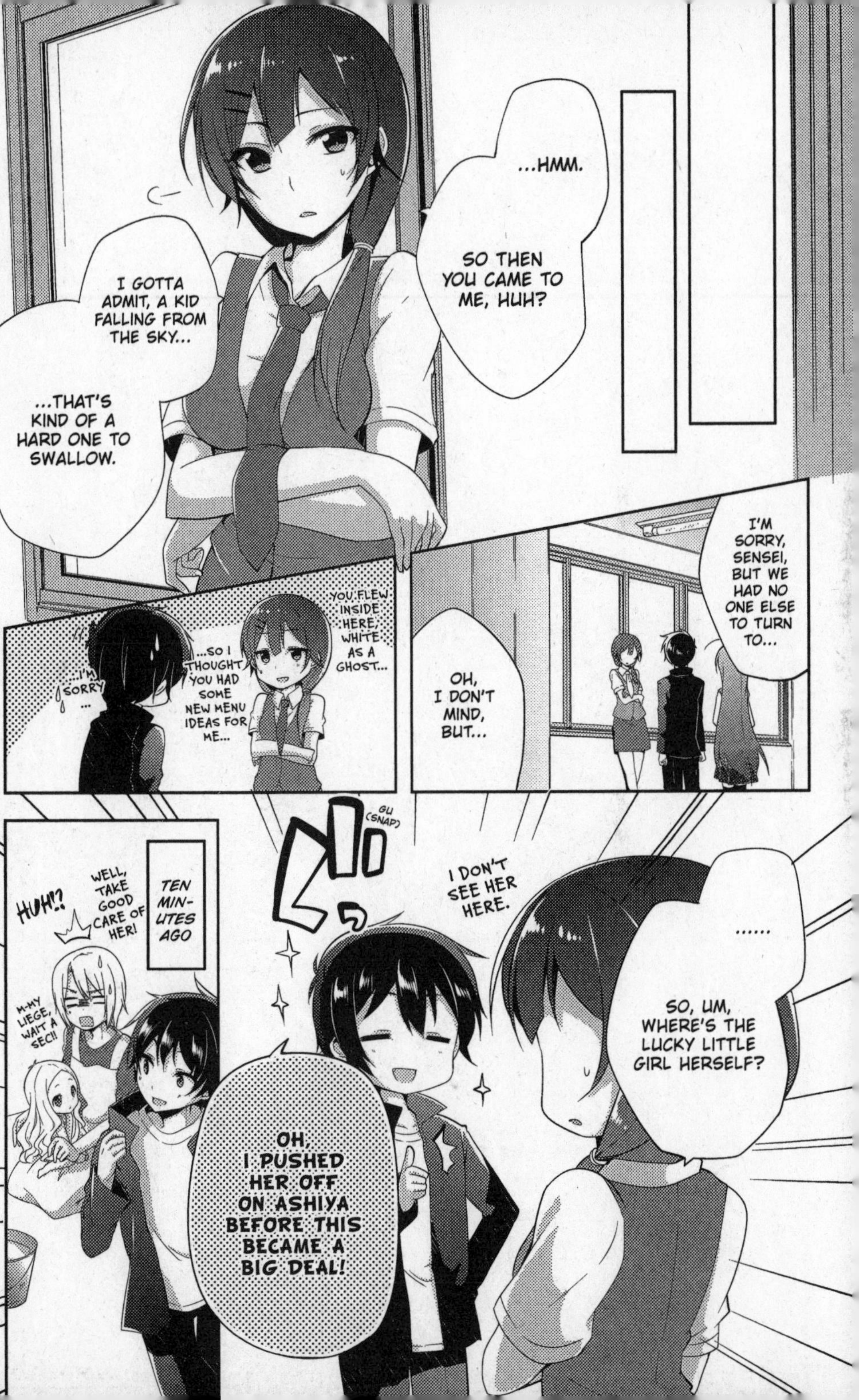
...HMM.
SO THEN YOU CAME TO ME, HUH?
I GOTTA ADMIT, A KID FALLING FROM THE SKY...
...THAT'S KIND OF A HARD ONE TO SWALLOW.
I'M SORRY, SENSEI, BUT WE HAD NO ONE ELSE TO TURN TO...
OH, I DON'T MIND, BUT...
YOU FLEW INSIDE HERE, WHITE AS A GHOST...
...SO I THOUGHT YOU HAD SOME NEW MENU IDEAS FOR ME...
...I'M SORRY...
......
SO, UM, WHERE'S THE LUCKY LITTLE GIRL HERSELF?
I DON'T SEE HER HERE.
GU (SNAP)
OH, I PUSHED HER OFF ON ASHIYA BEFORE THIS BECAME A BIG DEAL!
TEN MIN-UTES AGO
WELL, TAKE GOOD CARE OF HER!
HUH!?
M-MY LIEGE, WAIT A SEC!!

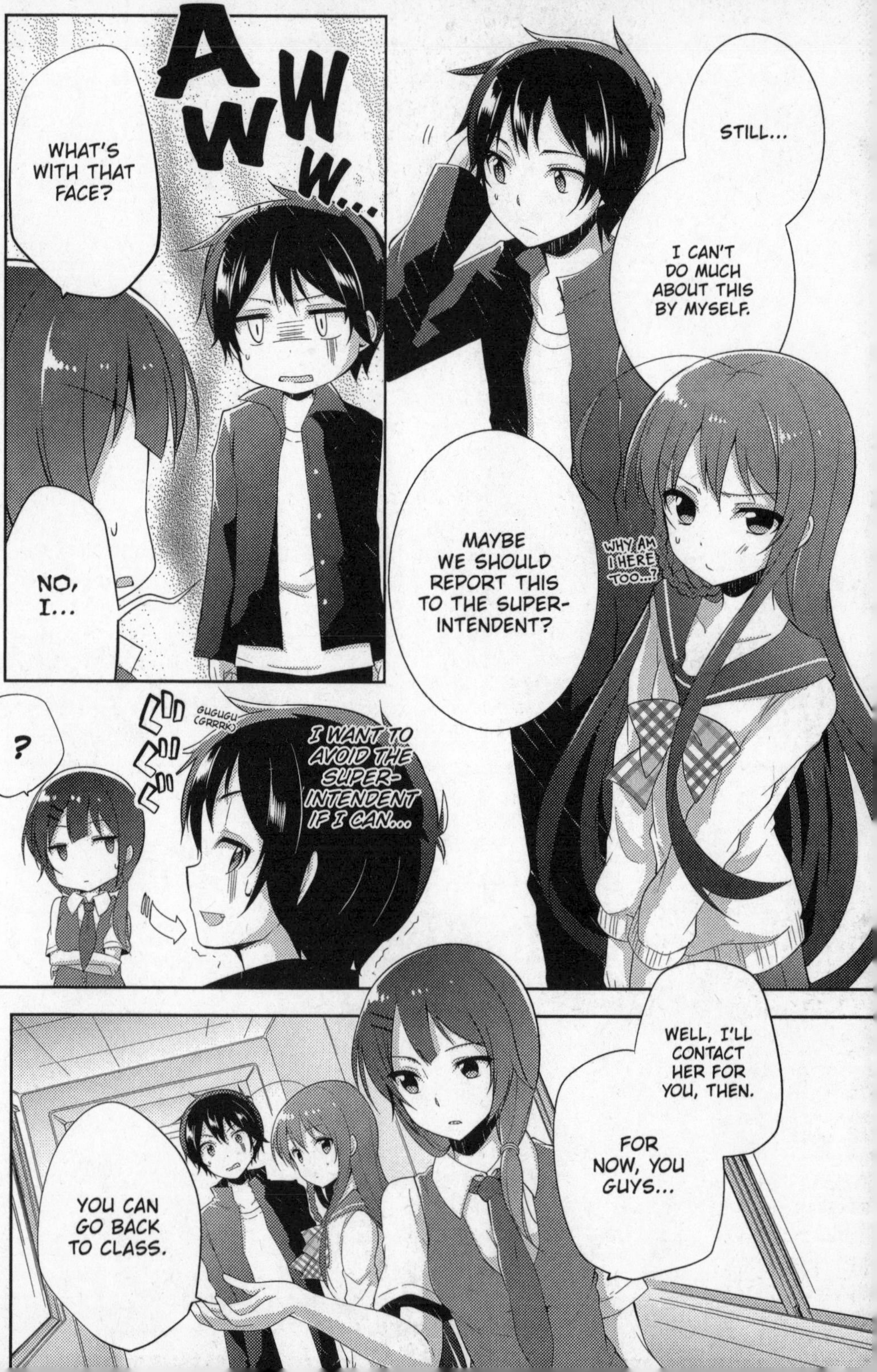
STILL...
I CAN'T DO MUCH ABOUT THIS BY MYSELF.
MAYBE WE SHOULD REPORT THIS TO THE SUPER-INTENDENT?
WHY AM I HERE TOO...?
AWWW...
WHAT'S WITH THAT FACE?
NO, I...
GUGUGU (GRRRK)
I WANT TO AVOID THE SUPER-INTENDENT IF I CAN...
?
WELL, I'LL CONTACT HER FOR YOU, THEN.
FOR NOW, YOU GUYS...
YOU CAN GO BACK TO CLASS.

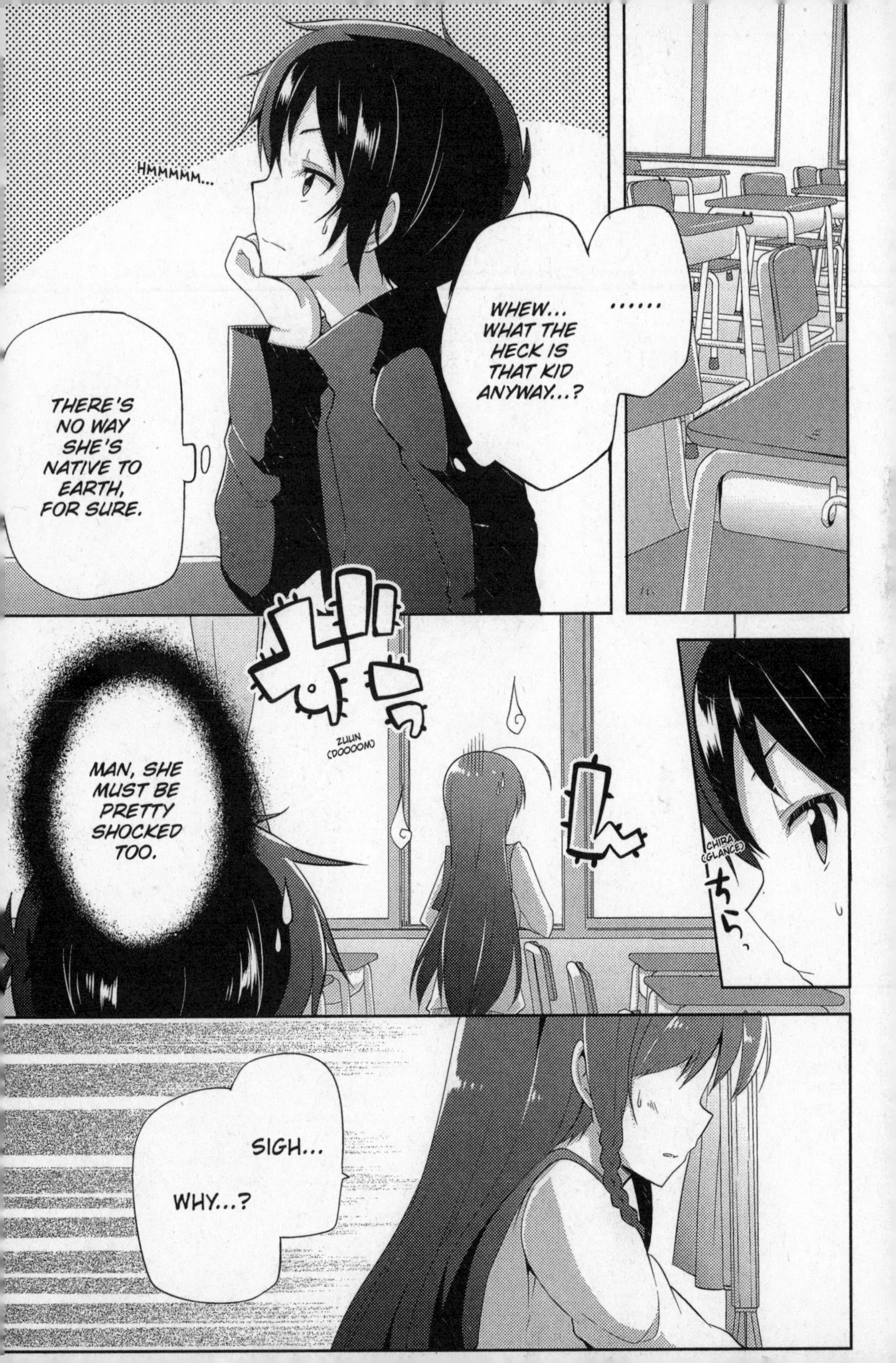
......
WHEW... WHAT THE HECK IS THAT KID ANYWAY...?
HMMMMM...
THERE'S NO WAY SHE'S NATIVE TO EARTH, FOR SURE.
CHIRA (GLANCE)
ZUUN (DOOOOM)
MAN, SHE MUST BE PRETTY SHOCKED TOO.
SIGH...
WHY...?

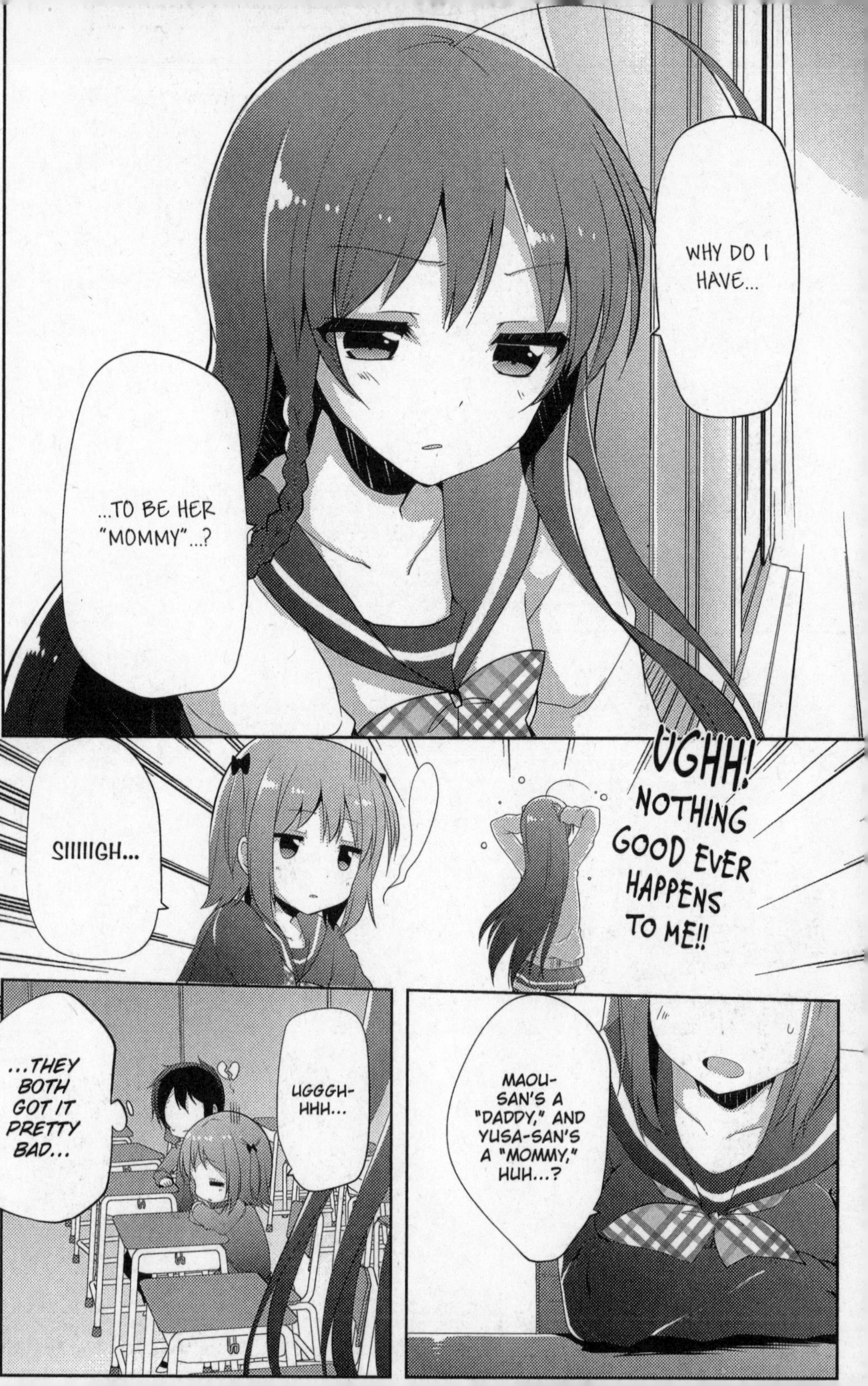
WHY DO I HAVE...
...TO BE HER "MOMMY"...?
UGHH! NOTHING GOOD EVER HAPPENS TO ME!!
SIIIIGH...
MAOU-SAN'S A "DADDY," AND YUSA-SAN'S A "MOMMY," HUH...?
UGGGH-HHH...
...THEY BOTH GOT IT PRETTY BAD...

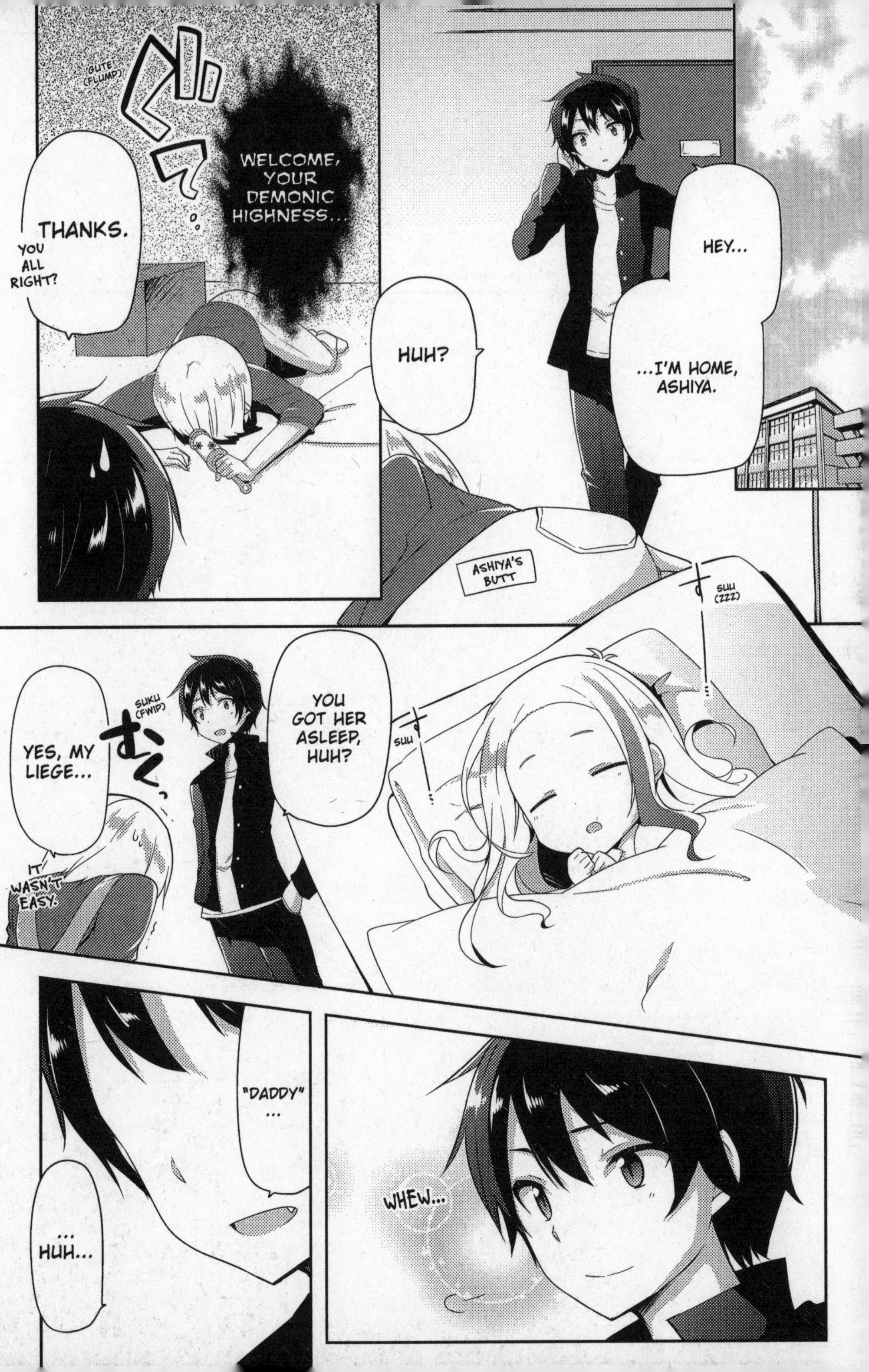
HEY...
...I'M HOME, ASHIYA.
HUH?
ASHIYA'S BUTT
SUU (ZZZ)
GUTE (FLUMP)
WELCOME, YOUR DEMONIC HIGHNESS...
THANKS.
YOU ALL RIGHT?
YOU GOT HER ASLEEP, HUH?
SUU
SUKU (FWIP)
YES, MY LIEGE...
IT WASN'T EASY.
WHEW...
"DADDY" ...
... HUH...

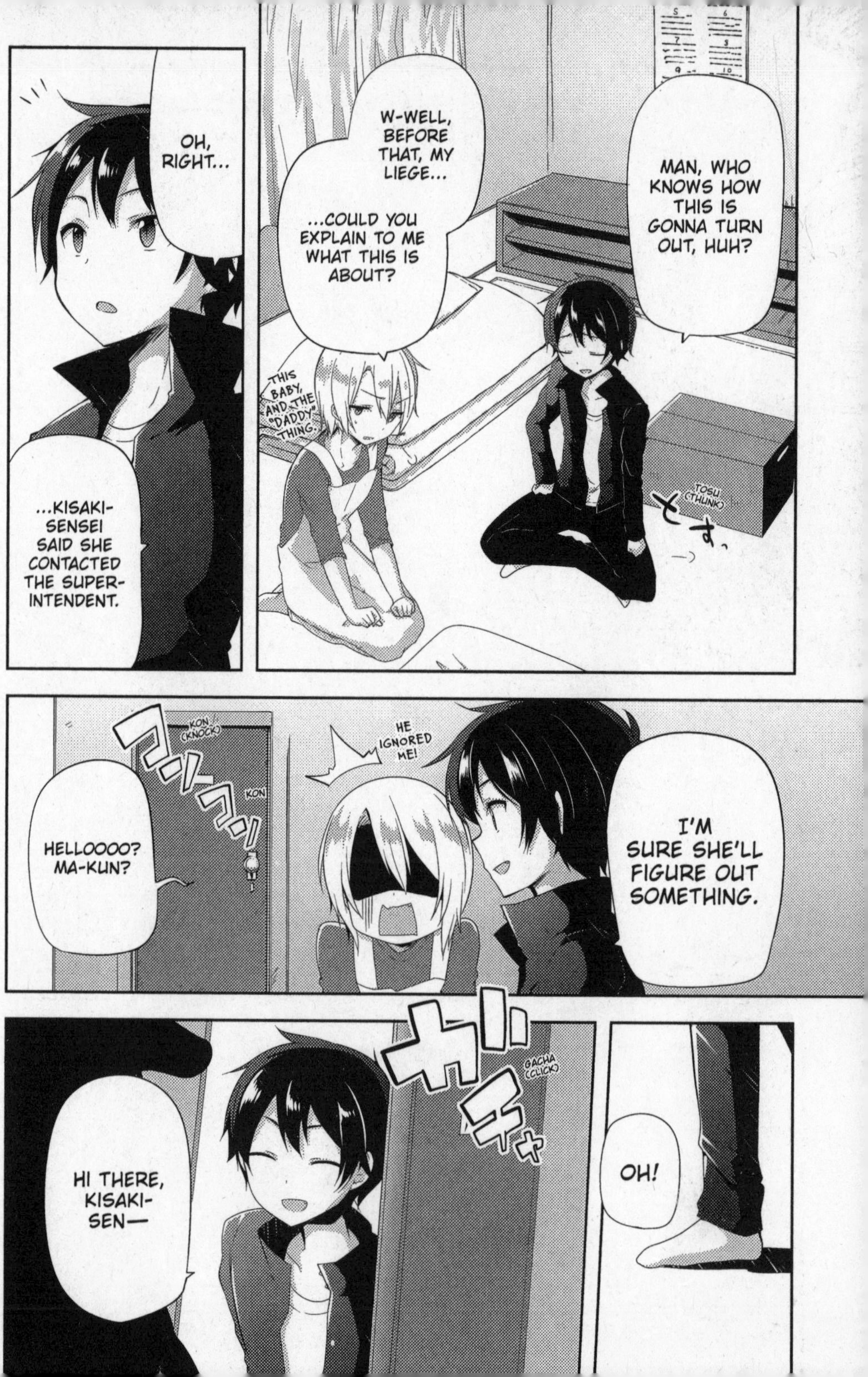
MAN, WHO KNOWS HOW THIS IS GONNA TURN OUT, HUH?
TOSU (THUNK)
W-WELL, BEFORE THAT, MY LIEGE...
...COULD YOU EXPLAIN TO ME WHAT THIS IS ABOUT?
THIS BABY, AND THE "DADDY" THING.
OH, RIGHT...
...KISAKI-SENSEI SAID SHE CONTACTED THE SUPER-INTENDENT.
I'M SURE SHE'LL FIGURE OUT SOMETHING.
HE IGNORED ME!
KON (KNOCK)
KON
HELLOOOO? MA-KUN?
OH!
GACHA (CLICK)
HI THERE, KISAKI-SEN—

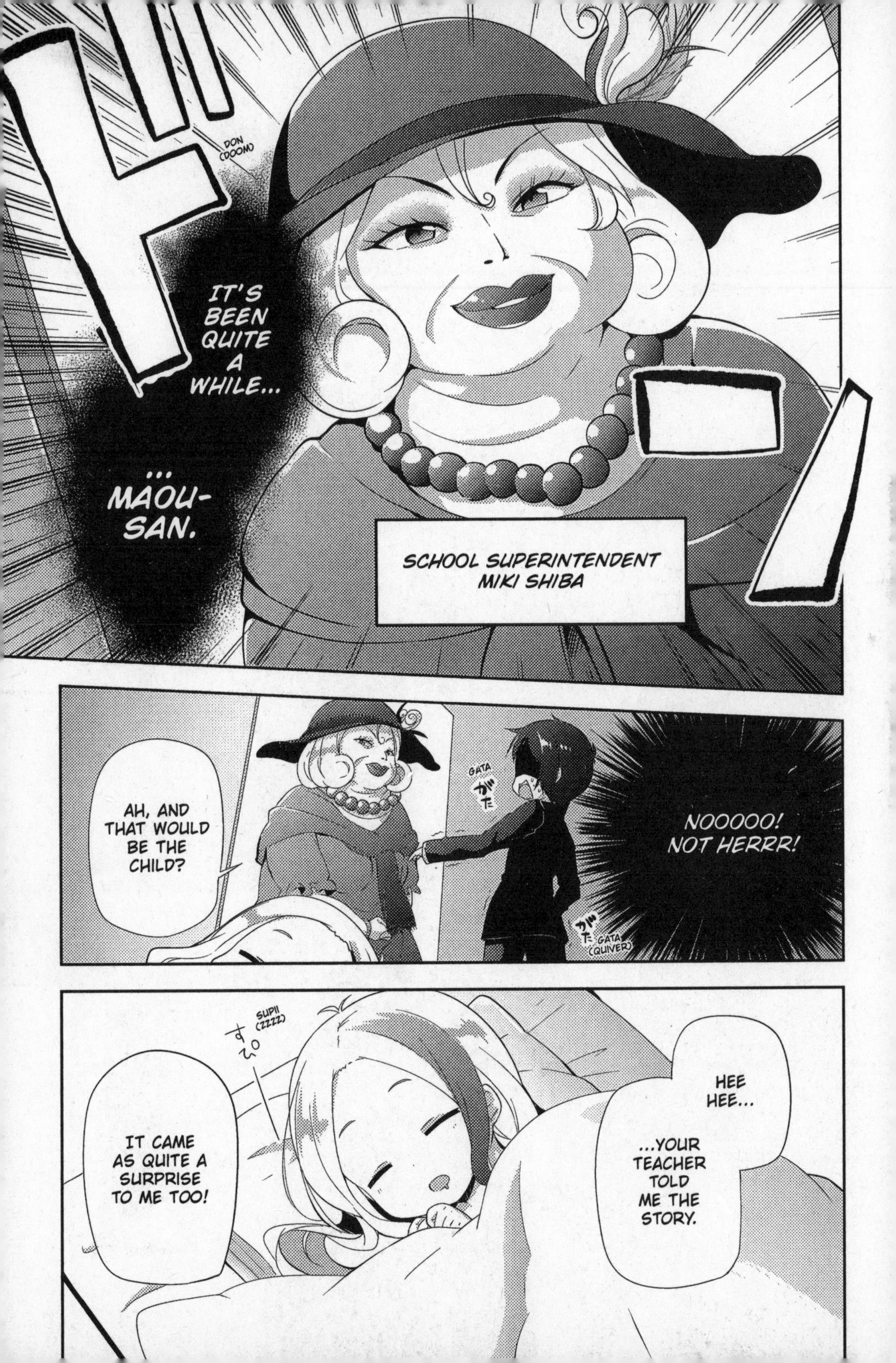
DON (DOOM)
IT'S BEEN QUITE A WHILE...
... MAOU-SAN.
SCHOOL SUPERINTENDENT MIKI SHIBA
NOOOOO! NOT HERRR!
GATA
がた
GATA (QUIVER)
がた
AH, AND THAT WOULD BE THE CHILD?
HEE HEE...
...YOUR TEACHER TOLD ME THE STORY.
SUPII (ZZZZ)
すぴ
IT CAME AS QUITE A SURPRISE TO ME TOO!

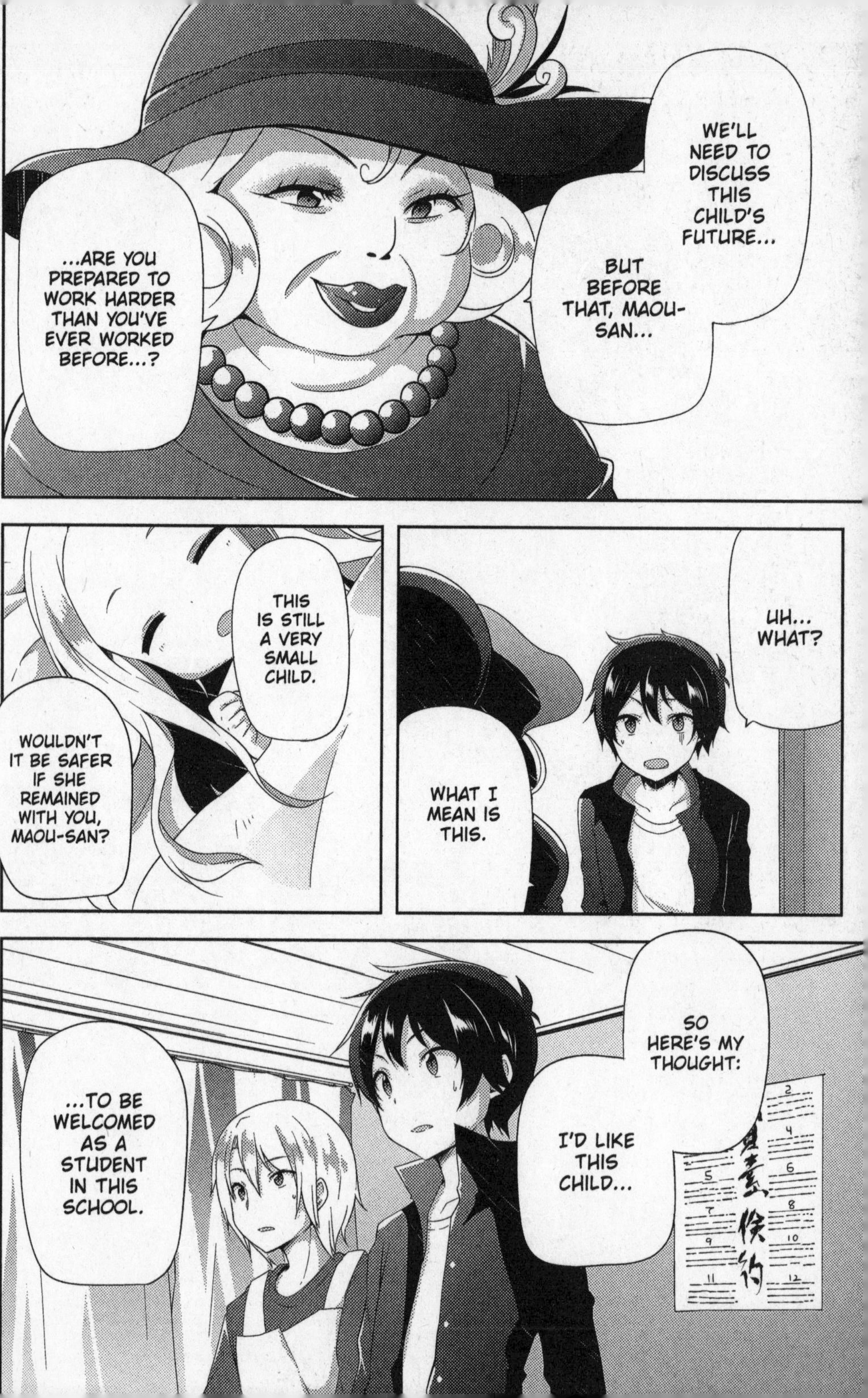
WE'LL NEED TO DISCUSS THIS CHILD'S FUTURE...
BUT BEFORE THAT, MAOU-SAN...
...ARE YOU PREPARED TO WORK HARDER THAN YOU'VE EVER WORKED BEFORE...?
UH... WHAT?
WHAT I MEAN IS THIS.
THIS IS STILL A VERY SMALL CHILD.
WOULDN'T IT BE SAFER IF SHE REMAINED WITH YOU, MAOU-SAN?
SO HERE'S MY THOUGHT:
I'D LIKE THIS CHILD...
...TO BE WELCOMED AS A STUDENT IN THIS SCHOOL.

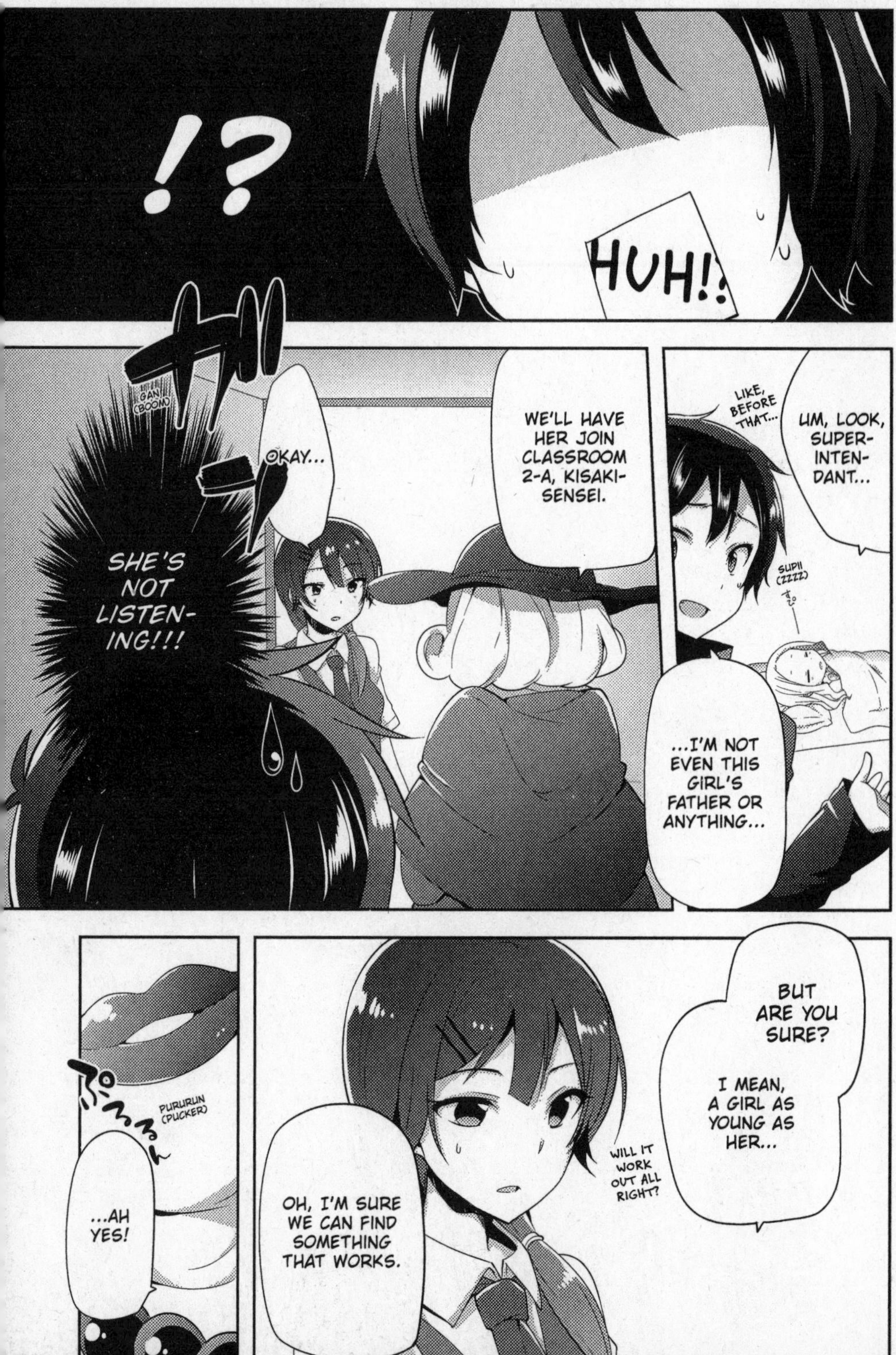
HUH!?
!?
UM, LOOK, SUPER-INTEN-DANT...
LIKE, BEFORE THAT...
SUPII (ZZZZ)
...I'M NOT EVEN THIS GIRL'S FATHER OR ANYTHING...
WE'LL HAVE HER JOIN CLASSROOM 2-A, KISAKI-SENSEI.
OKAY...
GAN (BOOM)
SHE'S NOT LISTEN-ING!!!
BUT ARE YOU SURE?
I MEAN, A GIRL AS YOUNG AS HER...
WILL IT WORK OUT ALL RIGHT?
OH, I'M SURE WE CAN FIND SOMETHING THAT WORKS.
PURURUN (PUCKER)
...AH YES!

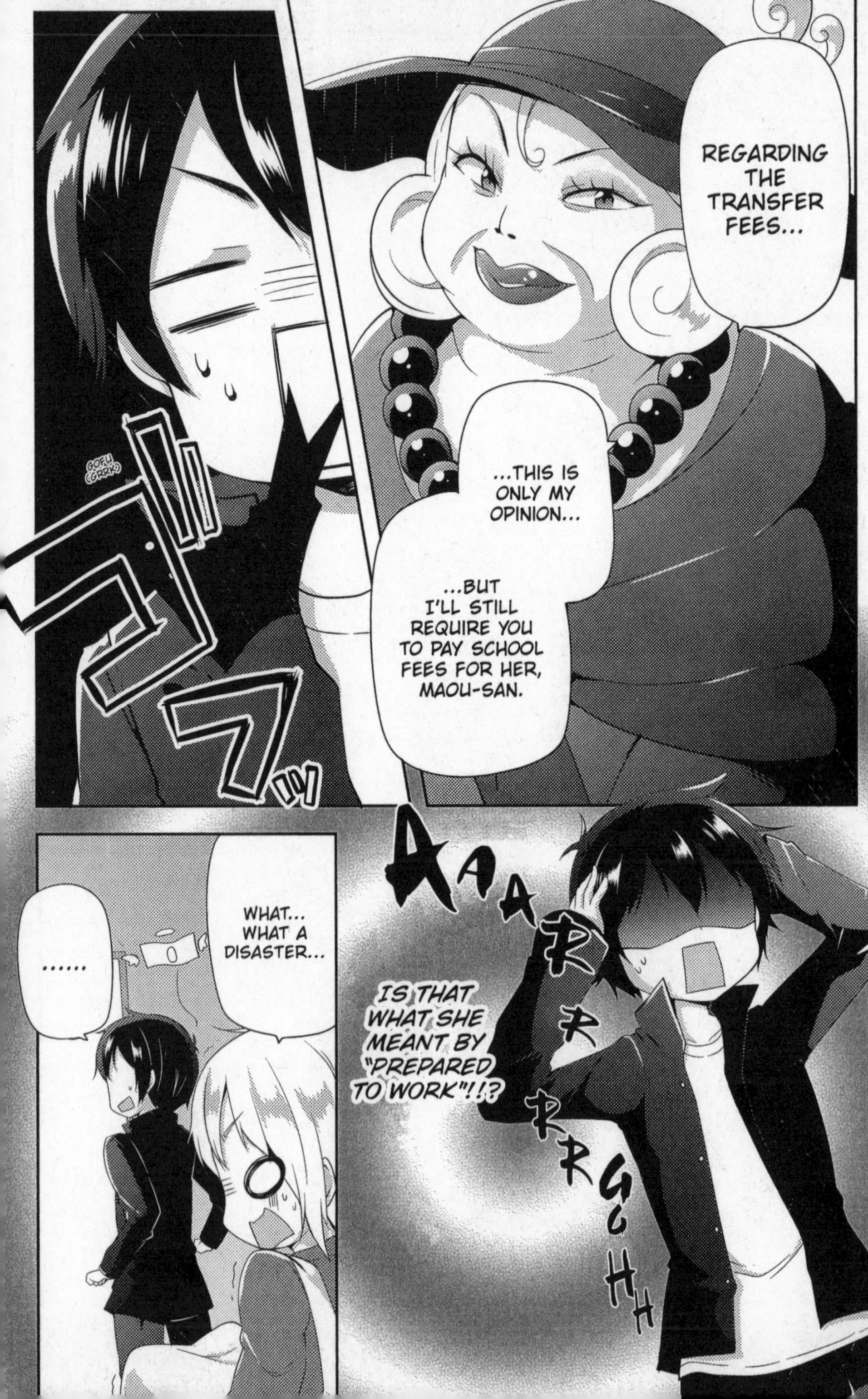
REGARDING THE TRANSFER FEES...
...THIS IS ONLY MY OPINION...
...BUT I'LL STILL REQUIRE YOU TO PAY SCHOOL FEES FOR HER, MAOU-SAN.
GOFU (GRRK)
AAARRRRGHH
IS THAT WHAT SHE MEANT BY "PREPARED TO WORK"!!?
WHAT... WHAT A DISASTER...
......

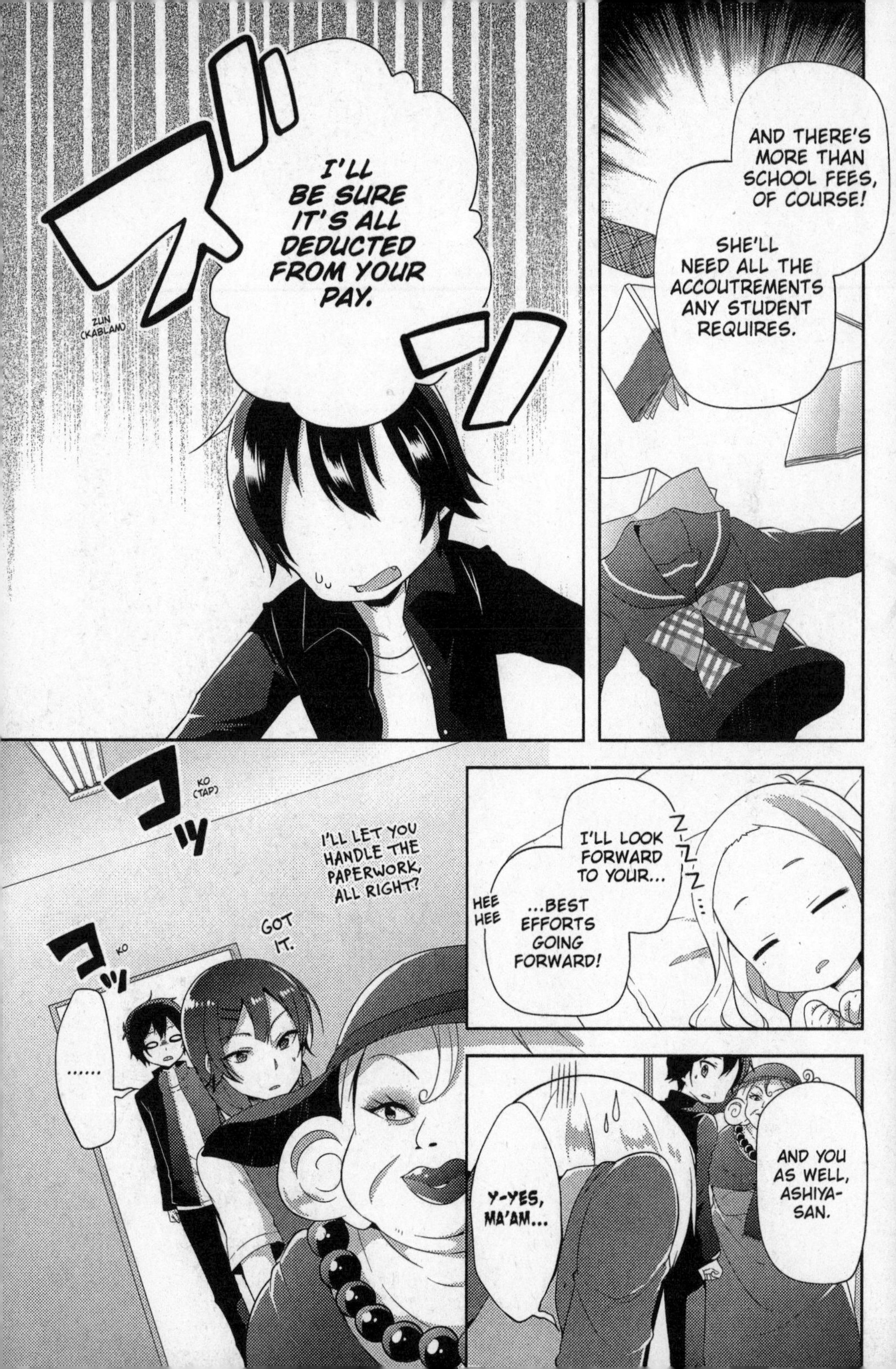
AND THERE'S MORE THAN SCHOOL FEES, OF COURSE!
SHE'LL NEED ALL THE ACCOUTREMENTS ANY STUDENT REQUIRES.
I'LL BE SURE IT'S ALL DEDUCTED FROM YOUR PAY.
ZUN (KABLAM)
I'LL LOOK FORWARD TO YOUR...
Z-Z-Z...
HEE HEE
...BEST EFFORTS GOING FORWARD!
AND YOU AS WELL, ASHIYA-SAN.
Y-YES, MA'AM...
KO (TAP)
I'LL LET YOU HANDLE THE PAPERWORK, ALL RIGHT?
GOT IT.
KO
......

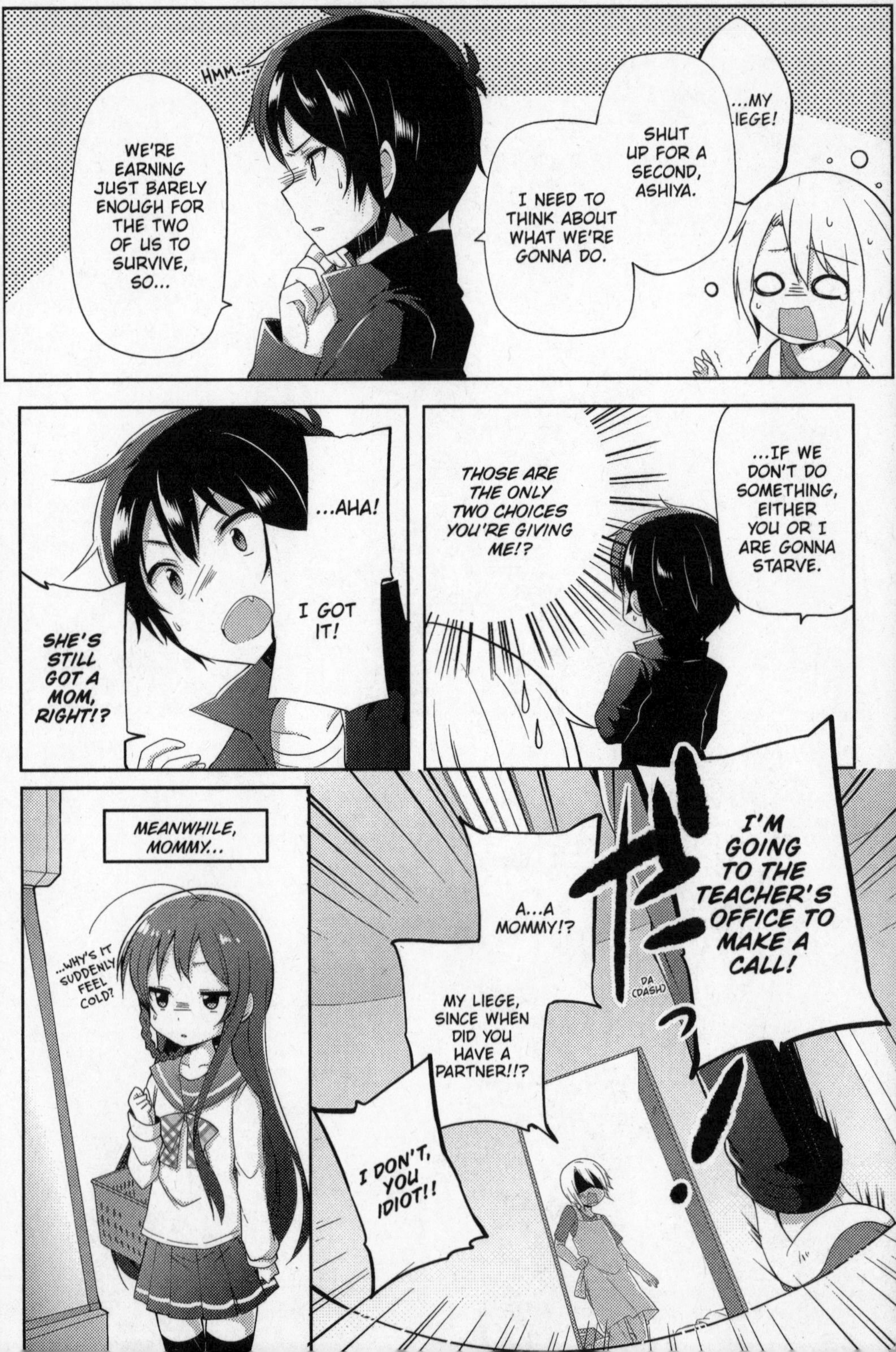
...MY LIEGE!
SHUT UP FOR A SECOND, ASHIYA.
I NEED TO THINK ABOUT WHAT WE'RE GONNA DO.
HMM...
WE'RE EARNING JUST BARELY ENOUGH FOR THE TWO OF US TO SURVIVE, SO...
...IF WE DON'T DO SOMETHING, EITHER YOU OR I ARE GONNA STARVE.
THOSE ARE THE ONLY TWO CHOICES YOU'RE GIVING ME!?
...AHA!
I GOT IT!
SHE'S STILL GOT A MOM, RIGHT!?
I'M GOING TO THE TEACHER'S OFFICE TO MAKE A CALL!
DA (DASH)
A...A MOMMY!?
MY LIEGE, SINCE WHEN DID YOU HAVE A PARTNER!!?
I DON'T, YOU IDIOT!!
MEANWHILE, MOMMY...
...WHY'S IT SUDDENLY FEEL COLD?

THE DEVIL IS A PART-TIMER! HIGH SCHOOL!

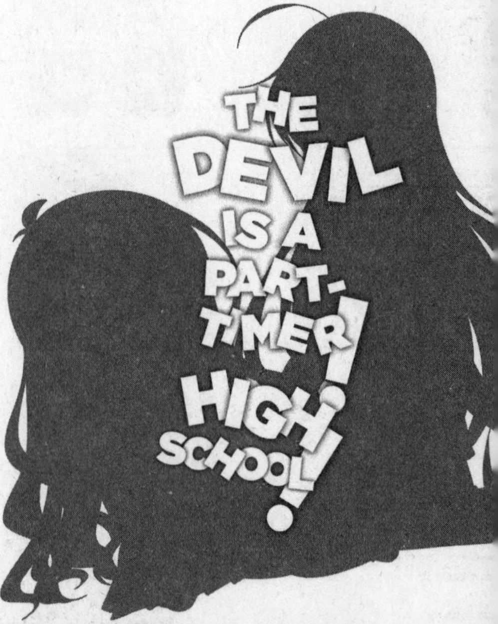
THE DEVIL IS A PART-TIMER! HIGH SCHOOL!

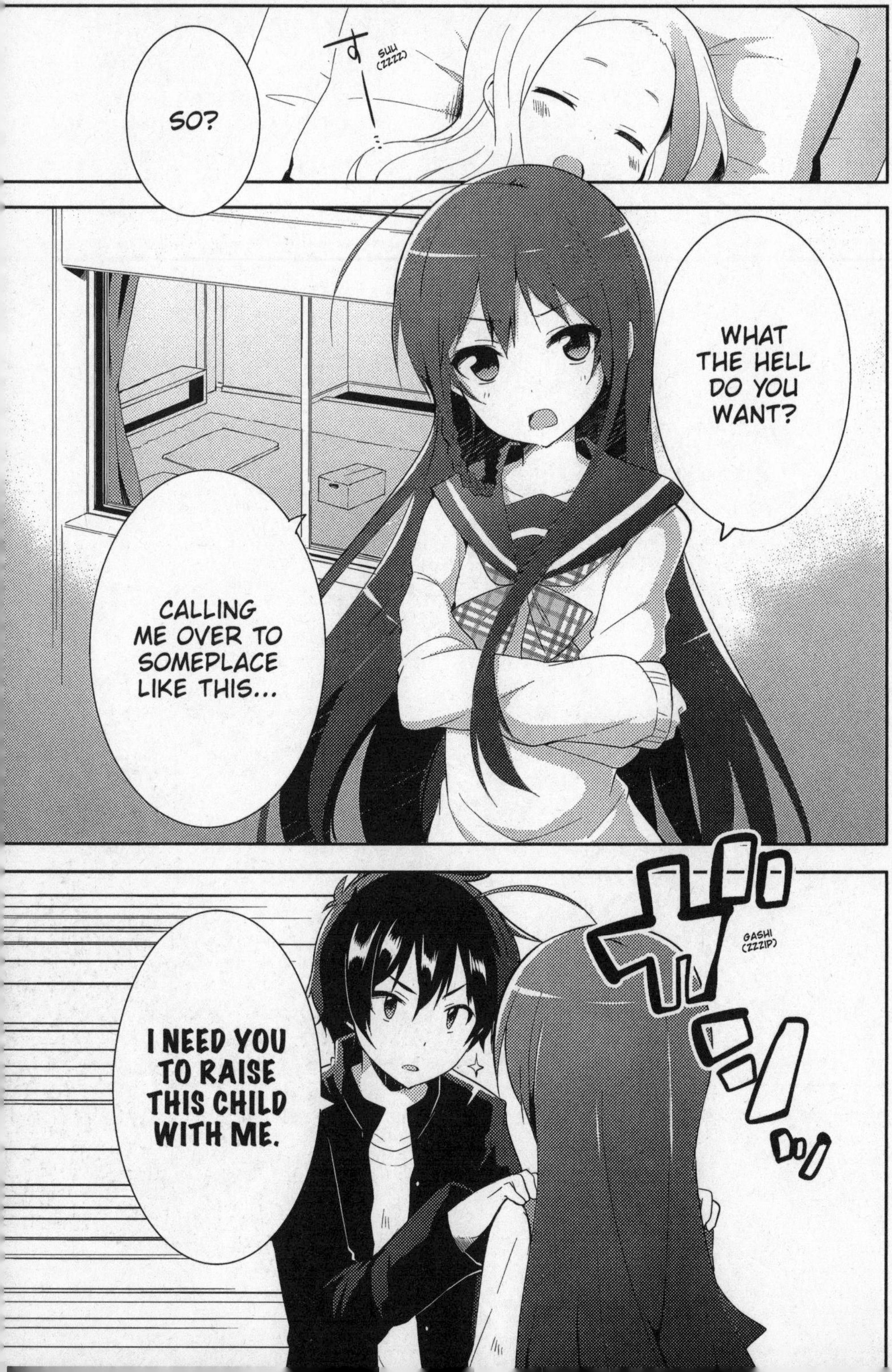
す
SUU (ZZZZ)
SO?
WHAT THE HELL DO YOU WANT?
CALLING ME OVER TO SOMEPLACE LIKE THIS...
GASHI (ZZZIP)
I NEED YOU TO RAISE THIS CHILD WITH ME.

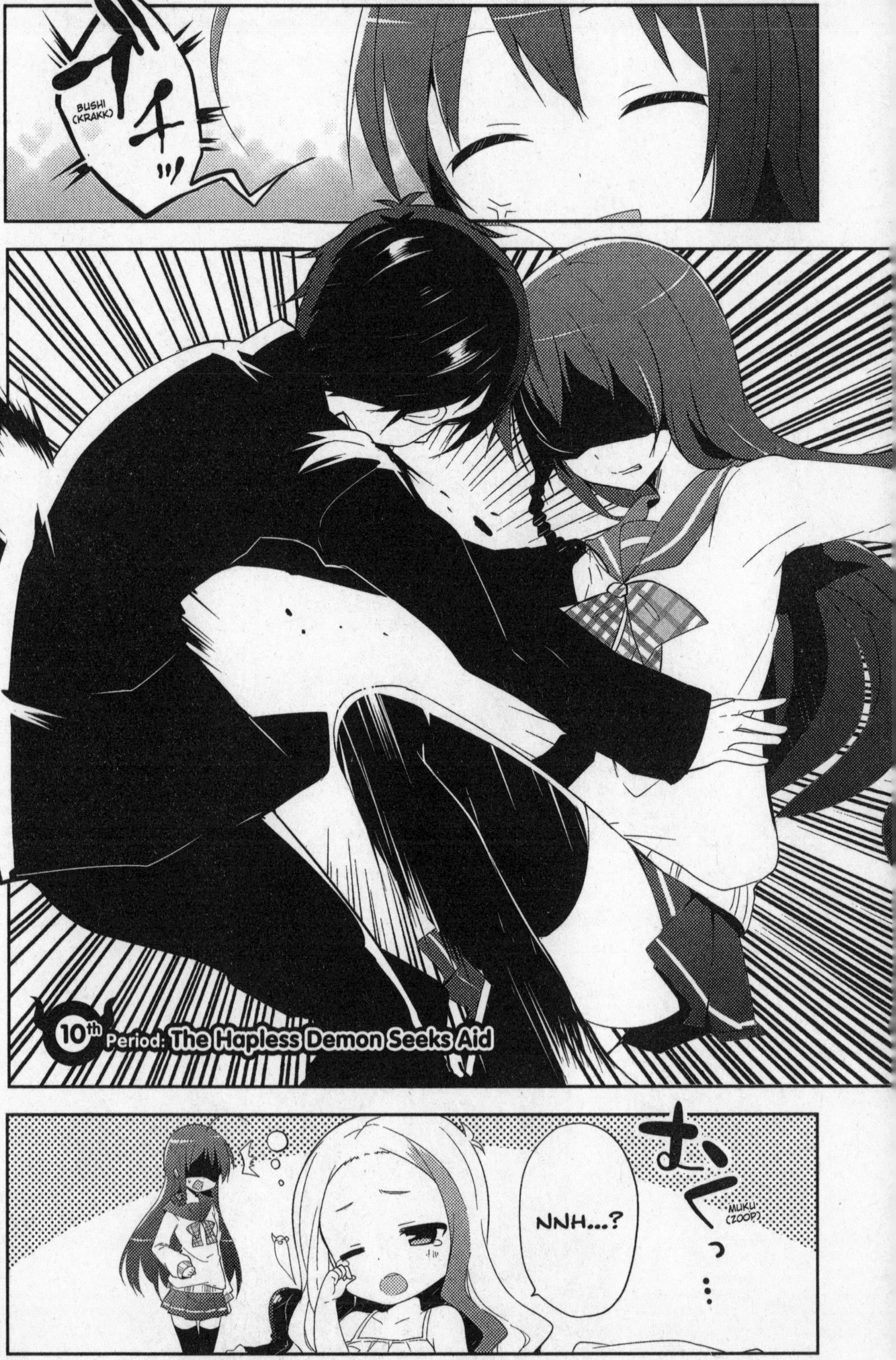
BUSHI (KRAKK)
10th Period: The Hapless Demon Seeks Aid
MUKU (ZOOP)
NNH...?

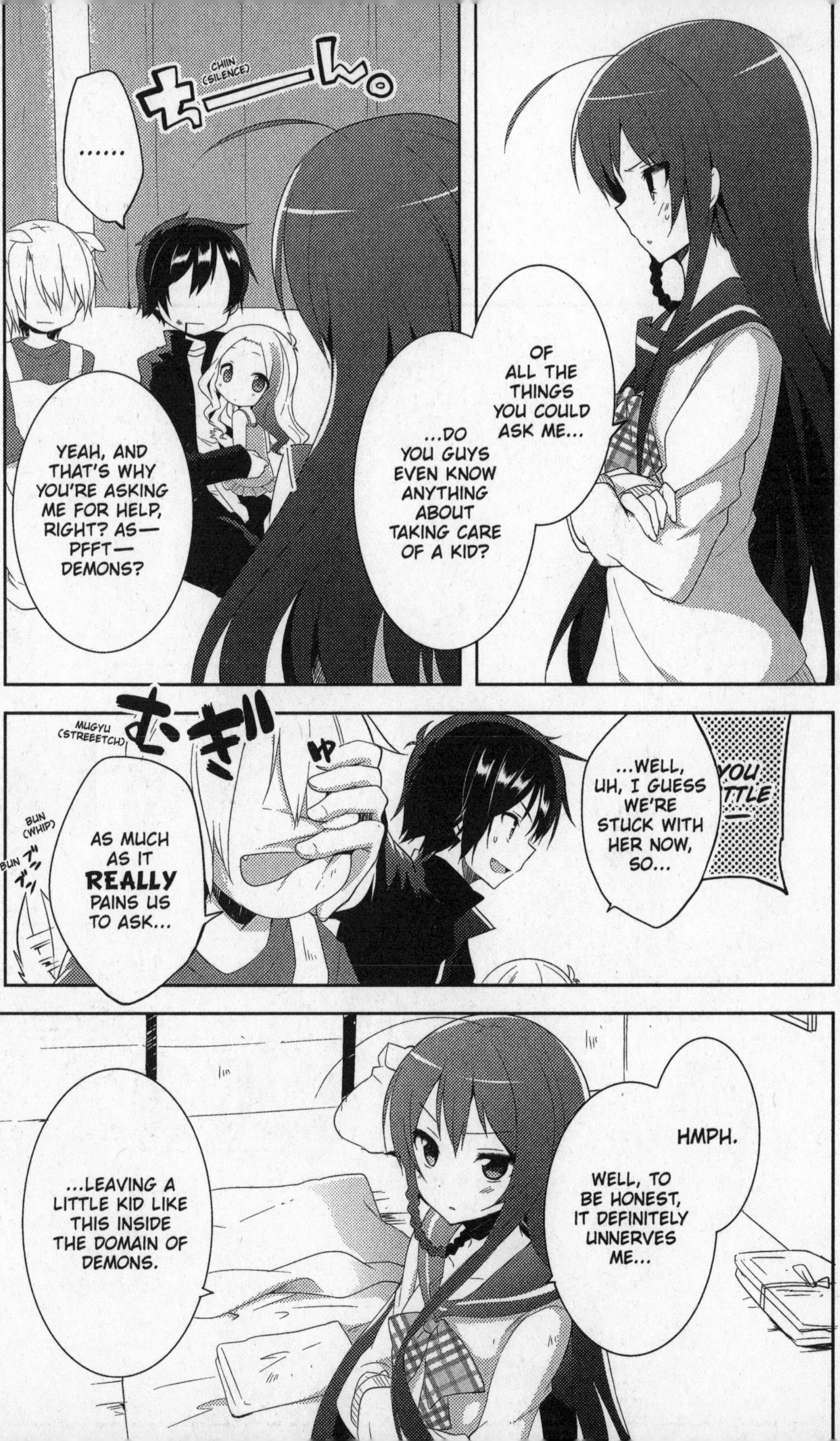

OF ALL THE THINGS YOU COULD ASK ME...
...DO YOU GUYS EVEN KNOW ANYTHING ABOUT TAKING CARE OF A KID?
CHIIN (SILENCE)
......
YEAH, AND THAT'S WHY YOU'RE ASKING ME FOR HELP, RIGHT? AS—PFFT—DEMONS?
...WELL, UH, I GUESS WE'RE STUCK WITH HER NOW, SO...
MUGYU (STREEETCH)
AS MUCH AS IT **REALLY** PAINS US TO ASK...
BUN (WHIP)
BUN
HMPH.
WELL, TO BE HONEST, IT DEFINITELY UNNERVES ME...
...LEAVING A LITTLE KID LIKE THIS INSIDE THE DOMAIN OF DEMONS.

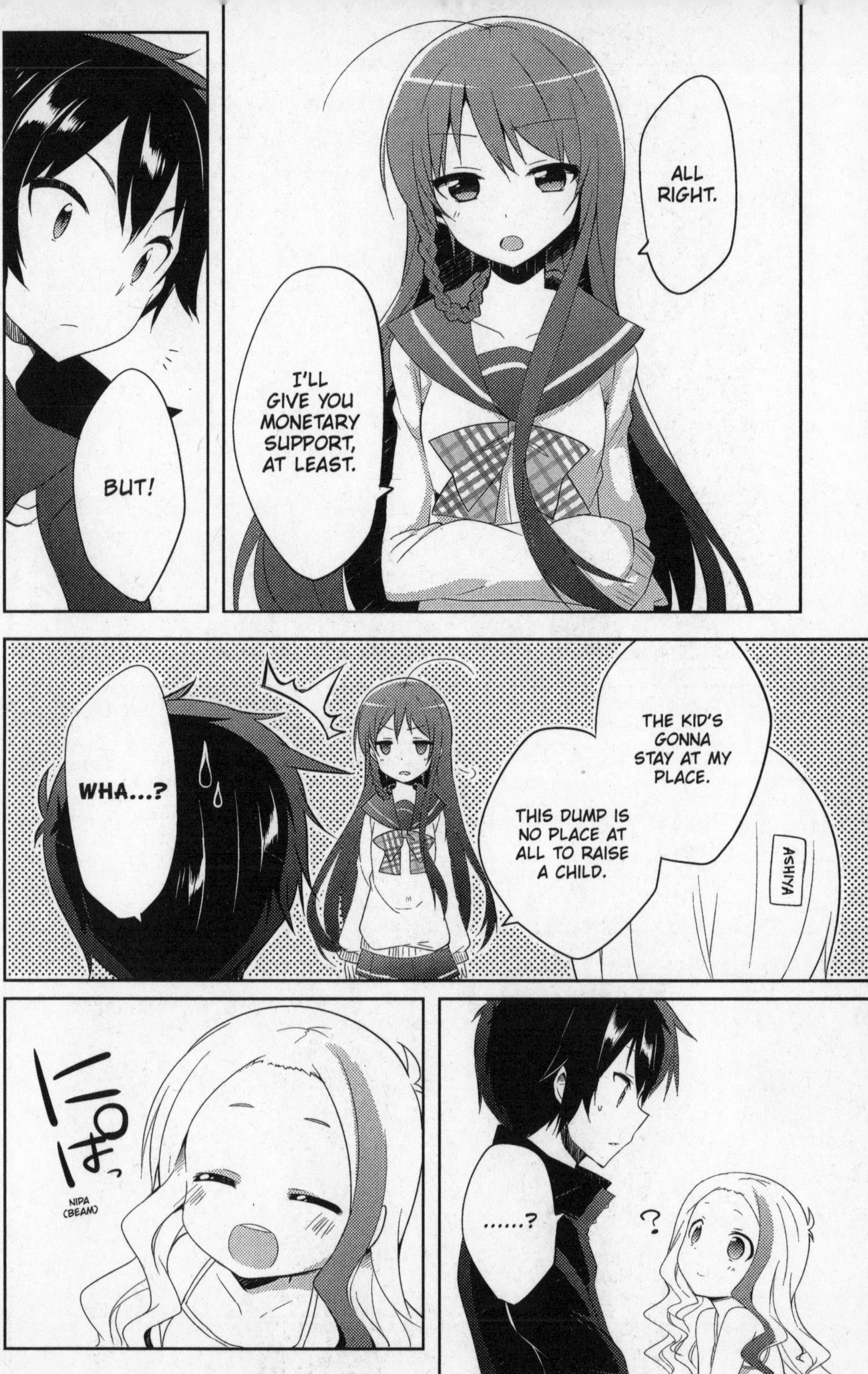
ALL RIGHT.
I'LL GIVE YOU MONETARY SUPPORT, AT LEAST.
BUT!
THE KID'S GONNA STAY AT MY PLACE.
THIS DUMP IS NO PLACE AT ALL TO RAISE A CHILD.
ASHIYA
WHA...?
......?
?
にぱっ
NIPA (BEAM)

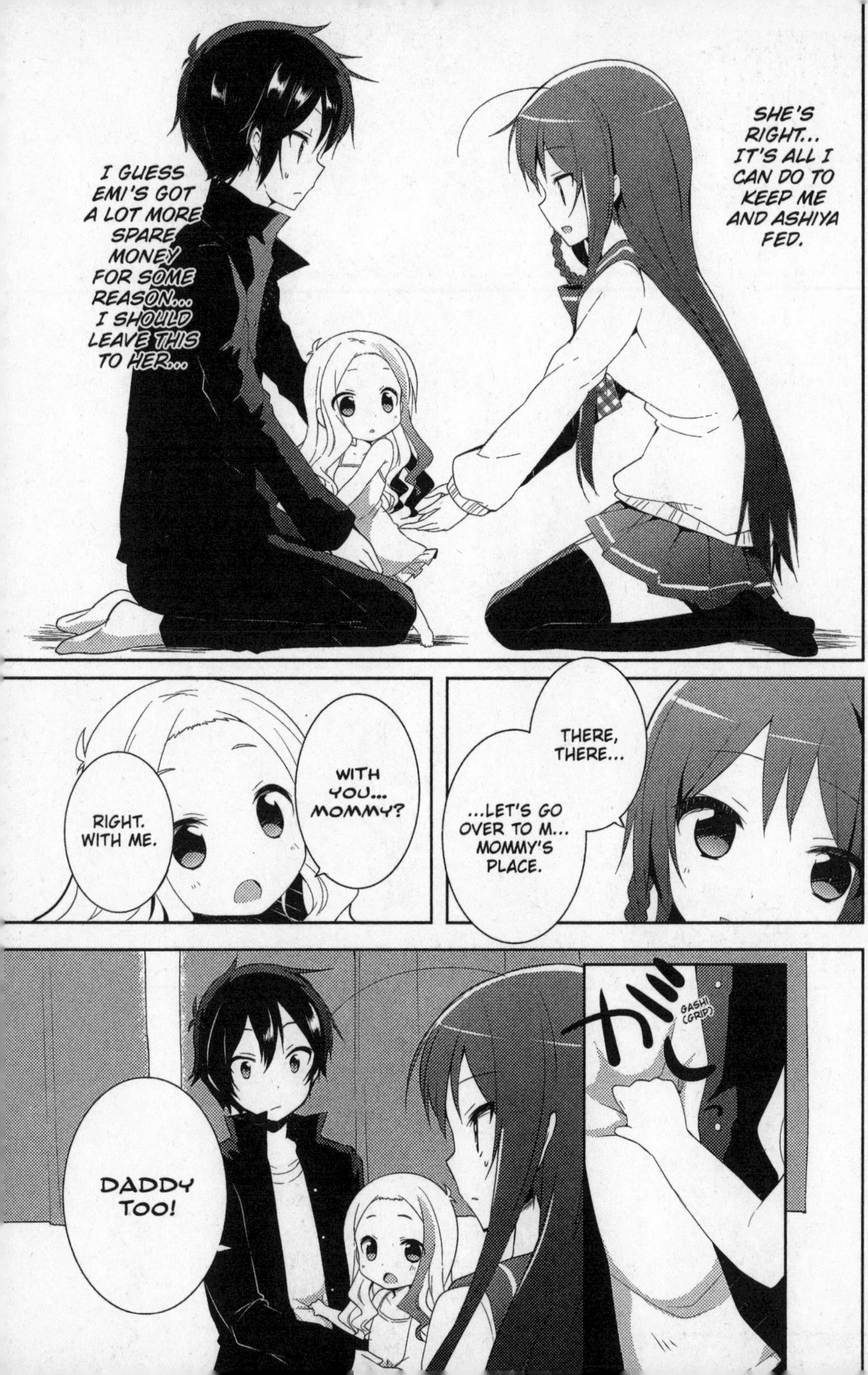
SHE'S RIGHT... IT'S ALL I CAN DO TO KEEP ME AND ASHIYA FED.
I GUESS EMI'S GOT A LOT MORE SPARE MONEY FOR SOME REASON... I SHOULD LEAVE THIS TO HER...
THERE, THERE...
...LET'S GO OVER TO M... MOMMY'S PLACE.
WITH YOU... MOMMY?
RIGHT. WITH ME.
GASHI (GRIP)
DADDY TOO!

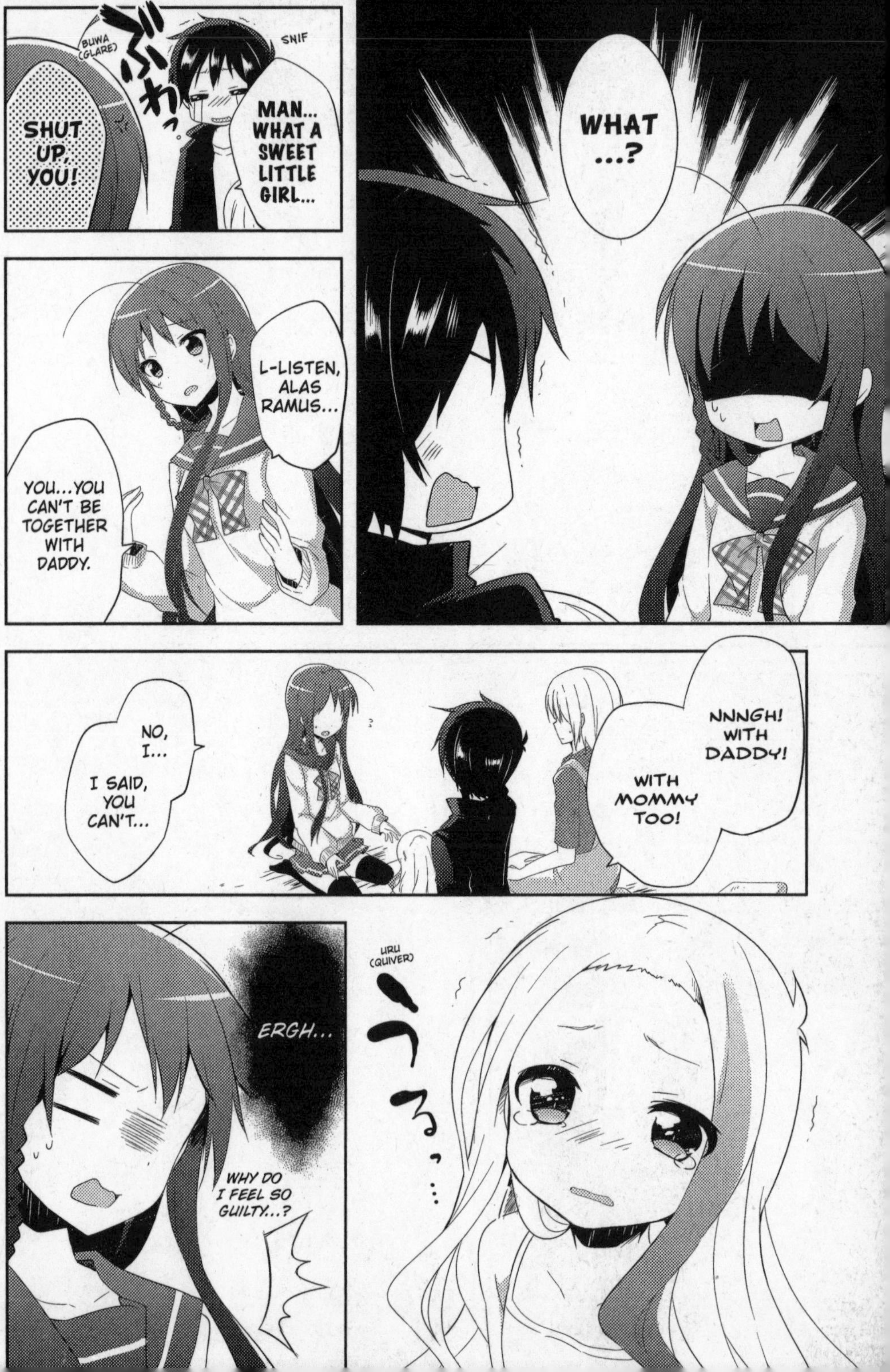
WHAT ...?
SNIF
MAN... WHAT A SWEET LITTLE GIRL...
BUWA (GLARE)
ぶわっ
SHUT UP, YOU!
L-LISTEN, ALAS RAMUS...
YOU...YOU CAN'T BE TOGETHER WITH DADDY.
NNNGH! WITH DADDY!
WITH MOMMY TOO!
NO, I...
I SAID, YOU CAN'T...
URU (QUIVER)
うる...
ERGH...
WHY DO I FEEL SO GUILTY...?

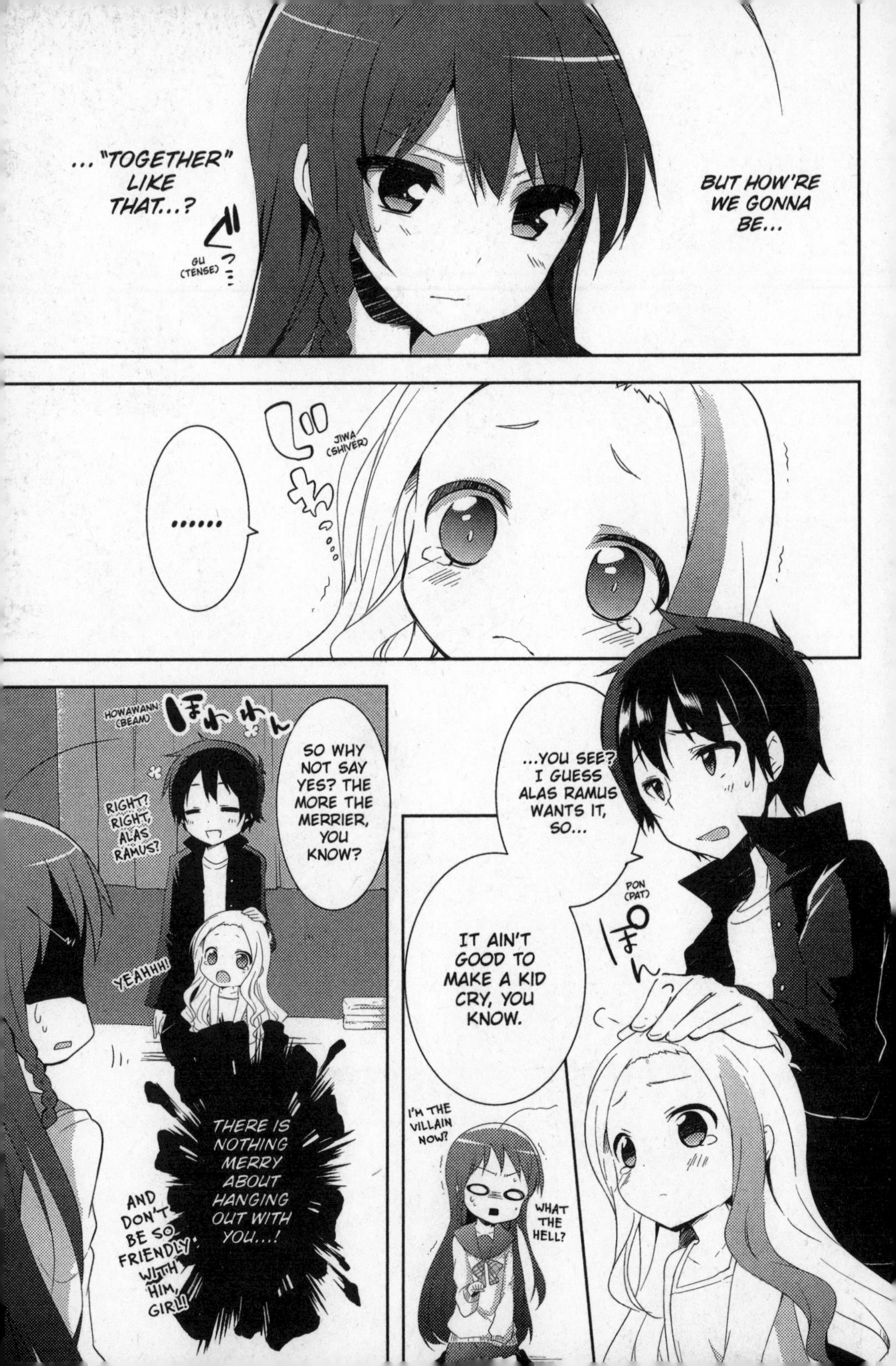
BUT HOW'RE WE GONNA BE...
..."TOGETHER" LIKE THAT...?
GU (TENSE)
JIWA (SHIVER)
......
...YOU SEE? I GUESS ALAS RAMUS WANTS IT, SO...
PON (PAT)
IT AIN'T GOOD TO MAKE A KID CRY, YOU KNOW.
I'M THE VILLAIN NOW?
WHAT THE HELL?
HOWAWANN (BEAM)
SO WHY NOT SAY YES? THE MORE THE MERRIER, YOU KNOW?
RIGHT? RIGHT, ALAS RAMUS?
YEAHHH!
THERE IS NOTHING MERRY ABOUT HANGING OUT WITH YOU...!
AND DON'T BE SO FRIENDLY WITH HIM, GIRL!!

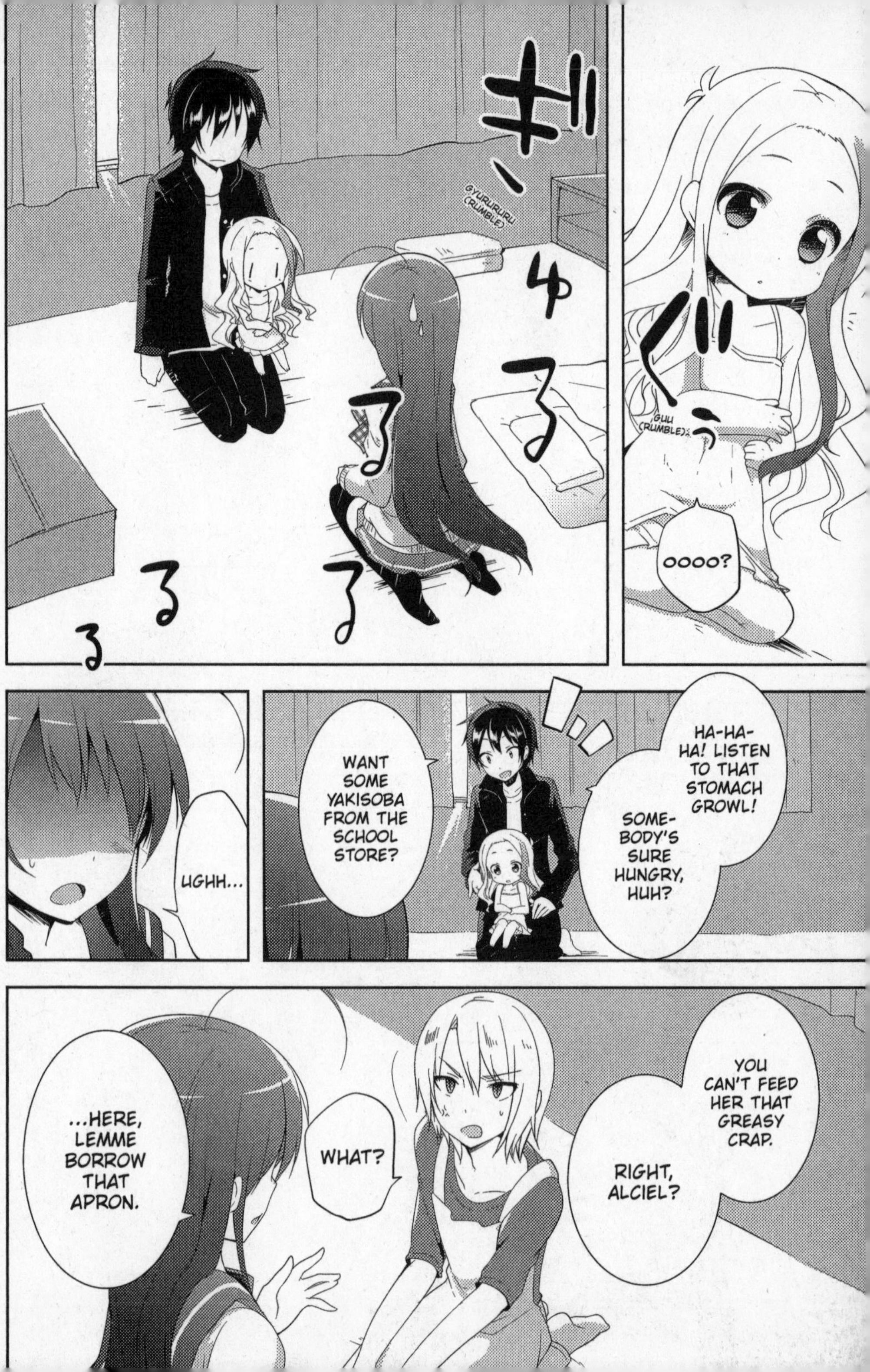
GUU (RUMBLE)
OOOO?
GYURURURU (RUMBLE)
HA-HA-HA! LISTEN TO THAT STOMACH GROWL!
SOME-BODY'S SURE HUNGRY, HUH?
WANT SOME YAKISOBA FROM THE SCHOOL STORE?
UGHH...
YOU CAN'T FEED HER THAT GREASY CRAP.
RIGHT, ALCIEL?
WHAT?
...HERE, LEMME BORROW THAT APRON.

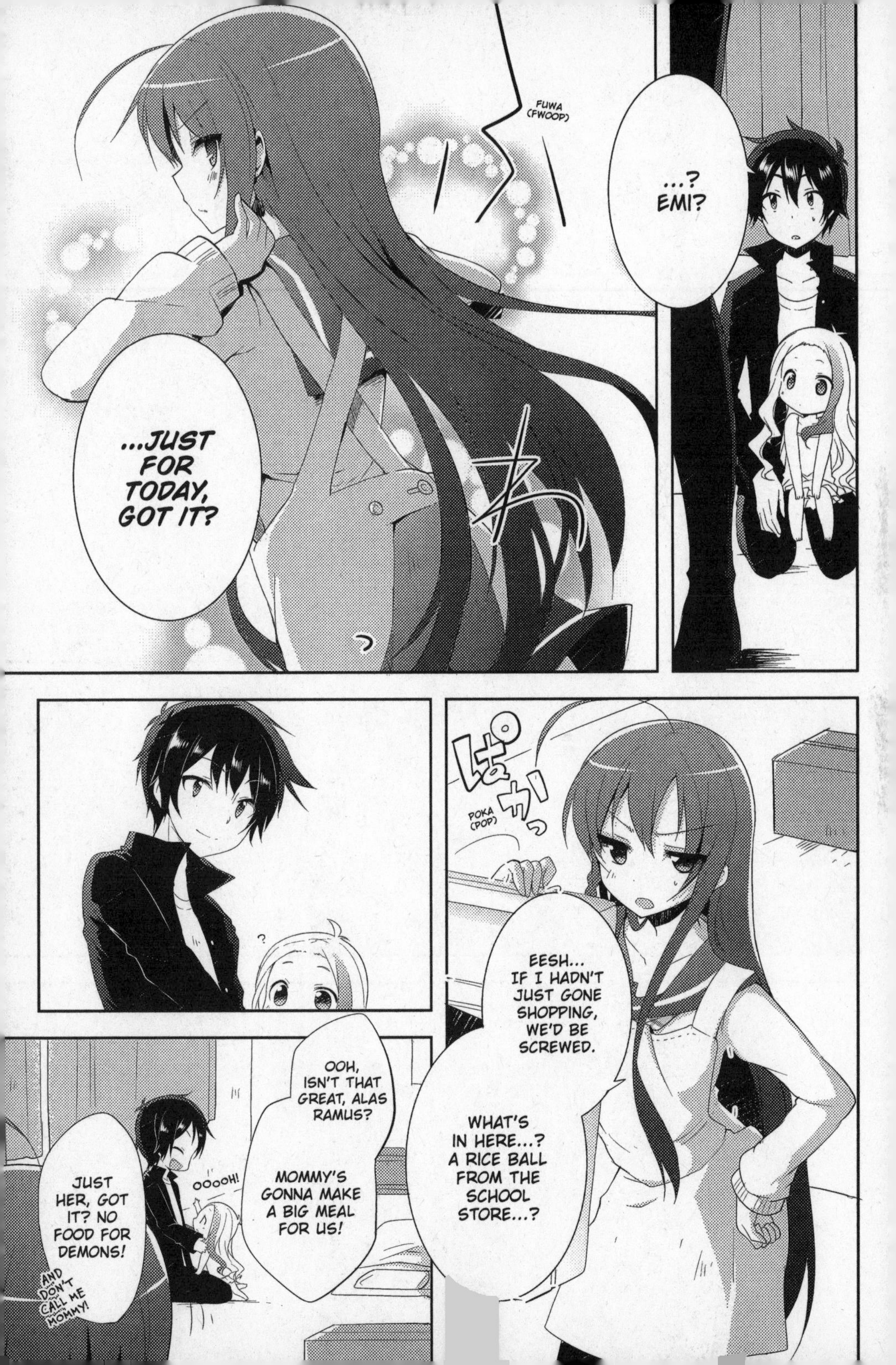
...? EMI?
FUWA (FWOOP)
...JUST FOR TODAY, GOT IT?
POKA (POP)
EESH... IF I HADN'T JUST GONE SHOPPING, WE'D BE SCREWED.
WHAT'S IN HERE...? A RICE BALL FROM THE SCHOOL STORE...?
?
OOH, ISN'T THAT GREAT, ALAS RAMUS?
MOMMY'S GONNA MAKE A BIG MEAL FOR US!
OOOOH!
JUST HER, GOT IT? NO FOOD FOR DEMONS!
AND DON'T CALL ME MOMMY!

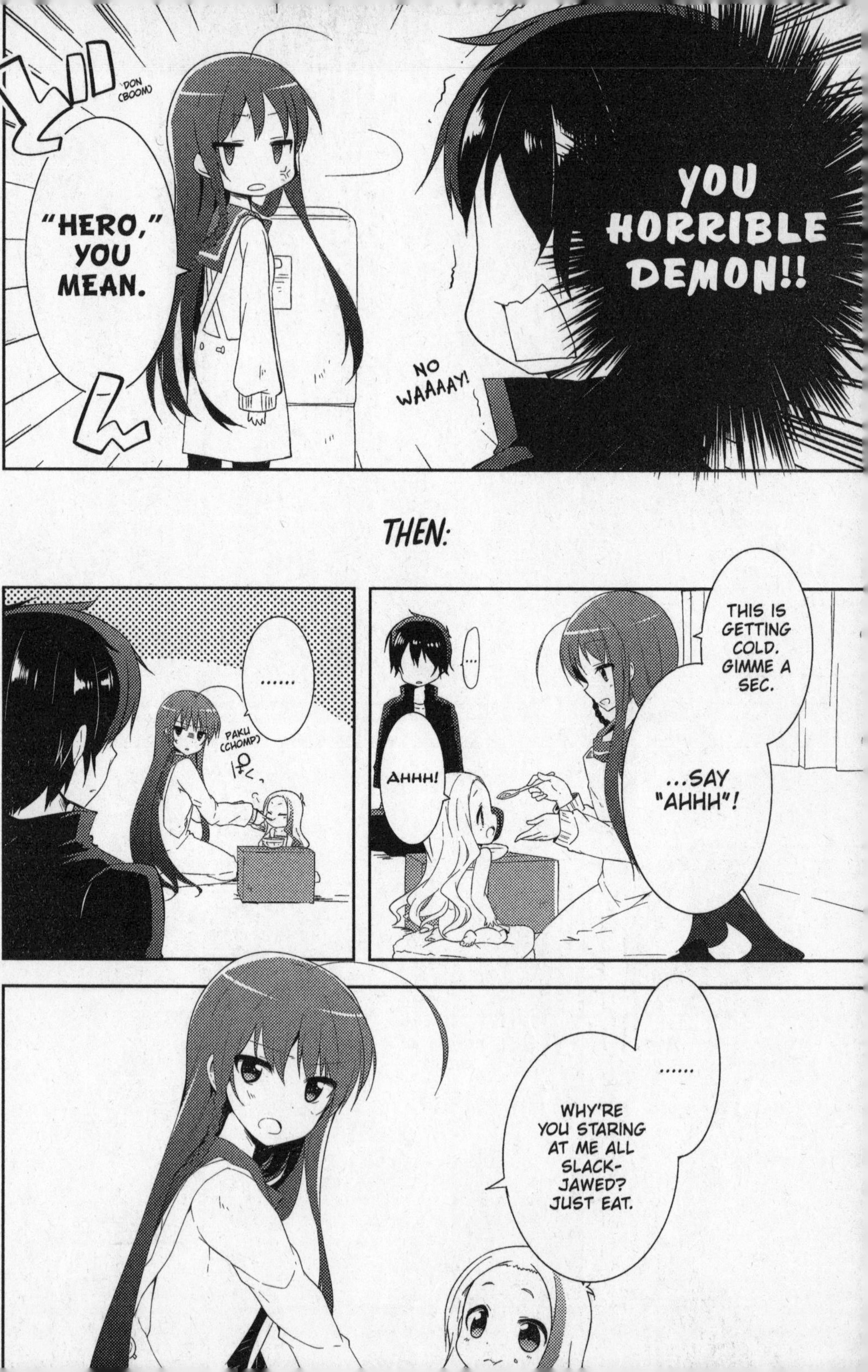
YOU HORRIBLE DEMON!!
NO WAAAAY!
DON (BOOM)
"HERO," YOU MEAN.
THEN:
THIS IS GETTING COLD. GIMME A SEC.
...SAY "AHHH"!
...
AHHH!
......
PAKU (CHOMP)
......
WHY'RE YOU STARING AT ME ALL SLACK-JAWED? JUST EAT.

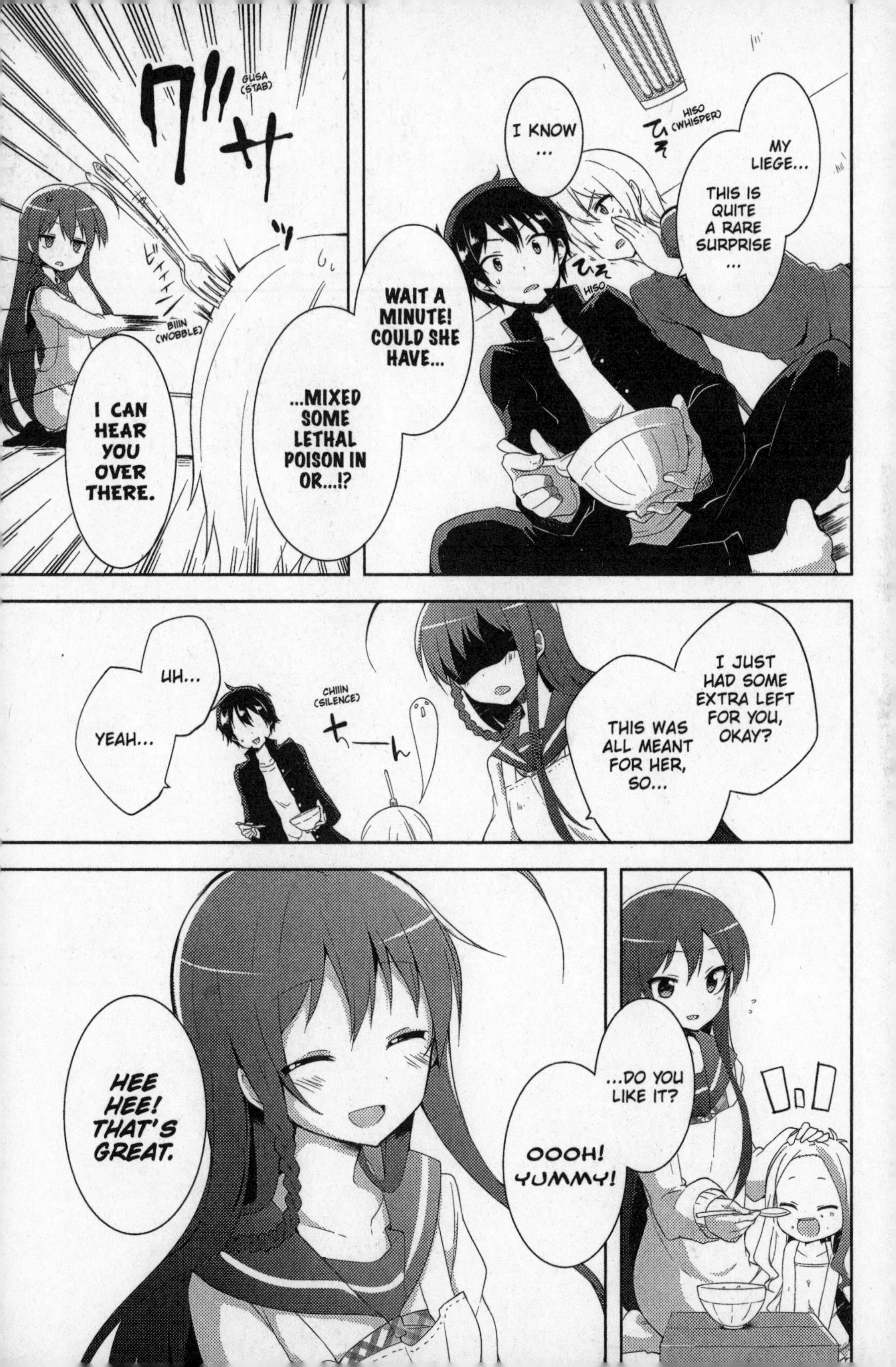
MY LIEGE... THIS IS QUITE A RARE SURPRISE ...
HISO (WHISPER)
I KNOW ...
HISO
WAIT A MINUTE! COULD SHE HAVE...
...MIXED SOME LETHAL POISON IN OR...!?
GUSA (STAB)
BIIIN (WOBBLE)
I CAN HEAR YOU OVER THERE.
I JUST HAD SOME EXTRA LEFT FOR YOU, OKAY?
THIS WAS ALL MEANT FOR HER, SO...
CHIIIN (SILENCE)
UH... YEAH...
...DO YOU LIKE IT?
OOOH! YUMMY!
HEE HEE! THAT'S GREAT.

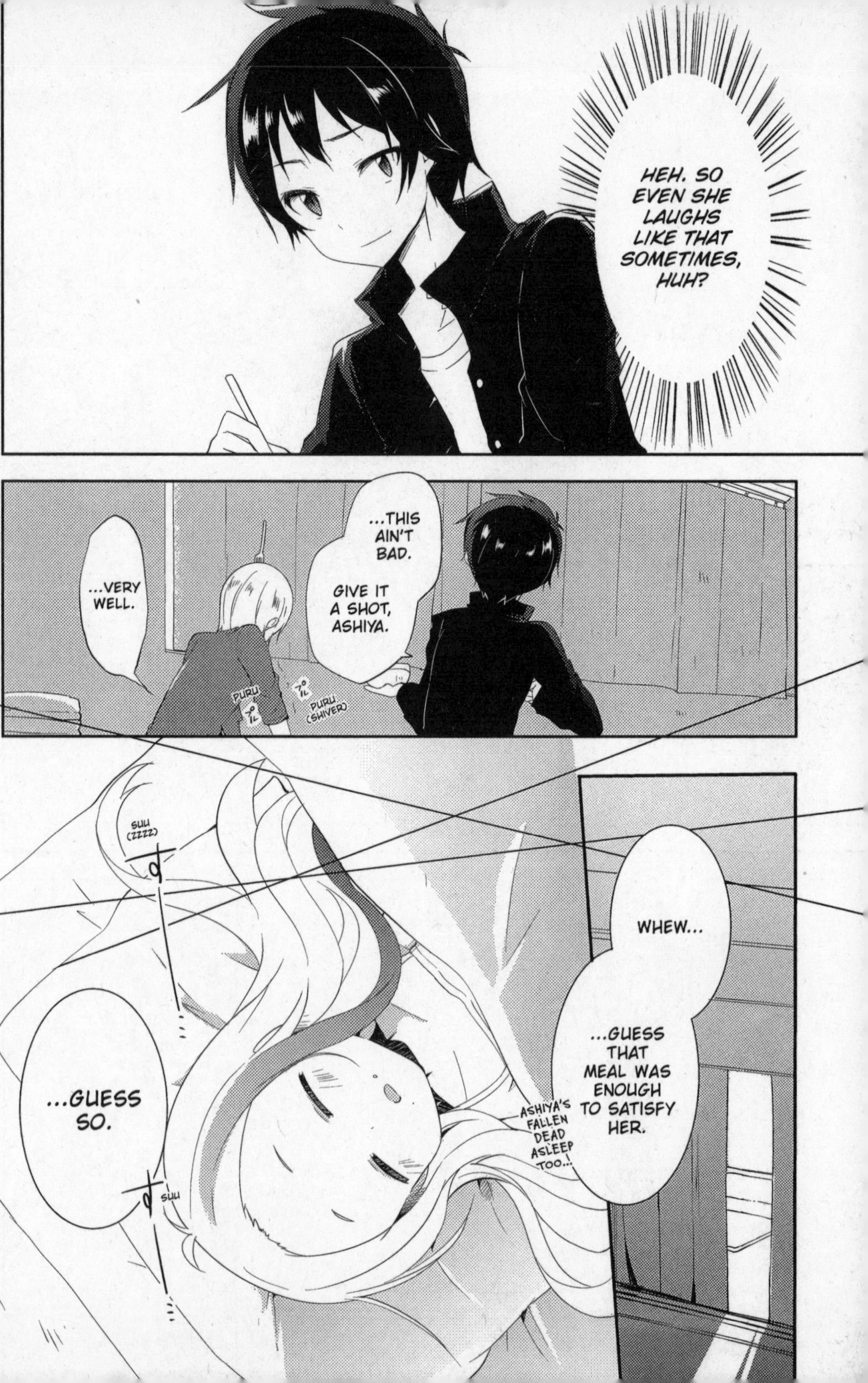
HEH. SO EVEN SHE LAUGHS LIKE THAT SOMETIMES, HUH?
...THIS AIN'T BAD.
GIVE IT A SHOT, ASHIYA.
...VERY WELL.
PURU
PURU (SHIVER)
WHEW...
...GUESS THAT MEAL WAS ENOUGH TO SATISFY HER.
ASHIYA'S FALLEN DEAD ASLEEP TOO..!
SUU (ZZZZ)
...GUESS SO.
SUU

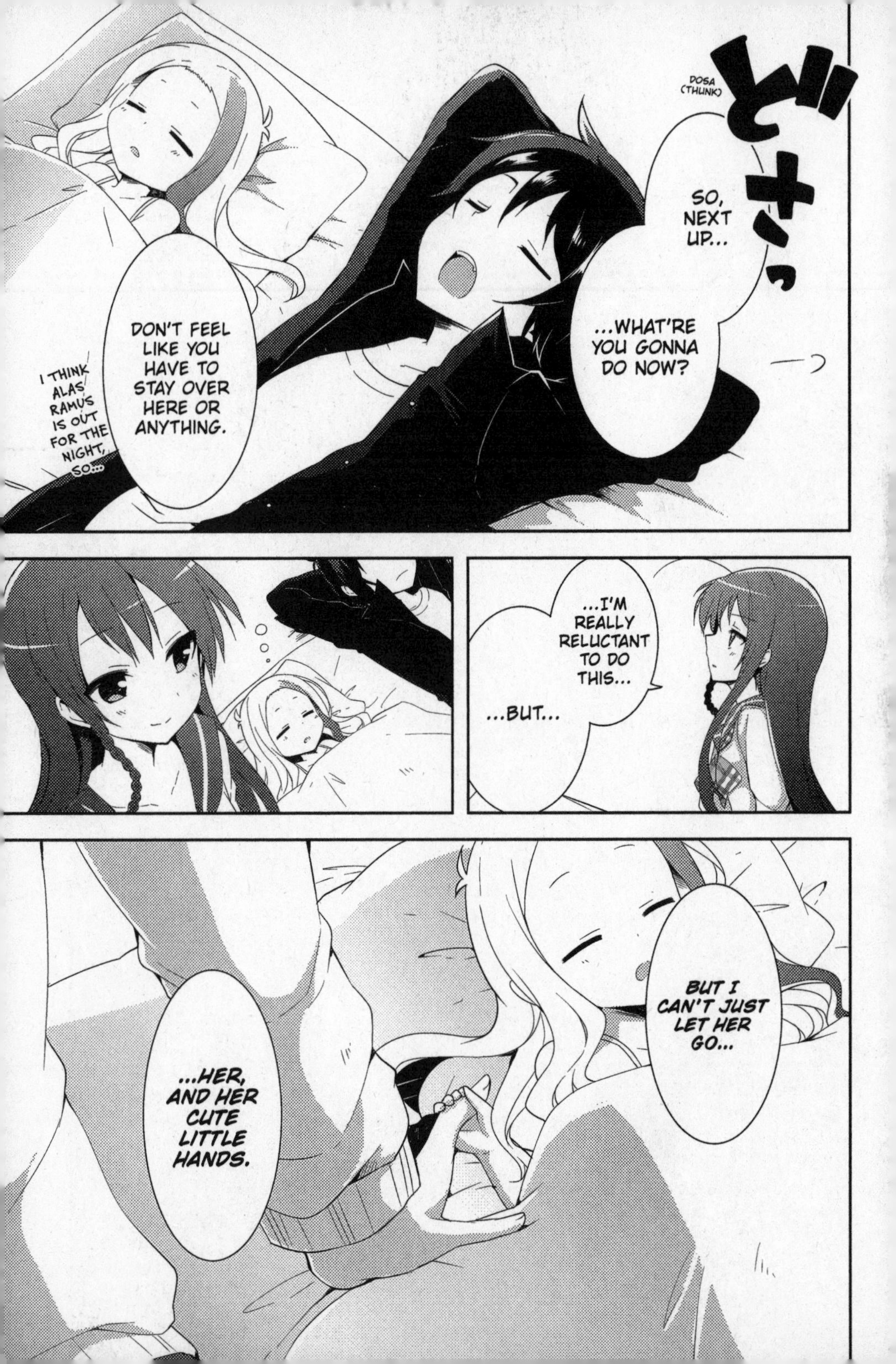
どさっ
DOSA (THUNK)
SO, NEXT UP...
...WHAT'RE YOU GONNA DO NOW?
DON'T FEEL LIKE YOU HAVE TO STAY OVER HERE OR ANYTHING.
I THINK ALAS RAMUS IS OUT FOR THE NIGHT, SO...
...I'M REALLY RELUCTANT TO DO THIS...
...BUT...
BUT I CAN'T JUST LET HER GO...
...HER, AND HER CUTE LITTLE HANDS.

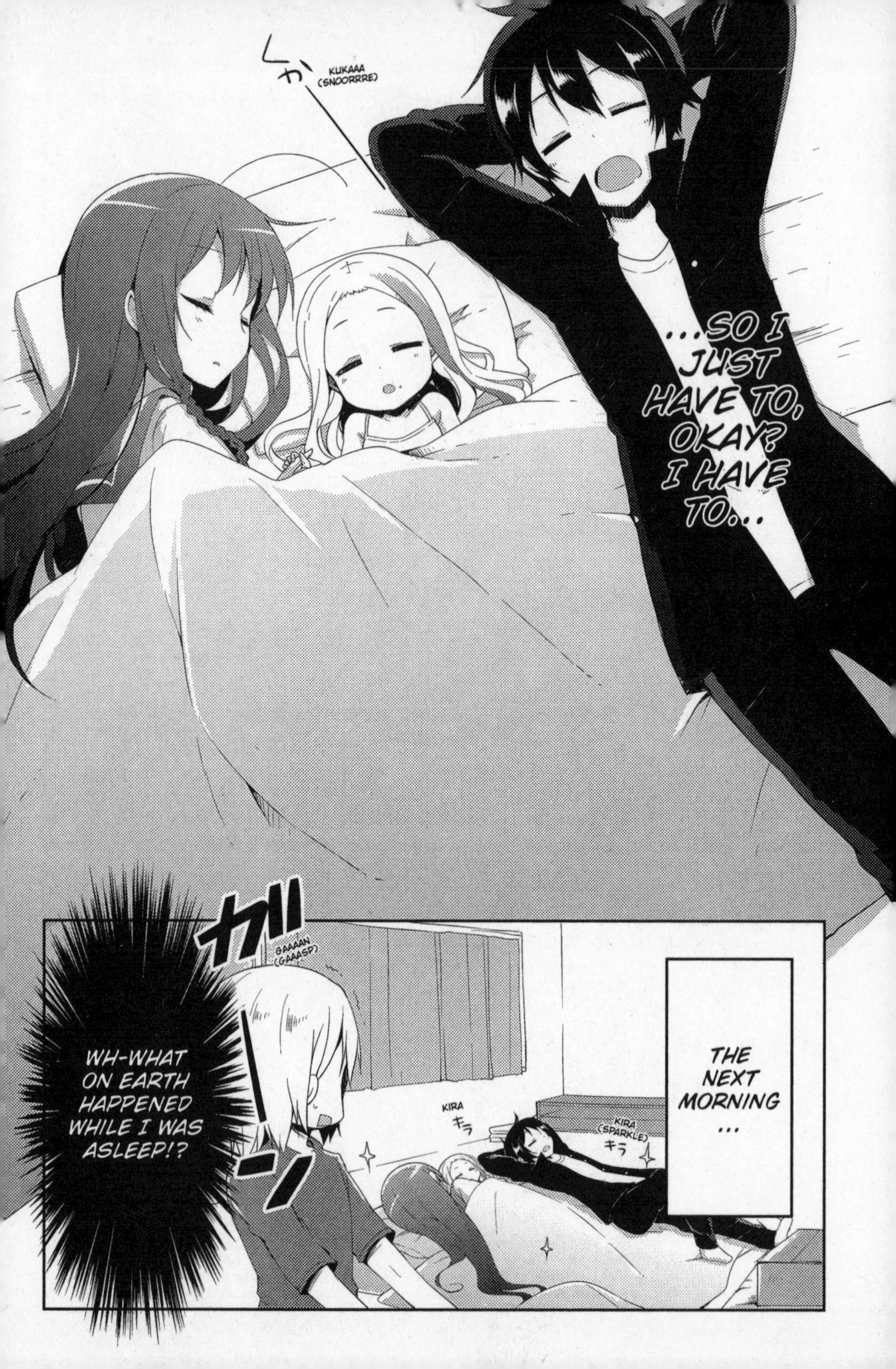

くか
KUKAAA (SNOORRRE)
...SO I JUST HAVE TO, OKAY? I HAVE TO...
THE NEXT MORNING...
KIRA (SPARKLE)
キラ
KIRA
キラ
GAAAAN (GAAASP)
WH-WHAT ON EARTH HAPPENED WHILE I WAS ASLEEP!?

THE DEVIL IS A PART-TIMER! HIGH SCHOOL!

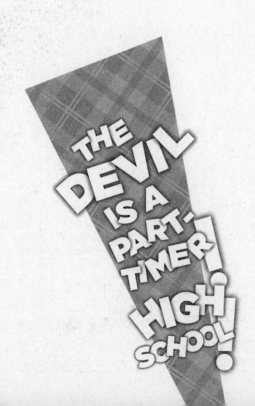

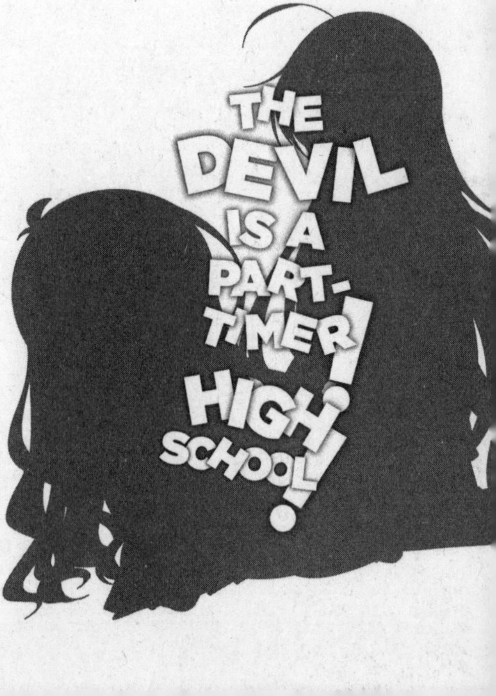
THE DEVIL IS A PART-TIMER!
HIGH SCHOOL!

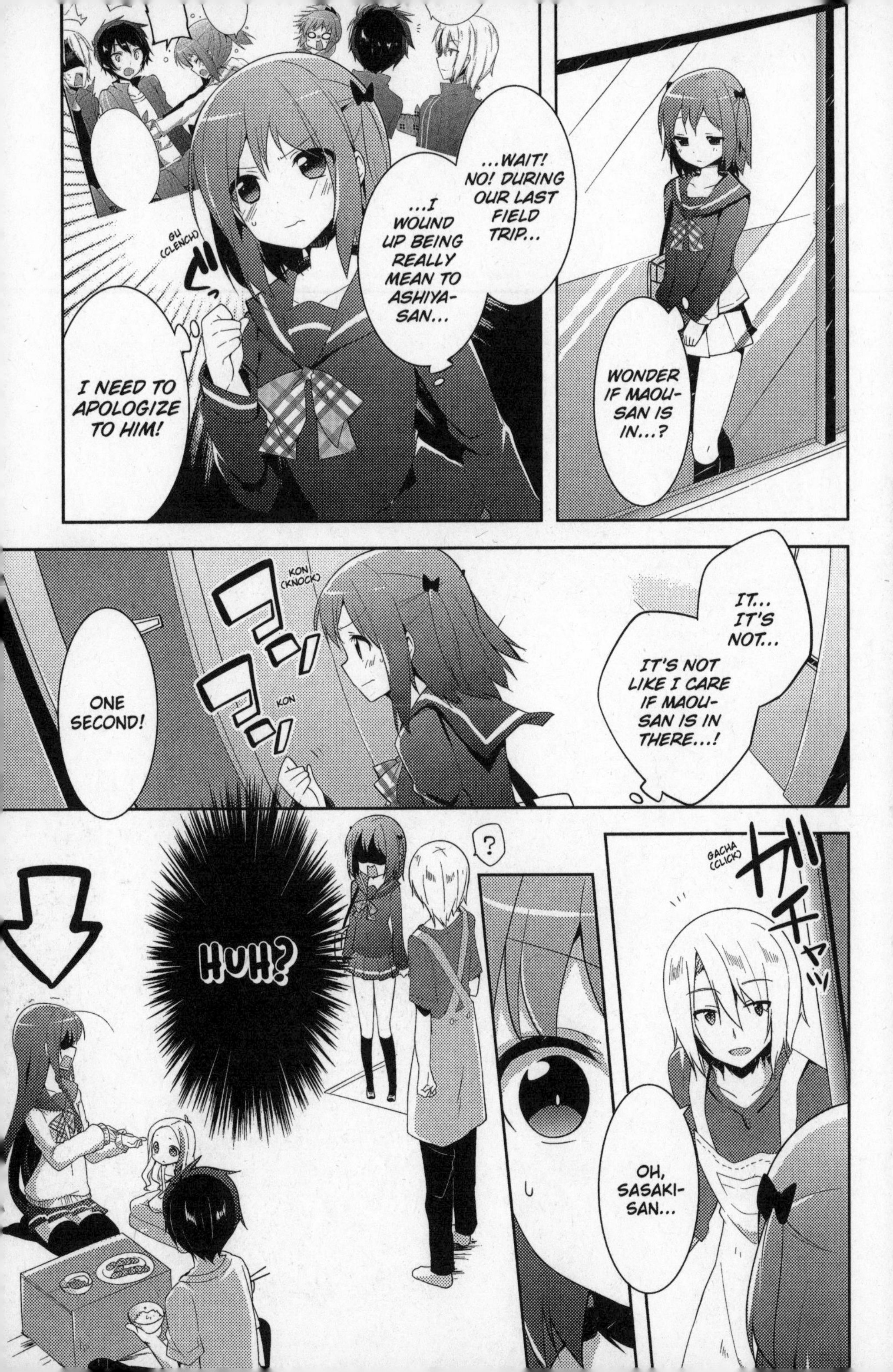
WONDER IF MAOU-SAN IS IN...?
...WAIT! NO! DURING OUR LAST FIELD TRIP...
...I WOUND UP BEING REALLY MEAN TO ASHIYA-SAN...
GU (CLENCH)
I NEED TO APOLOGIZE TO HIM!
IT... IT'S NOT...
IT'S NOT LIKE I CARE IF MAOU-SAN IS IN THERE...!
KON (KNOCK)
KON
ONE SECOND!
GACHA (CLICK)
OH, SASAKI-SAN...
?
HUH?

11th Period: The Udon-Selling Girl Relies on the Devil King

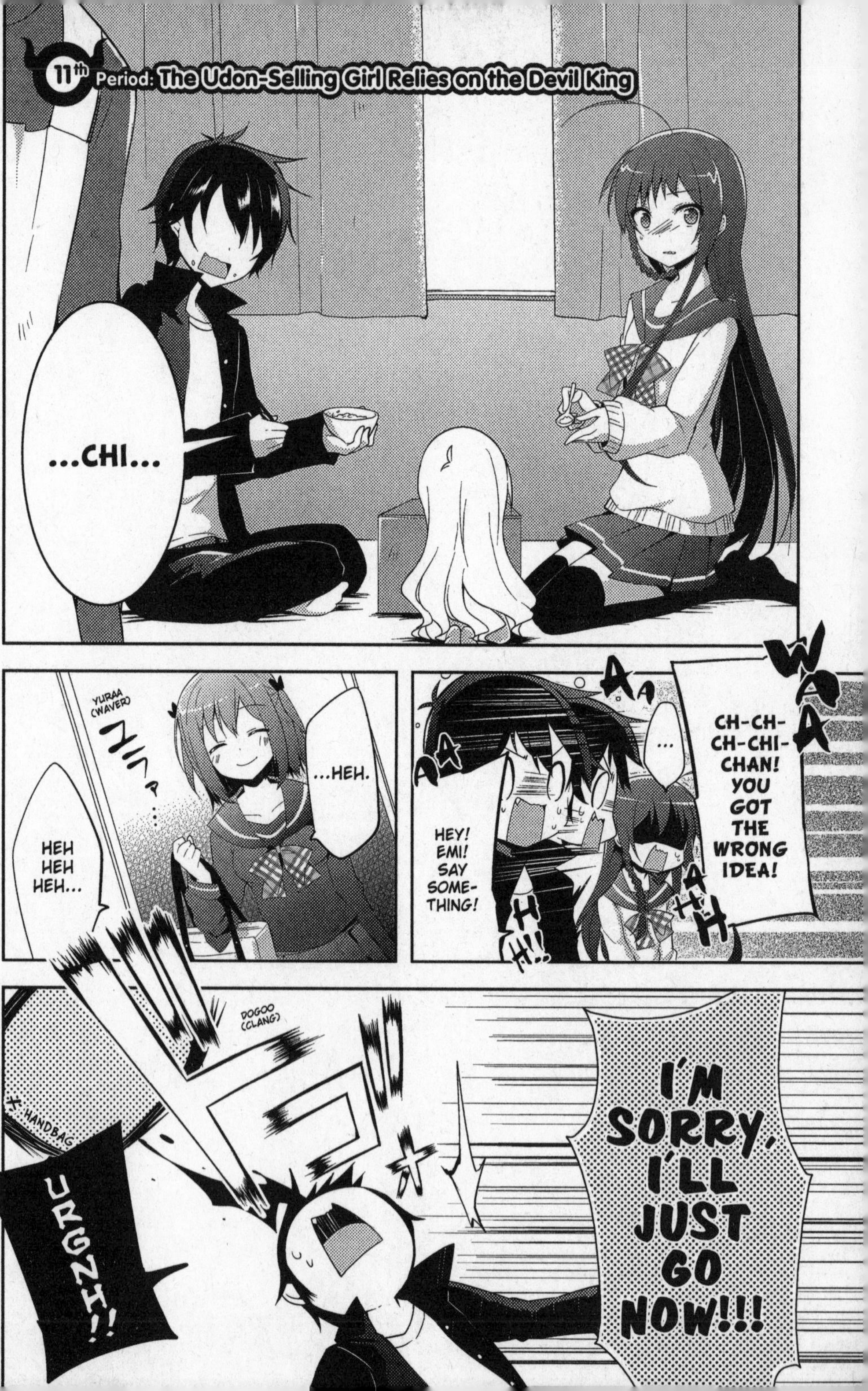
...CHI...
WAAAA
CH-CH-CH-CHI-CHAN! YOU GOT THE WRONG IDEA!
...
HEY! EMI! SAY SOMETHING!
AAHHH!!
YURAA (WAVER)
...HEH.
HEH HEH HEH...
I'M SORRY, I'LL JUST GO NOW!!!
DOGOO (CLANG)
*: HANDBAG
URGNH!!

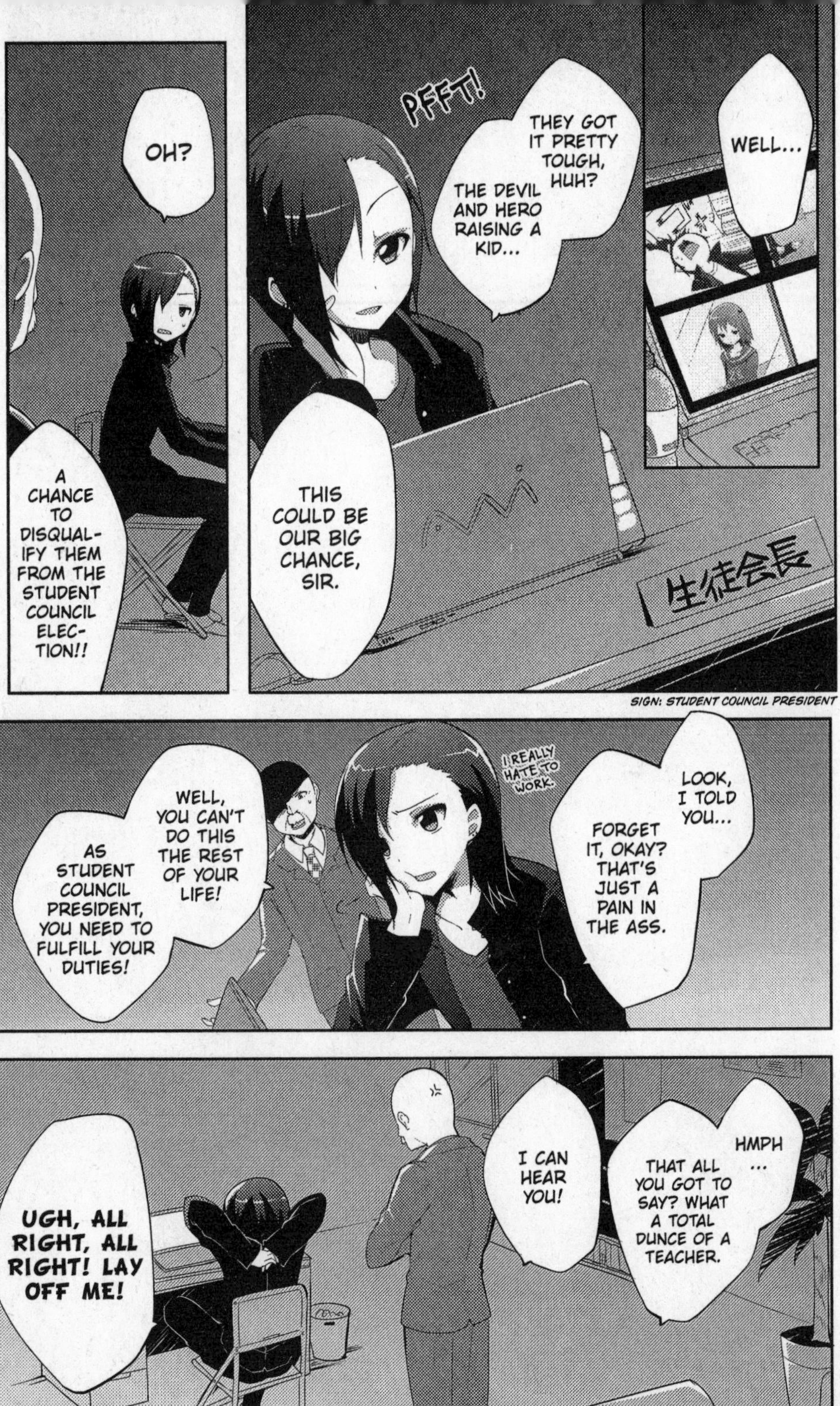

WELL...
PFFT!
THEY GOT IT PRETTY TOUGH, HUH?
THE DEVIL AND HERO RAISING A KID...
THIS COULD BE OUR BIG CHANCE, SIR.
生徒会長
OH?
A CHANCE TO DISQUAL-IFY THEM FROM THE STUDENT COUNCIL ELEC-TION!!
SIGN: STUDENT COUNCIL PRESIDENT
LOOK, I TOLD YOU...
FORGET IT, OKAY? THAT'S JUST A PAIN IN THE ASS.
I REALLY HATE TO WORK.
WELL, YOU CAN'T DO THIS THE REST OF YOUR LIFE!
AS STUDENT COUNCIL PRESIDENT, YOU NEED TO FULFILL YOUR DUTIES!
HMPH...
THAT ALL YOU GOT TO SAY? WHAT A TOTAL DUNCE OF A TEACHER.
I CAN HEAR YOU!
UGH, ALL RIGHT, ALL RIGHT! LAY OFF ME!

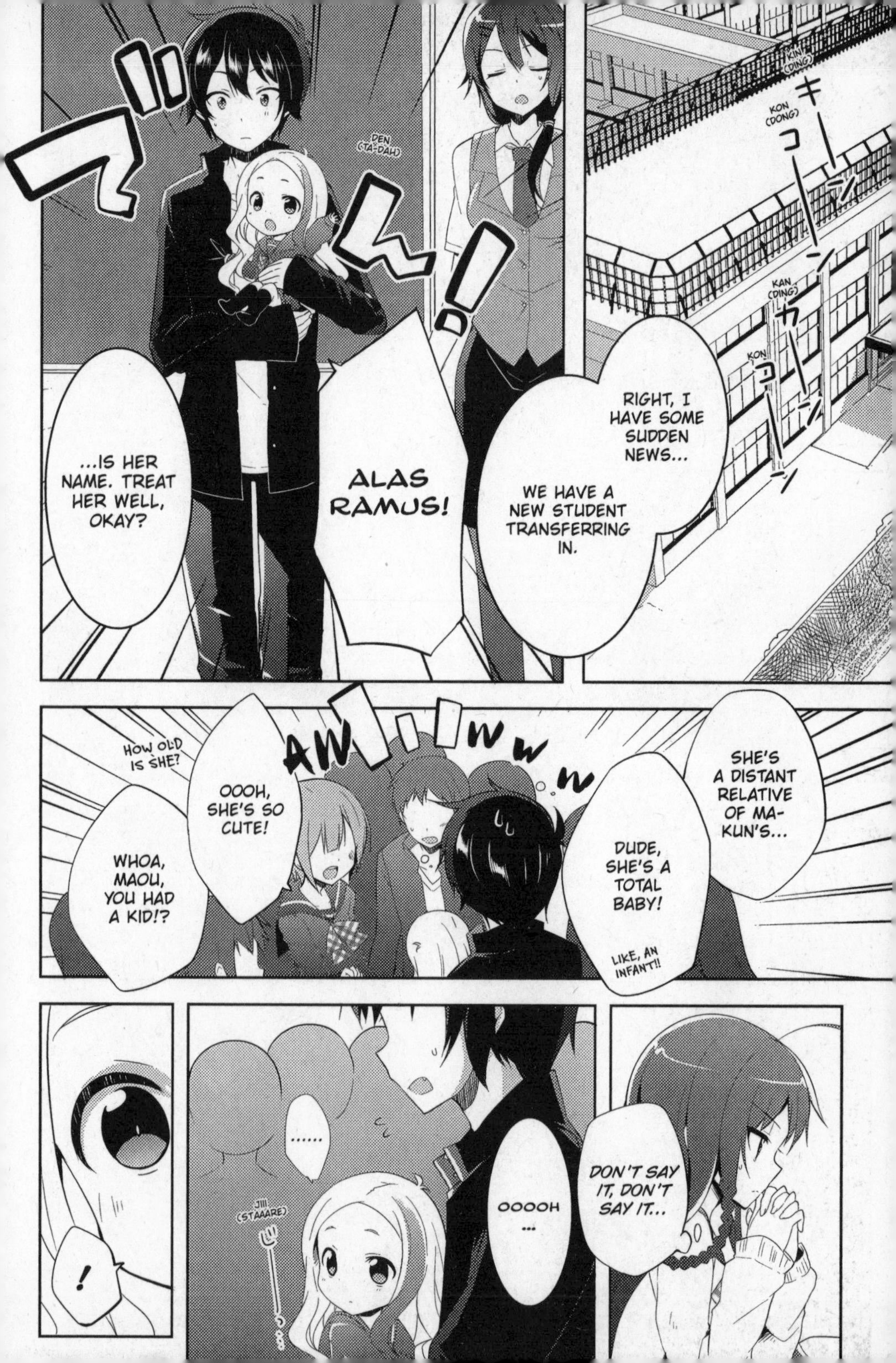
KIN (DING)
KON (DONG)
KAN (DING)
KON
RIGHT, I HAVE SOME SUDDEN NEWS...
WE HAVE A NEW STUDENT TRANSFERRING IN.
DEN (TA-DAH)
ALAS RAMUS!
...IS HER NAME. TREAT HER WELL, OKAY?
SHE'S A DISTANT RELATIVE OF MA-KUN'S...
DUDE, SHE'S A TOTAL BABY!
LIKE, AN INFANT!!
AWWWW
OOOH, SHE'S SO CUTE!
HOW OLD IS SHE?
WHOA, MAOU, YOU HAD A KID!?
DON'T SAY IT, DON'T SAY IT...
OOOOH ...
......
JIII (STAAARE)
!

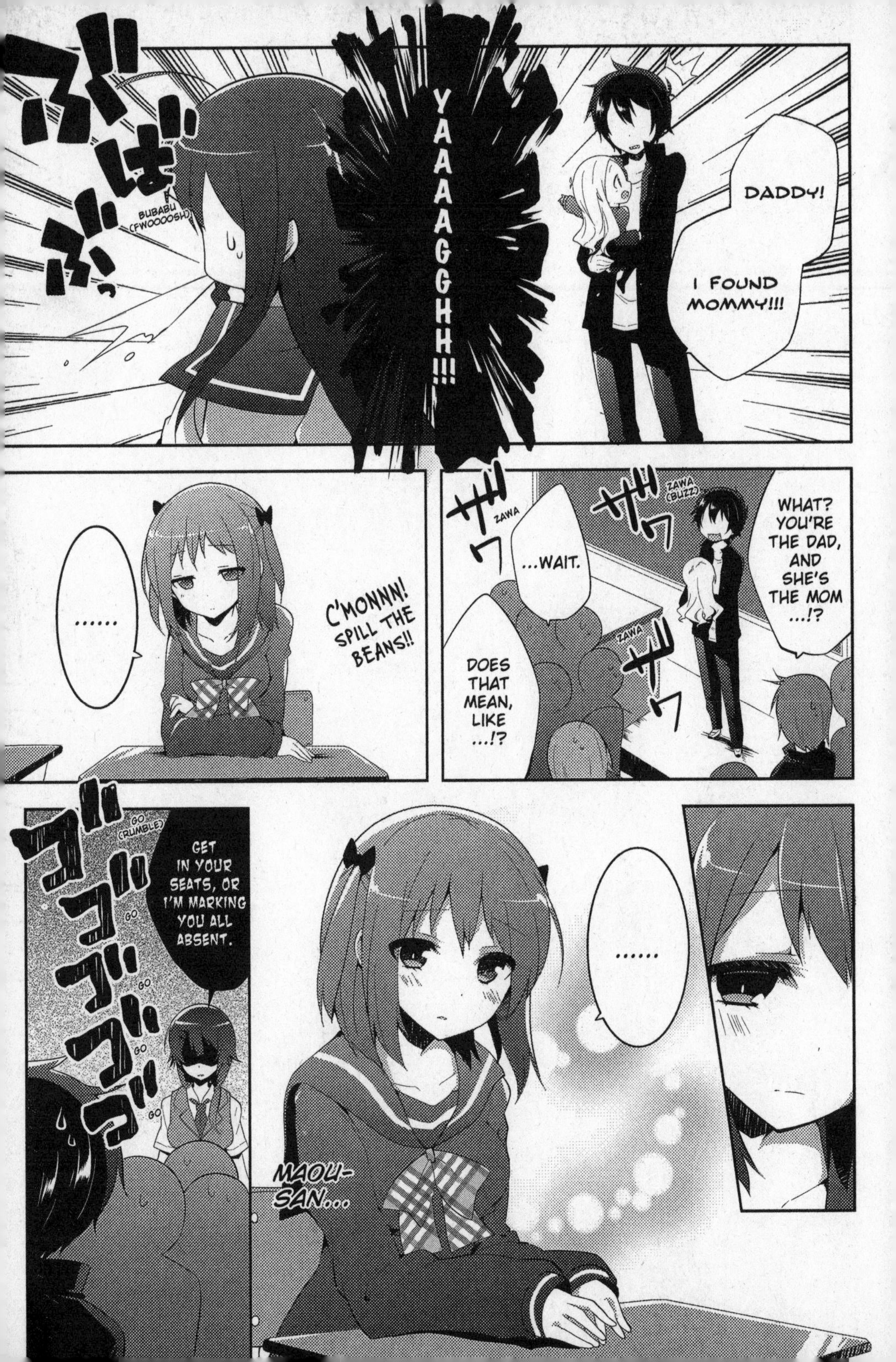
DADDY!
I FOUND MOMMY!!!
YAAAAGGHH!!!
BUBABU (FWOOOOSH)
WHAT? YOU'RE THE DAD, AND SHE'S THE MOM ...!?
ZAWA (BUZZ)
...WAIT.
ZAWA
ZAWA
DOES THAT MEAN, LIKE ...!?
C'MONNN! SPILL THE BEANS!!
......
......
......
MAOU-SAN...
GET IN YOUR SEATS, OR I'M MARKING YOU ALL ABSENT.
GO (RUMBLE)
GO
GO
GO
GO

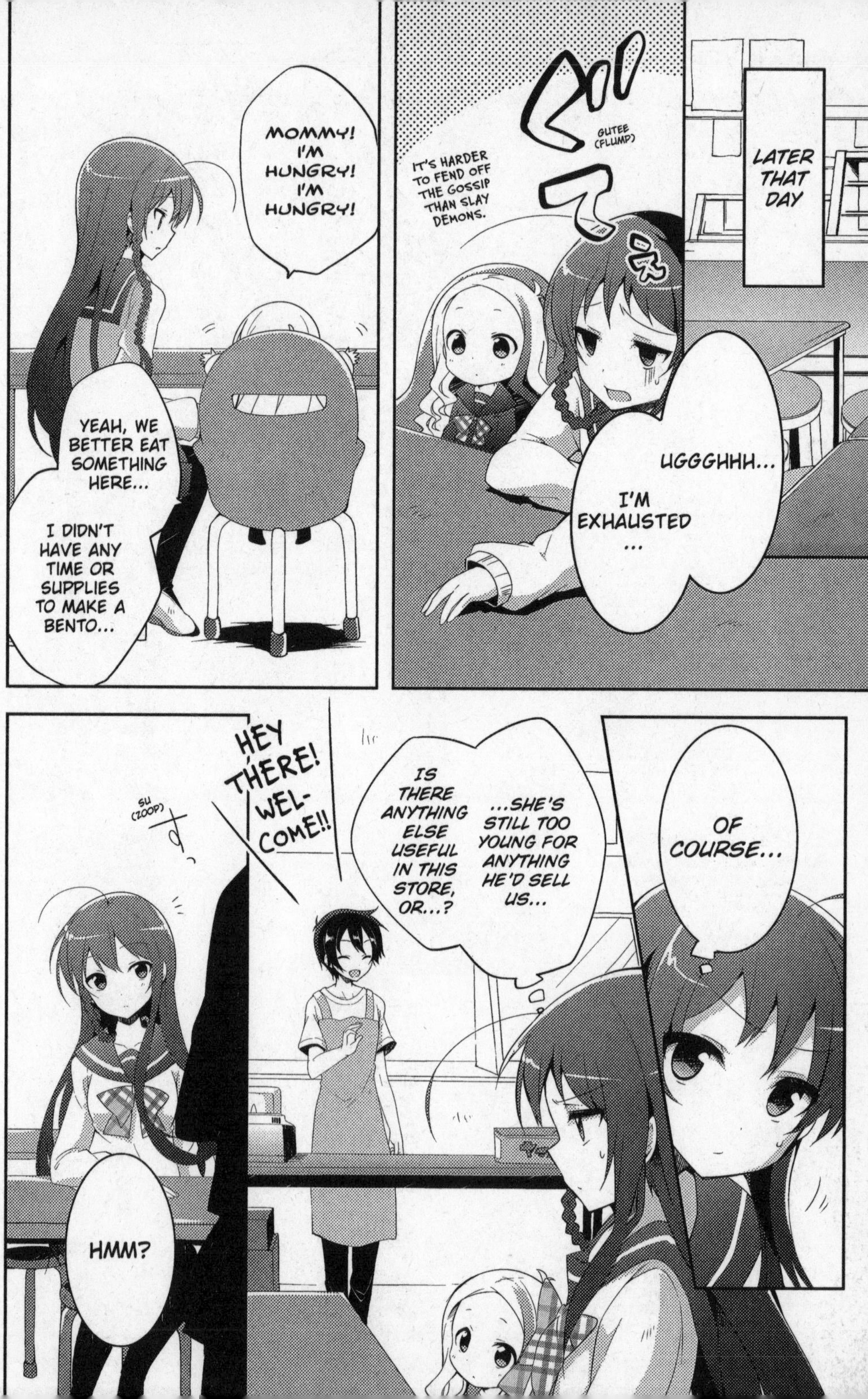
LATER THAT DAY
GUTEE (FLUMP)
IT'S HARDER TO FEND OFF THE GOSSIP THAN SLAY DEMONS.
UGGGHHH...
I'M EXHAUSTED...
MOMMY! I'M HUNGRY! I'M HUNGRY!
YEAH, WE BETTER EAT SOMETHING HERE...
I DIDN'T HAVE ANY TIME OR SUPPLIES TO MAKE A BENTO...
OF COURSE...
IS THERE ANYTHING ELSE USEFUL IN THIS STORE, OR...?
...SHE'S STILL TOO YOUNG FOR ANYTHING HE'D SELL US...
HEY THERE! WEL-COME!!
SU (ZOOP)
HMM?

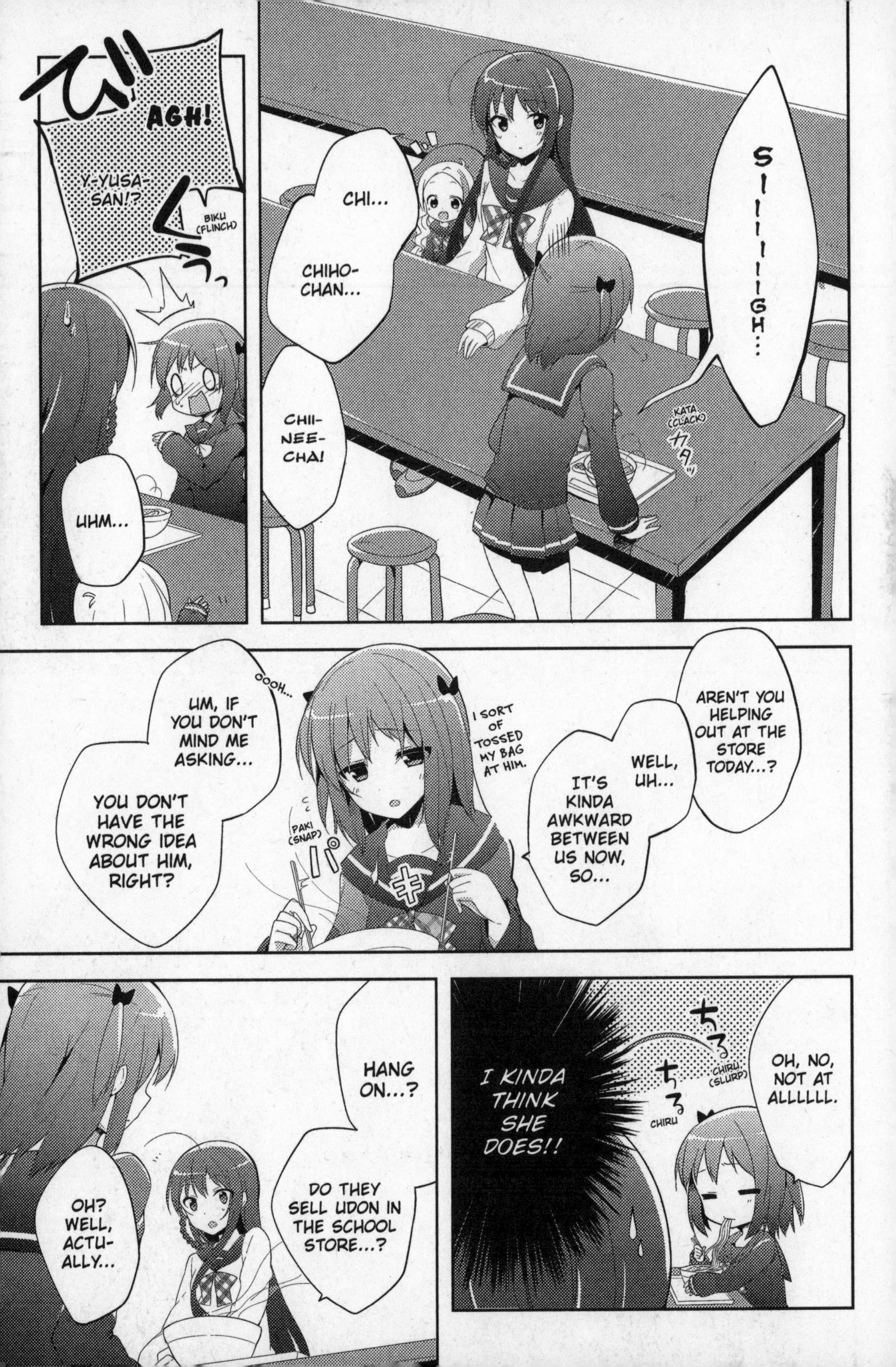
SIIIIIIGH...
KATA (CLACK)
CHI...
CHIHO-CHAN...
CHII-NEE-CHA!
AGH!
Y-YUSA-SAN!?
BIKU (FLINCH)
UHM...
AREN'T YOU HELPING OUT AT THE STORE TODAY...?
WELL, UH...
IT'S KINDA AWKWARD BETWEEN US NOW, SO...
I SORT OF TOSSED MY BAG AT HIM.
PAKI (SNAP)
OOOH...
UM, IF YOU DON'T MIND ME ASKING...
YOU DON'T HAVE THE WRONG IDEA ABOUT HIM, RIGHT?
OH, NO, NOT AT ALLLLLL.
CHIRU (SLURP)
CHIRU
I KINDA THINK SHE DOES!!
HANG ON...?
DO THEY SELL UDON IN THE SCHOOL STORE...?
OH? WELL, ACTU-ALLY...

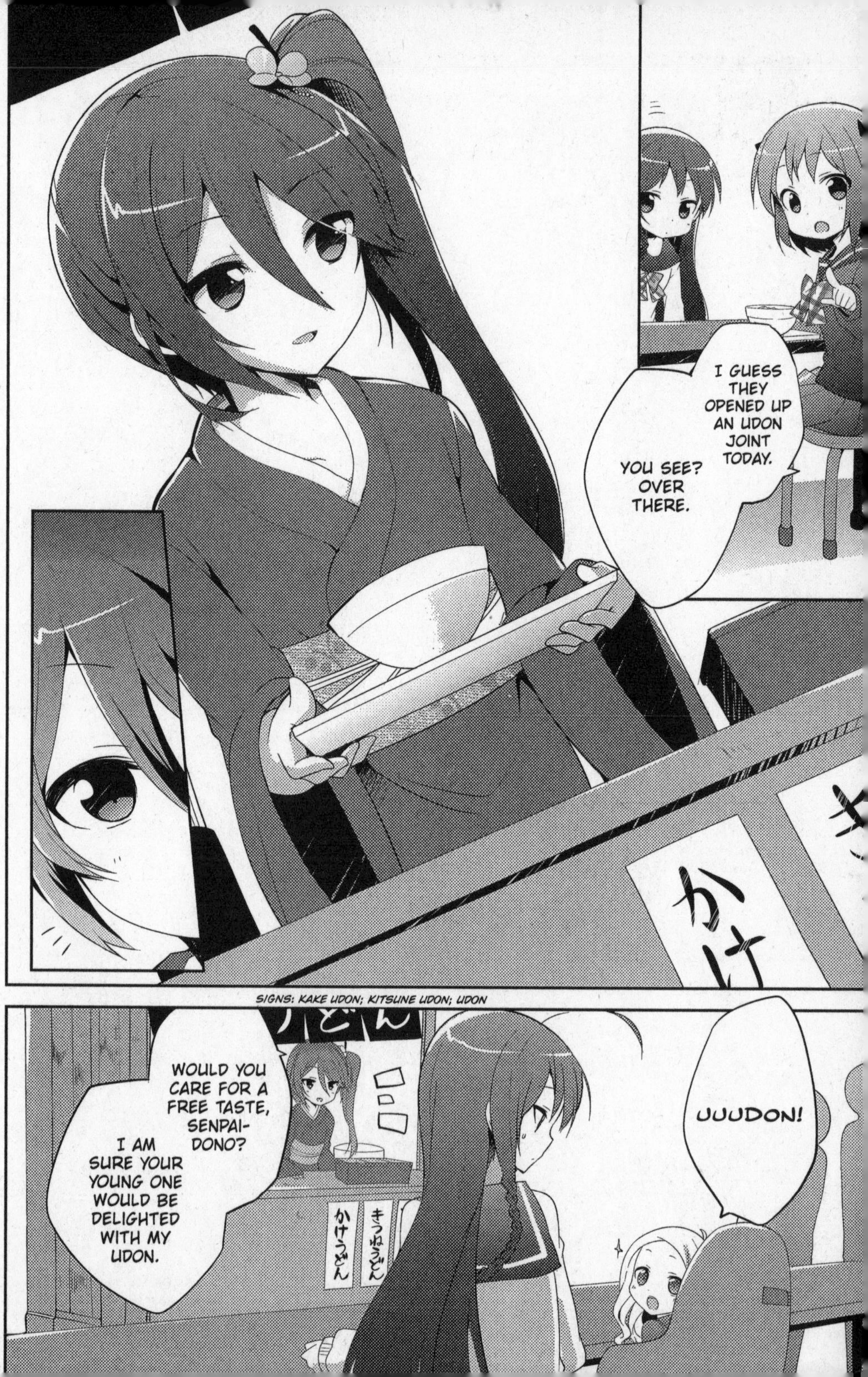

I GUESS THEY OPENED UP AN UDON JOINT TODAY.
YOU SEE? OVER THERE.
SIGNS: KAKE UDON; KITSUNE UDON; UDON
UUUDON!
WOULD YOU CARE FOR A FREE TASTE, SENPAI-DONO?
I AM SURE YOUR YOUNG ONE WOULD BE DELIGHTED WITH MY UDON.

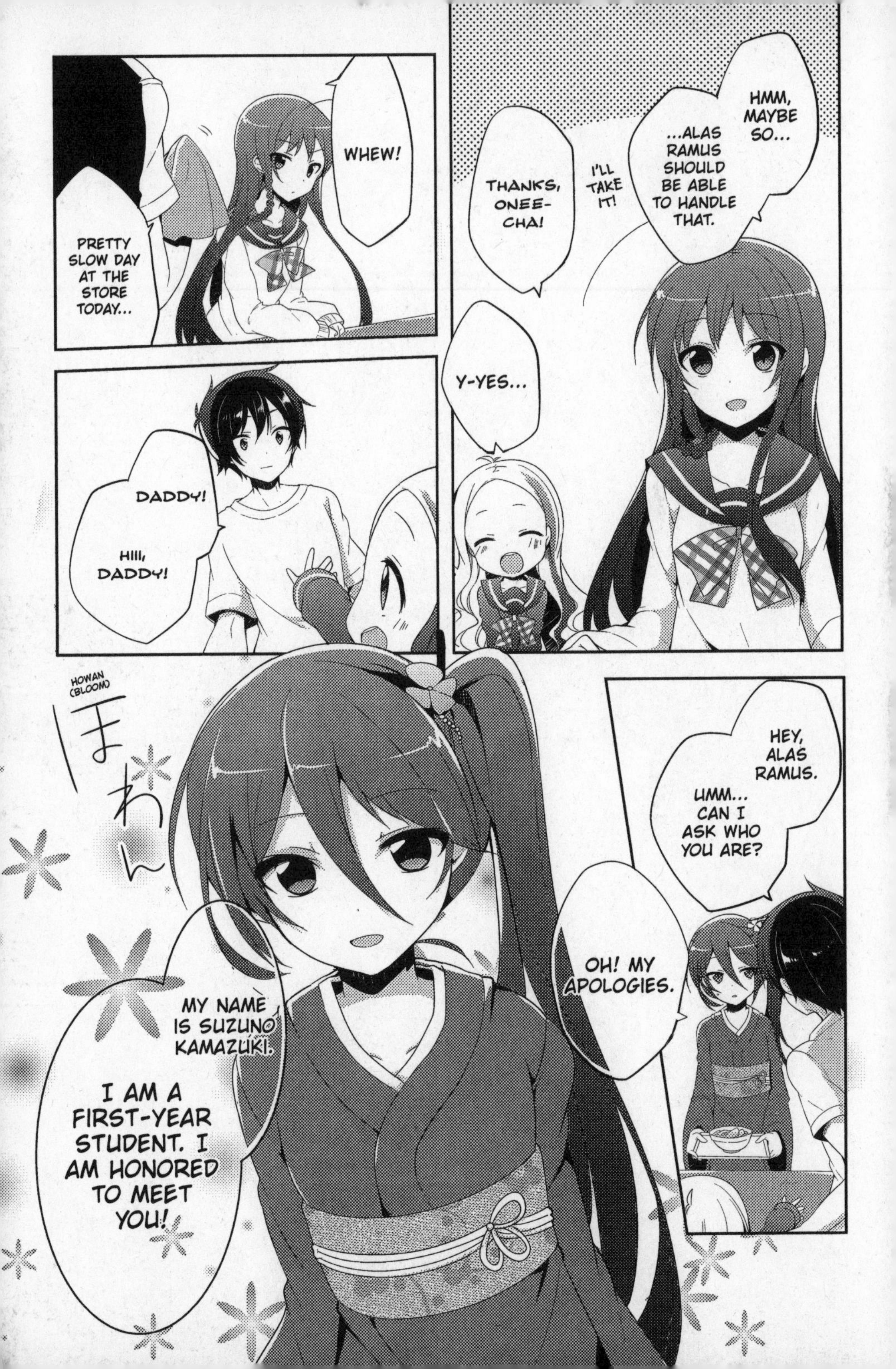
HMM, MAYBE SO...
...ALAS RAMUS SHOULD BE ABLE TO HANDLE THAT.
I'LL TAKE IT!
THANKS, ONEE-CHA!
Y-YES...
WHEW!
PRETTY SLOW DAY AT THE STORE TODAY...
DADDY!
HIII, DADDY!
HEY, ALAS RAMUS.
UMM... CAN I ASK WHO YOU ARE?
OH! MY APOLOGIES.
HOWAN (BLOOM)
ほわん
MY NAME IS SUZUNO KAMAZUKI.
I AM A FIRST-YEAR STUDENT. I AM HONORED TO MEET YOU!

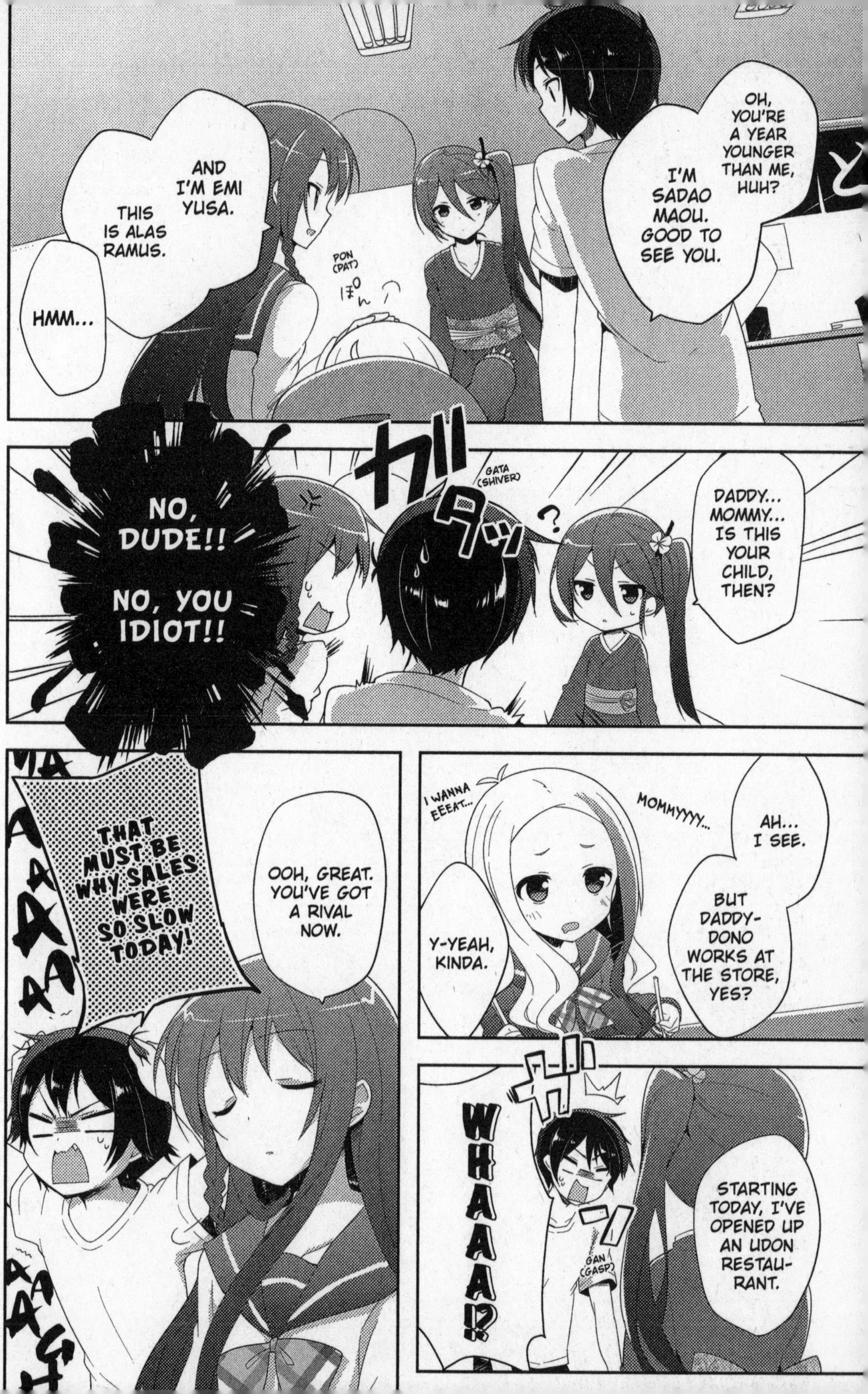
OH, YOU'RE A YEAR YOUNGER THAN ME, HUH?
I'M SADAO MAOU. GOOD TO SEE YOU.
PON (PAT)
ぽん
AND I'M EMI YUSA.
THIS IS ALAS RAMUS.
HMM...
DADDY... MOMMY... IS THIS YOUR CHILD, THEN?
?
GATA (SHIVER)
ガタッ
NO, DUDE!!
NO, YOU IDIOT!!
AH... I SEE.
MOMMYYYY...
BUT DADDY-DONO WORKS AT THE STORE, YES?
I WANNA EEEAT...
Y-YEAH, KINDA.
STARTING TODAY, I'VE OPENED UP AN UDON RESTAURANT.
ガーン
GAN (GASP)
WHAAAA!?
OOH, GREAT. YOU'VE GOT A RIVAL NOW.
THAT MUST BE WHY SALES WERE SO SLOW TODAY!

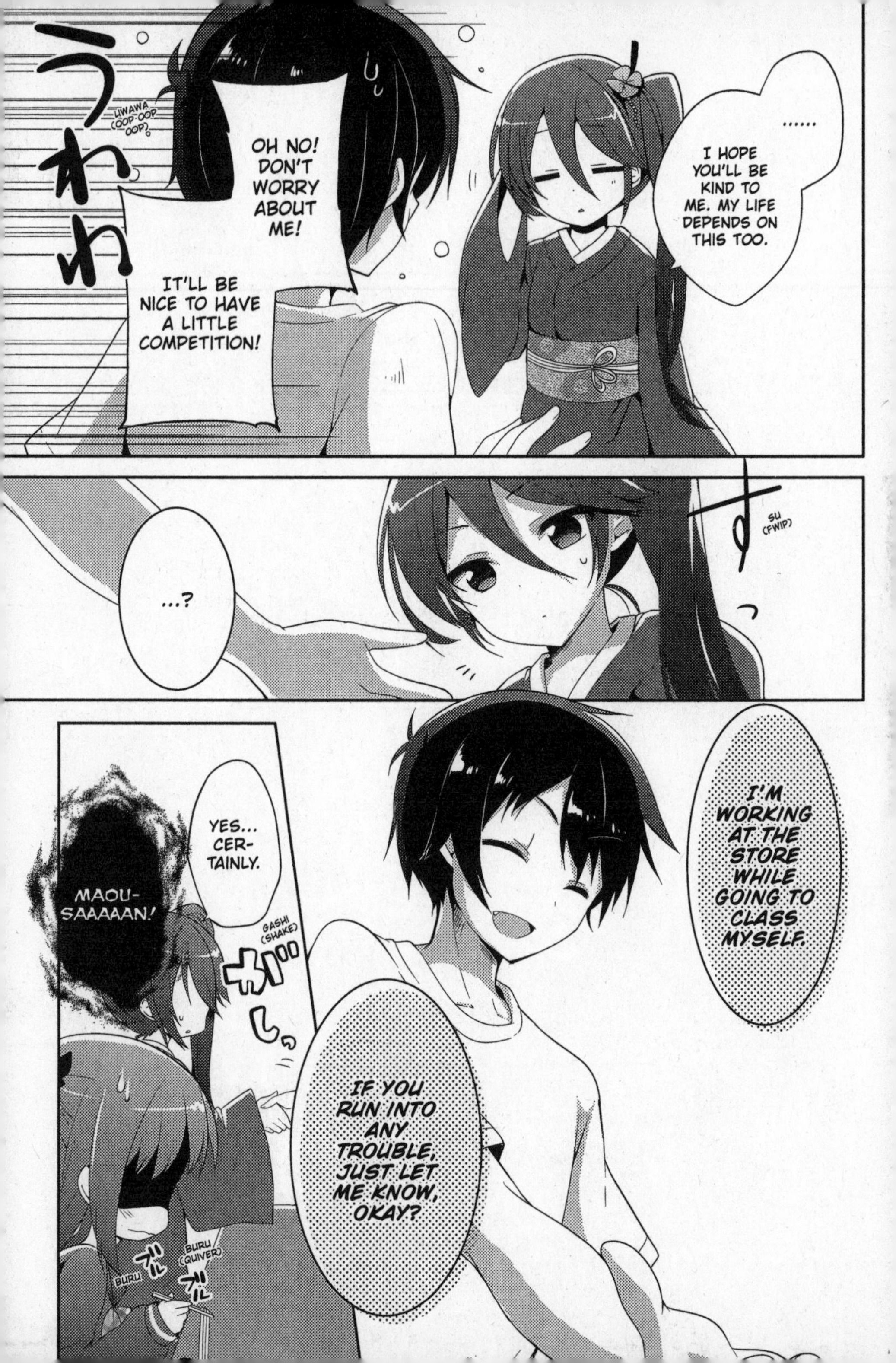
......
I HOPE YOU'LL BE KIND TO ME. MY LIFE DEPENDS ON THIS TOO.
OH NO! DON'T WORRY ABOUT ME!
IT'LL BE NICE TO HAVE A LITTLE COMPETITION!
うわわ
UWAWA (OOP-OOP OOP)
す
SU (FWIP)
...?
I'M WORKING AT THE STORE WHILE GOING TO CLASS MYSELF.
IF YOU RUN INTO ANY TROUBLE, JUST LET ME KNOW, OKAY?
YES... CERTAINLY.
GASHI (SHAKE)
MAOU-SAAAAAN!
BURU (QUIVER)
BURU

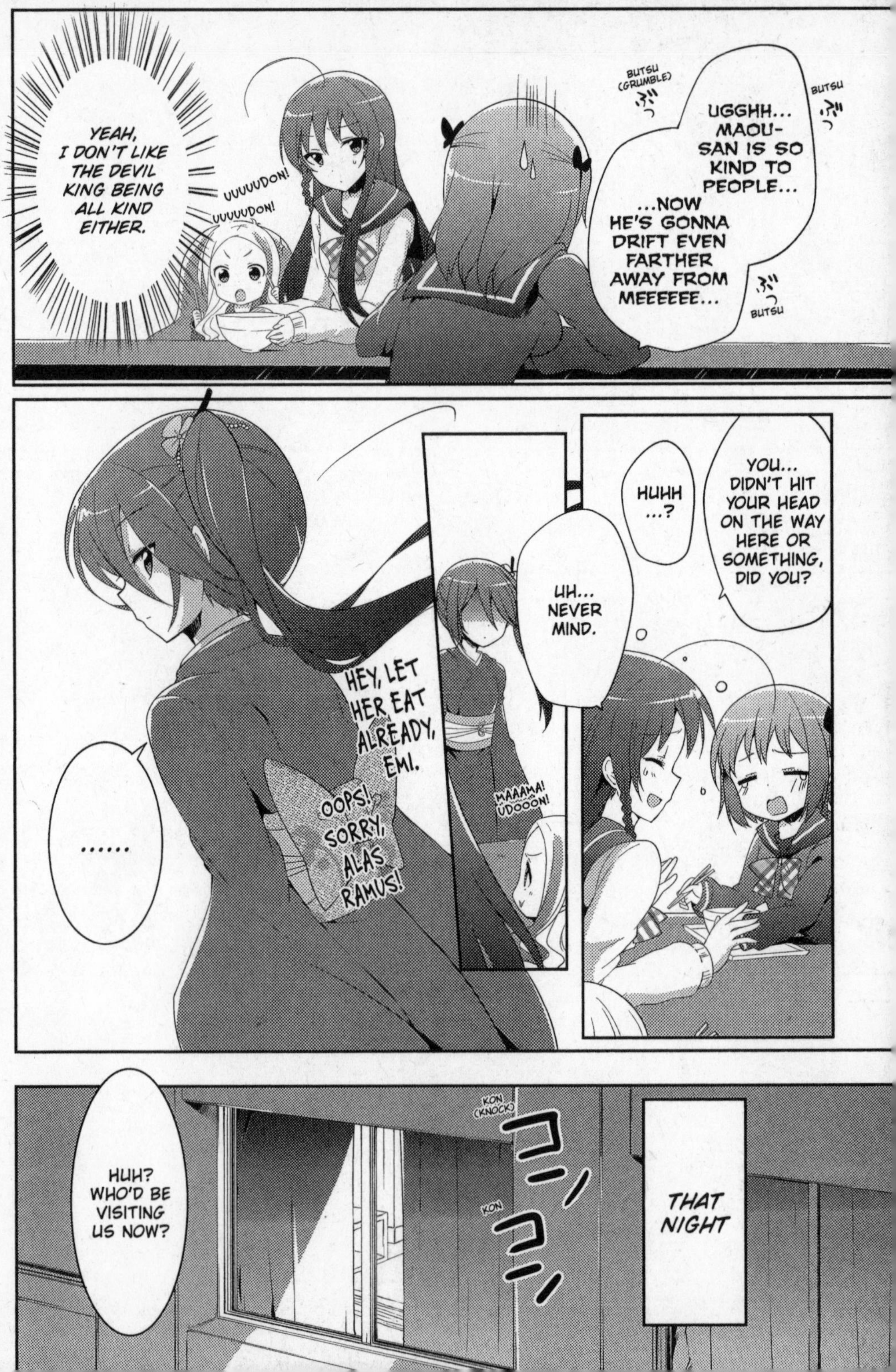
BUTSU (GRUMBLE)
ぶつ
BUTSU
ぶつ
UGGHH... MAOU-SAN IS SO KIND TO PEOPLE...
...NOW HE'S GONNA DRIFT EVEN FARTHER AWAY FROM MEEEEEE...
ぶつ
BUTSU
UUUUUDON!
UUUUUDON!
YEAH, I DON'T LIKE THE DEVIL KING BEING ALL KIND EITHER.
YOU... DIDN'T HIT YOUR HEAD ON THE WAY HERE OR SOMETHING, DID YOU?
HUHH ...?
UH... NEVER MIND.
MAAAMA! UDOOON!
HEY, LET HER EAT ALREADY, EMI.
OOPS! SORRY, ALAS RAMUS!
......
THAT NIGHT
KON (KNOCK)
コン
KON
コン
HUH? WHO'D BE VISITING US NOW?

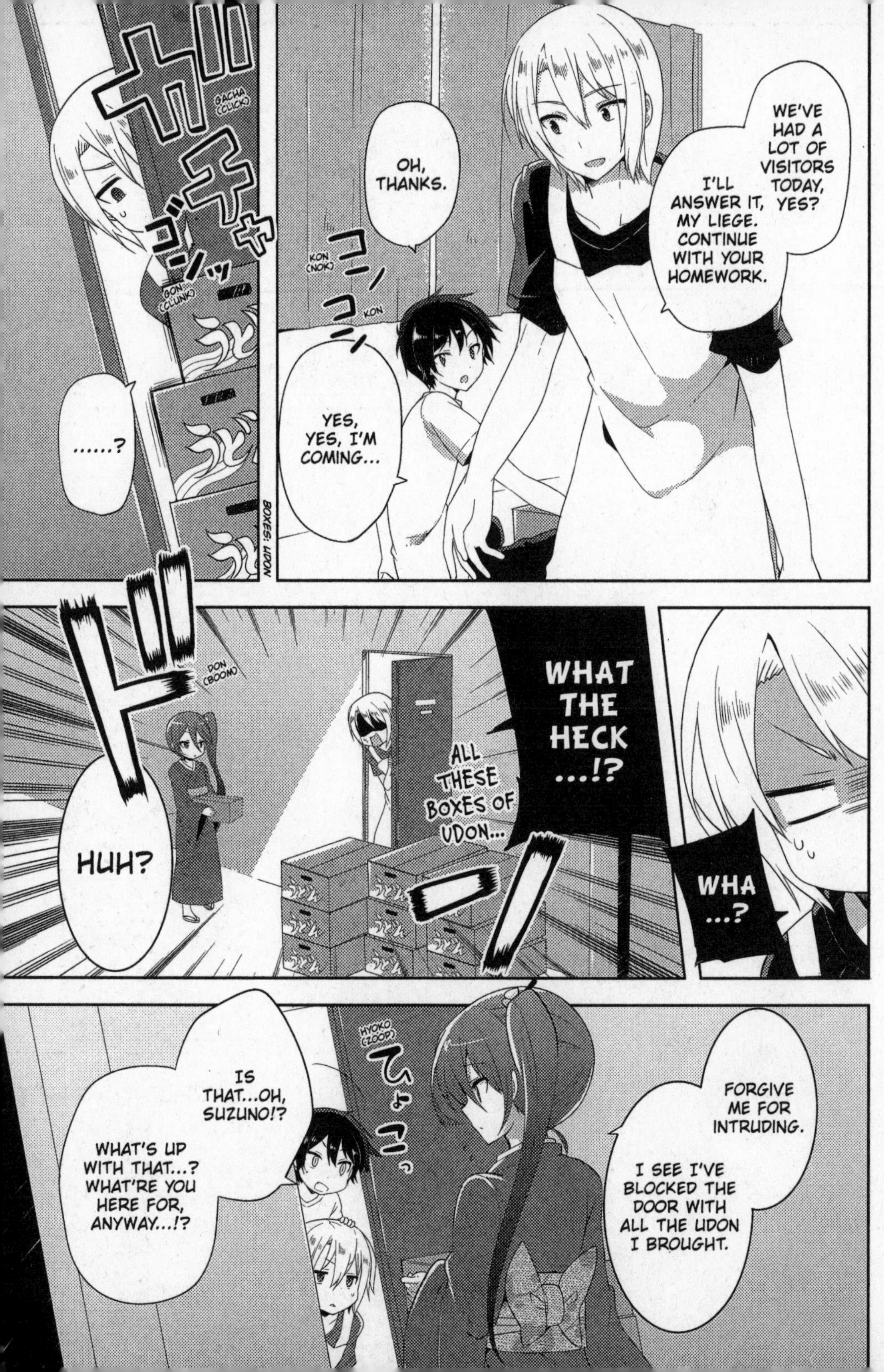
WE'VE HAD A LOT OF VISITORS TODAY, YES?
I'LL ANSWER IT, MY LIEGE. CONTINUE WITH YOUR HOMEWORK.
OH, THANKS.
KON (NOK)
KON
YES, YES, I'M COMING...
GACHA (CLICK)
GON (CLUNK)
......?
BOXES: UDON
WHA ...?
WHAT THE HECK ...!?
ALL THESE BOXES OF UDON...
DON (BOOM)
HUH?
HYOKO (ZOOP)
FORGIVE ME FOR INTRUDING.
I SEE I'VE BLOCKED THE DOOR WITH ALL THE UDON I BROUGHT.
IS THAT...OH, SUZUNO!?
WHAT'S UP WITH THAT...? WHAT'RE YOU HERE FOR, ANYWAY...!?

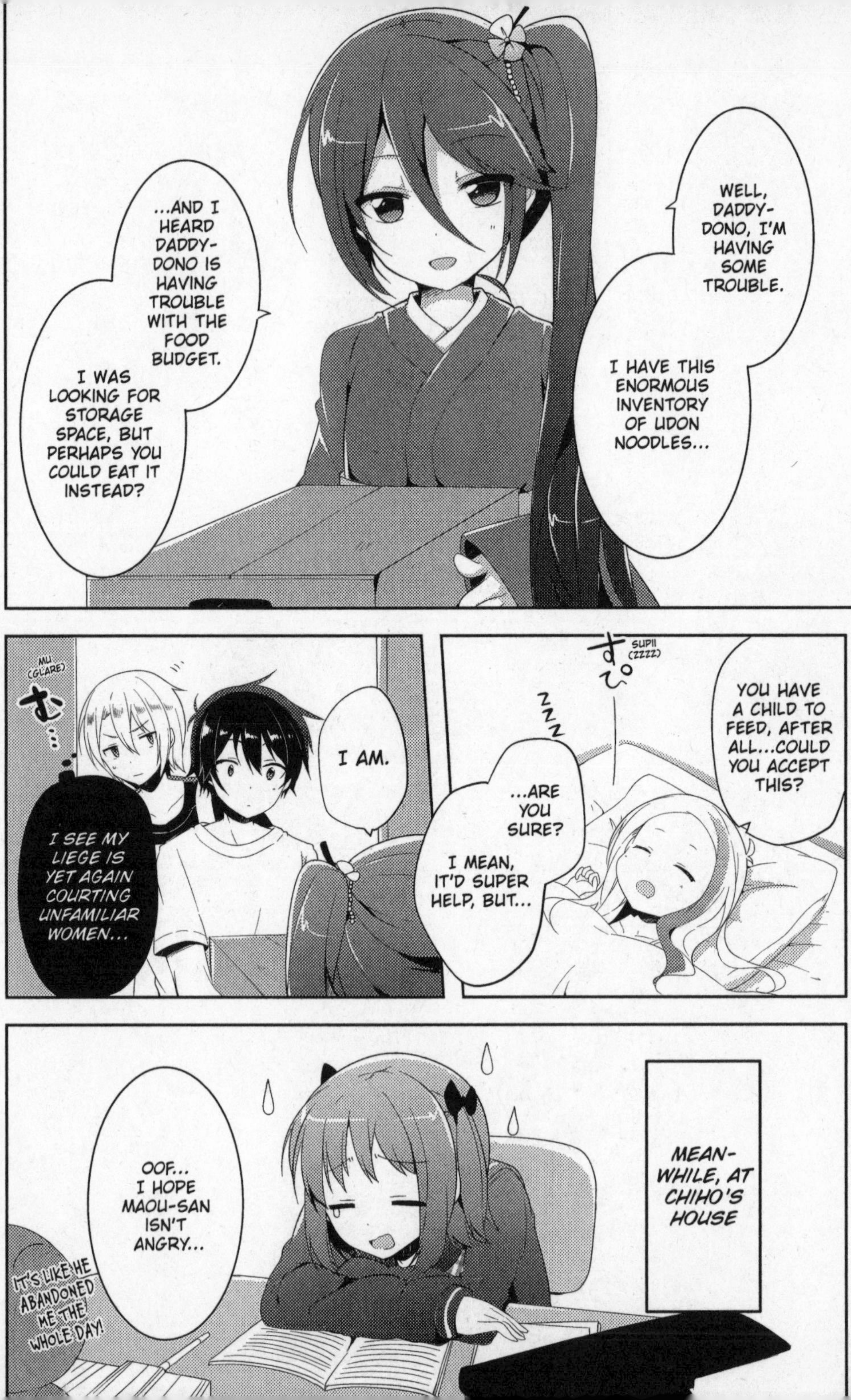
WELL, DADDY-DONO, I'M HAVING SOME TROUBLE.
I HAVE THIS ENORMOUS INVENTORY OF UDON NOODLES...
...AND I HEARD DADDY-DONO IS HAVING TROUBLE WITH THE FOOD BUDGET.
I WAS LOOKING FOR STORAGE SPACE, BUT PERHAPS YOU COULD EAT IT INSTEAD?
YOU HAVE A CHILD TO FEED, AFTER ALL...COULD YOU ACCEPT THIS?
SUPII (ZZZZ)
ZZZ
...ARE YOU SURE?
I MEAN, IT'D SUPER HELP, BUT...
I AM.
MU (GLARE)
I SEE MY LIEGE IS YET AGAIN COURTING UNFAMILIAR WOMEN...
MEAN-WHILE, AT CHIHO'S HOUSE
OOF... I HOPE MAOU-SAN ISN'T ANGRY...
IT'S LIKE HE ABANDONED ME THE WHOLE DAY!

THE DEVIL IS A PART-TIMER! HIGH SCHOOL!

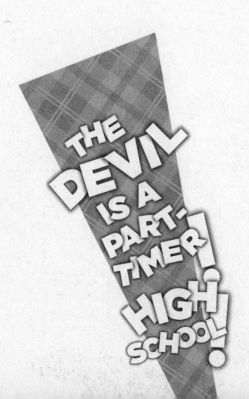

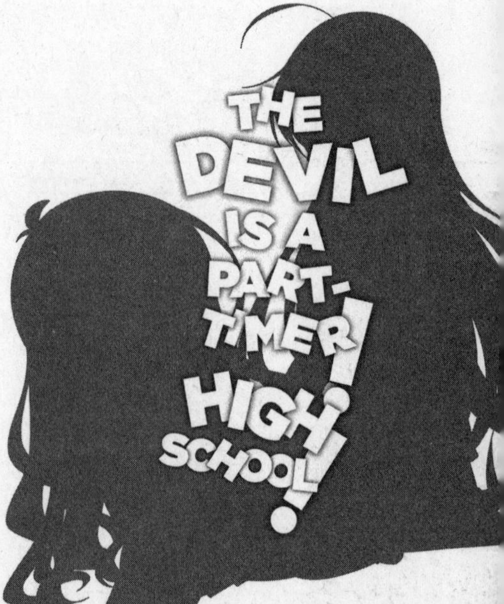
THE DEVIL IS A PART-TIMER! HIGH SCHOOL!

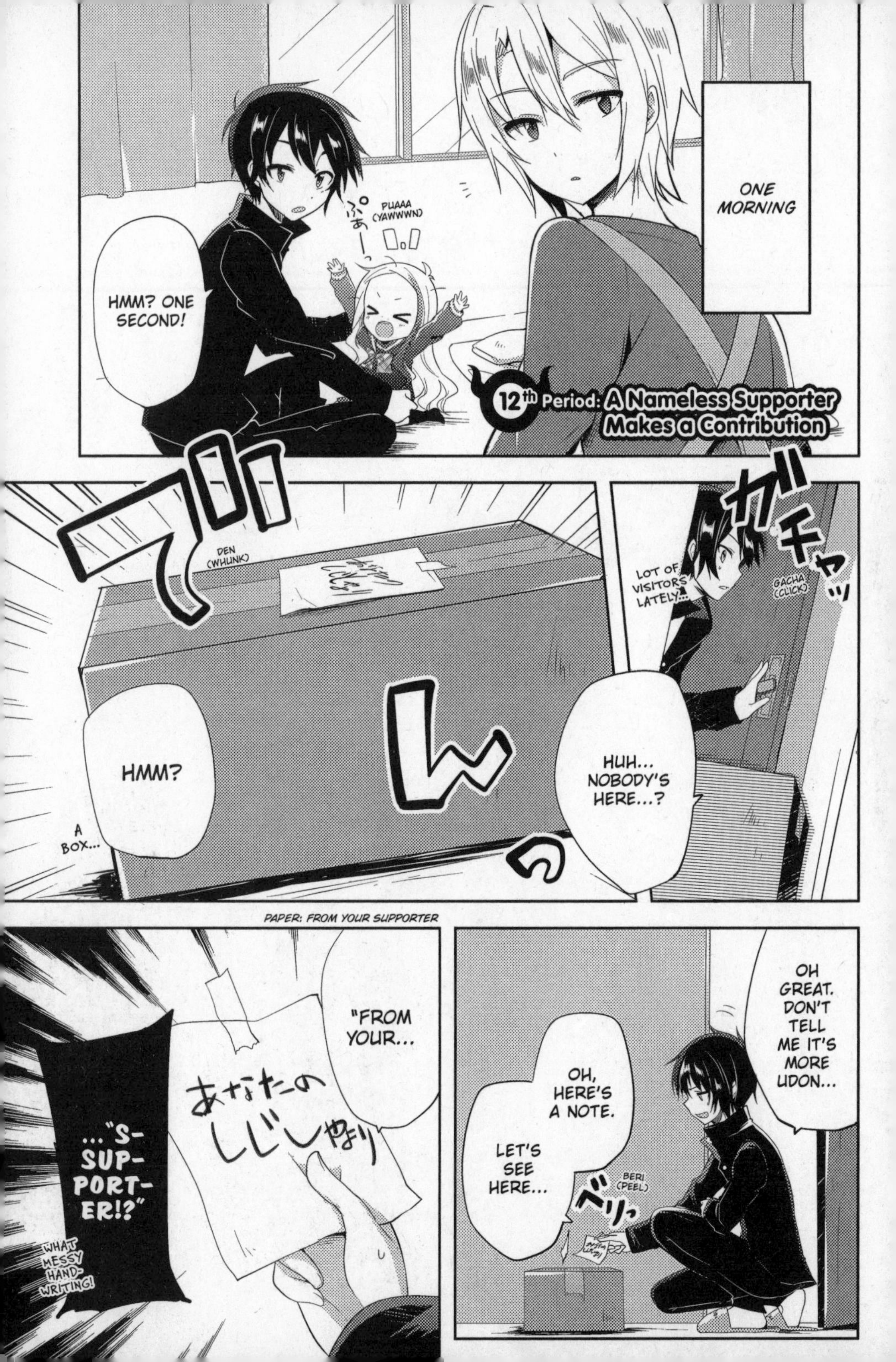
ONE MORNING
12th Period: A Nameless Supporter Makes a Contribution
ぷあーっ
PUAAA (YAWWWN)
HMM? ONE SECOND!
ガチャッ
GACHA (CLICK)
LOT OF VISITORS LATELY...
HUH... NOBODY'S HERE...?
でんっ
DEN (WHUNK)
HMM?
A BOX...
PAPER: FROM YOUR SUPPORTER
OH GREAT. DON'T TELL ME IT'S MORE UDON...
OH, HERE'S A NOTE.
LET'S SEE HERE...
べりっ
BERI (PEEL)
"FROM YOUR...
あなたの しじしゃより
..."S-SUP-PORT-ER!?"
WHAT MESSY HAND-WRITING!

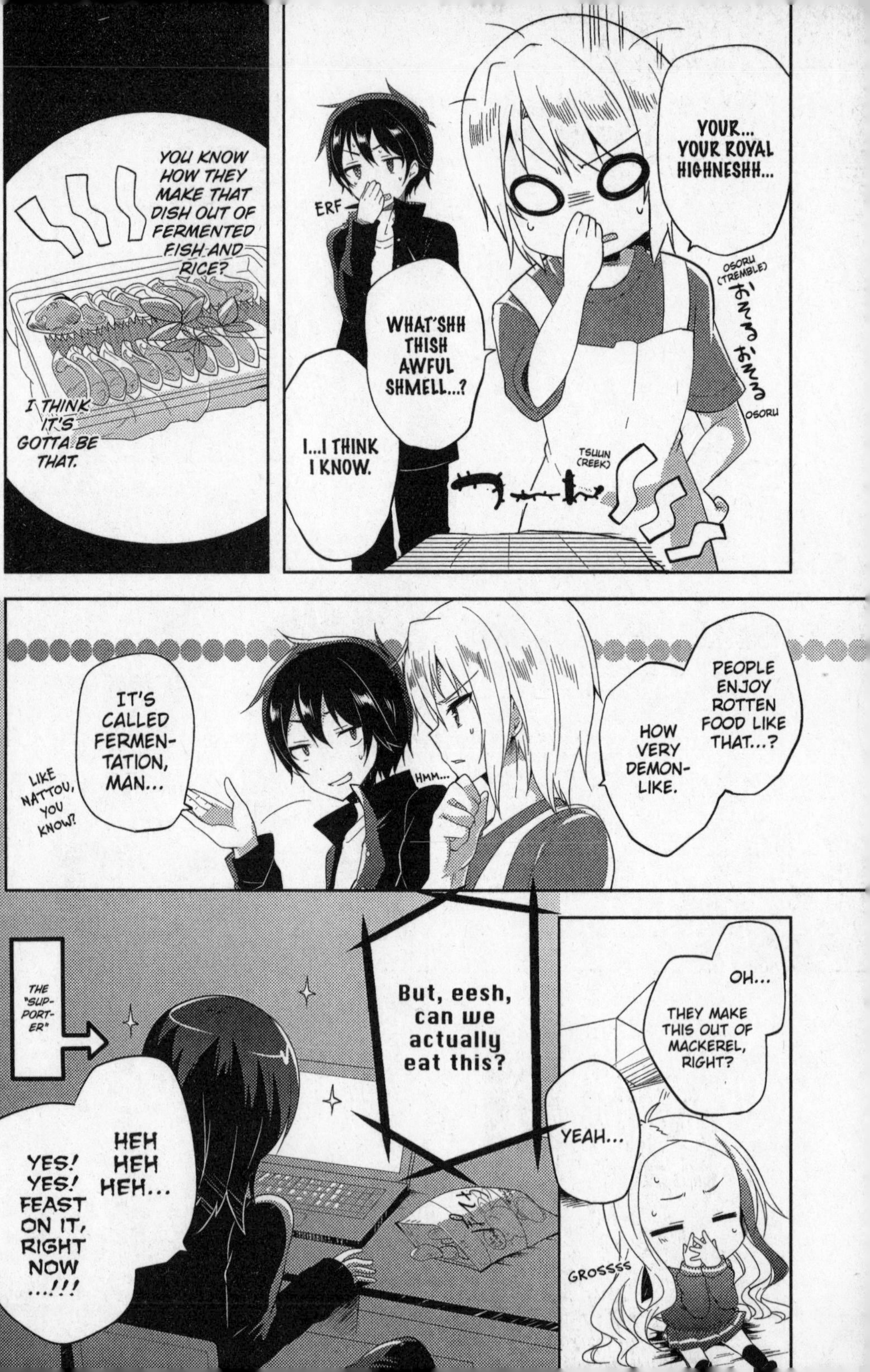
YOUR... YOUR ROYAL HIGHNESHH...
OSORU (TREMBLE)
おそるおそる
OSORU
ERF
WHAT'SHH THISH AWFUL SHMELL...?
TSUUN (REEK)
I...I THINK I KNOW.
YOU KNOW HOW THEY MAKE THAT DISH OUT OF FERMENTED FISH AND RICE?
I THINK IT'S GOTTA BE THAT.
PEOPLE ENJOY ROTTEN FOOD LIKE THAT...?
HOW VERY DEMON-LIKE.
HMM...
IT'S CALLED FERMENTATION, MAN...
LIKE NATTOU, YOU KNOW?
OH...
THEY MAKE THIS OUT OF MACKEREL, RIGHT?
YEAH...
GROSSSS
But, eesh, can we actually eat this?
THE "SUPPORTER"
HEH HEH HEH...
YES! YES! FEAST ON IT, RIGHT NOW...!!!

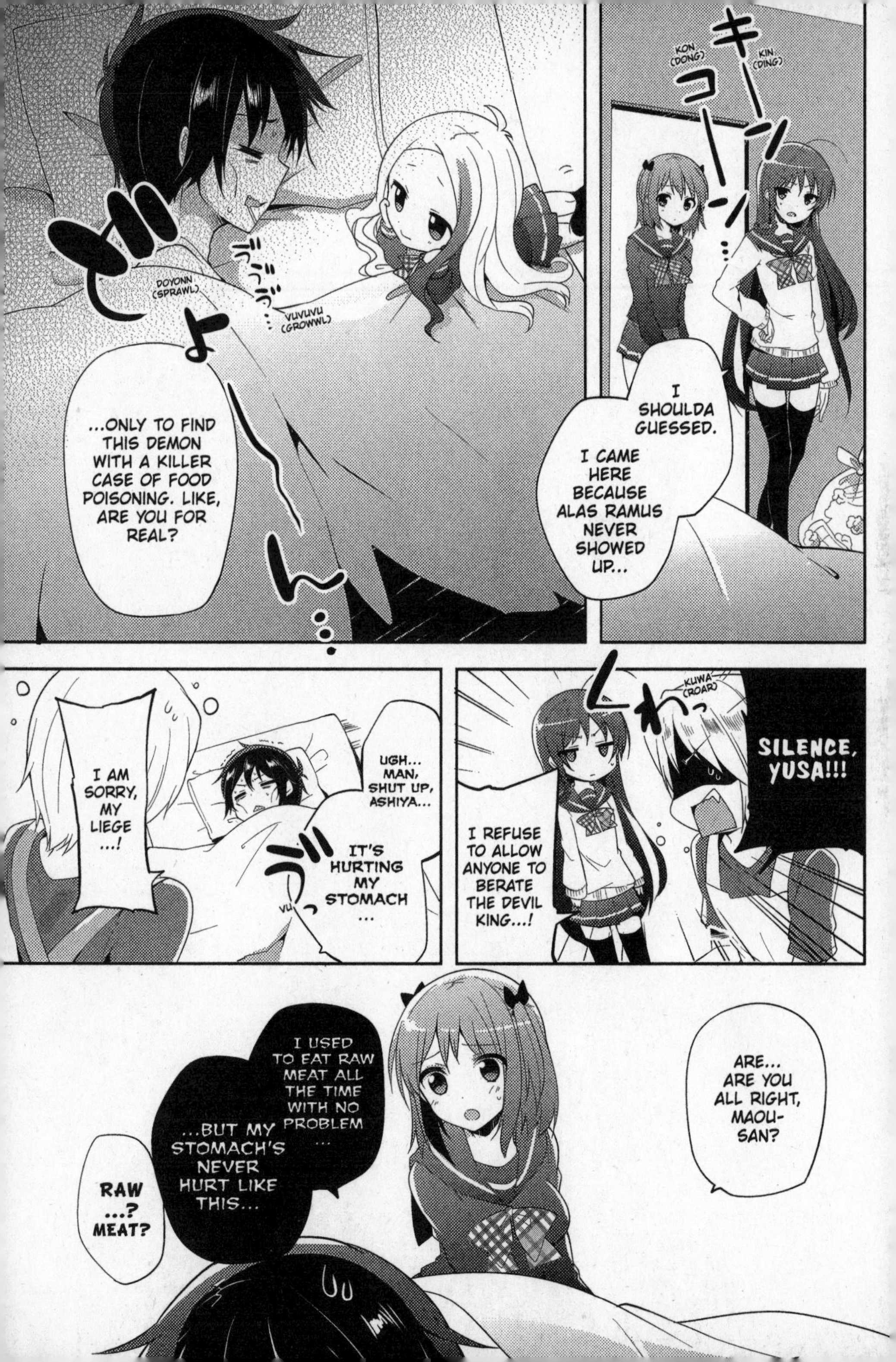
KIN (DING)
KON (DONG)
I SHOULDA GUESSED.
I CAME HERE BECAUSE ALAS RAMUS NEVER SHOWED UP...
DOYONN (SPRAWL)
VUVUVU (GROWWL)
...ONLY TO FIND THIS DEMON WITH A KILLER CASE OF FOOD POISONING. LIKE, ARE YOU FOR REAL?
KUWA (ROAR)
SILENCE, YUSA!!!
I REFUSE TO ALLOW ANYONE TO BERATE THE DEVIL KING...!
UGH... MAN, SHUT UP, ASHIYA...
IT'S HURTING MY STOMACH...
VU
I AM SORRY, MY LIEGE...!
ARE... ARE YOU ALL RIGHT, MAOU-SAN?
I USED TO EAT RAW MEAT ALL THE TIME WITH NO PROBLEM...
...BUT MY STOMACH'S NEVER HURT LIKE THIS...
RAW...? MEAT?

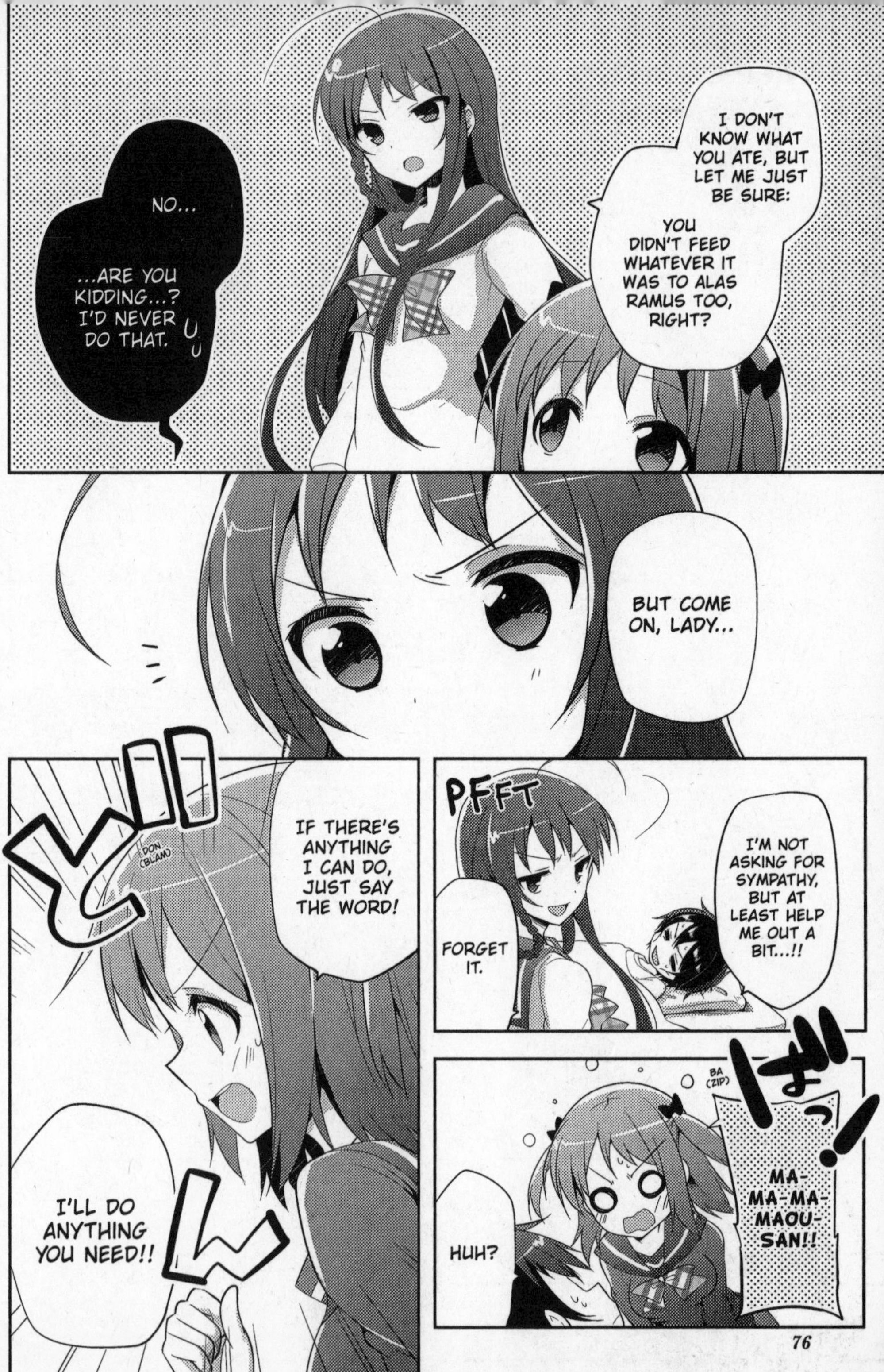
I DON'T KNOW WHAT YOU ATE, BUT LET ME JUST BE SURE:
YOU DIDN'T FEED WHATEVER IT WAS TO ALAS RAMUS TOO, RIGHT?
NO...
...ARE YOU KIDDING...? I'D NEVER DO THAT.
BUT COME ON, LADY...
PFFT
I'M NOT ASKING FOR SYMPATHY, BUT AT LEAST HELP ME OUT A BIT...!!
FORGET IT.
BA (ZIP)
MA-MA-MA-MAOU-SAN!!
HUH?
DON (BLAM)
IF THERE'S ANYTHING I CAN DO, JUST SAY THE WORD!
I'LL DO ANYTHING YOU NEED!!

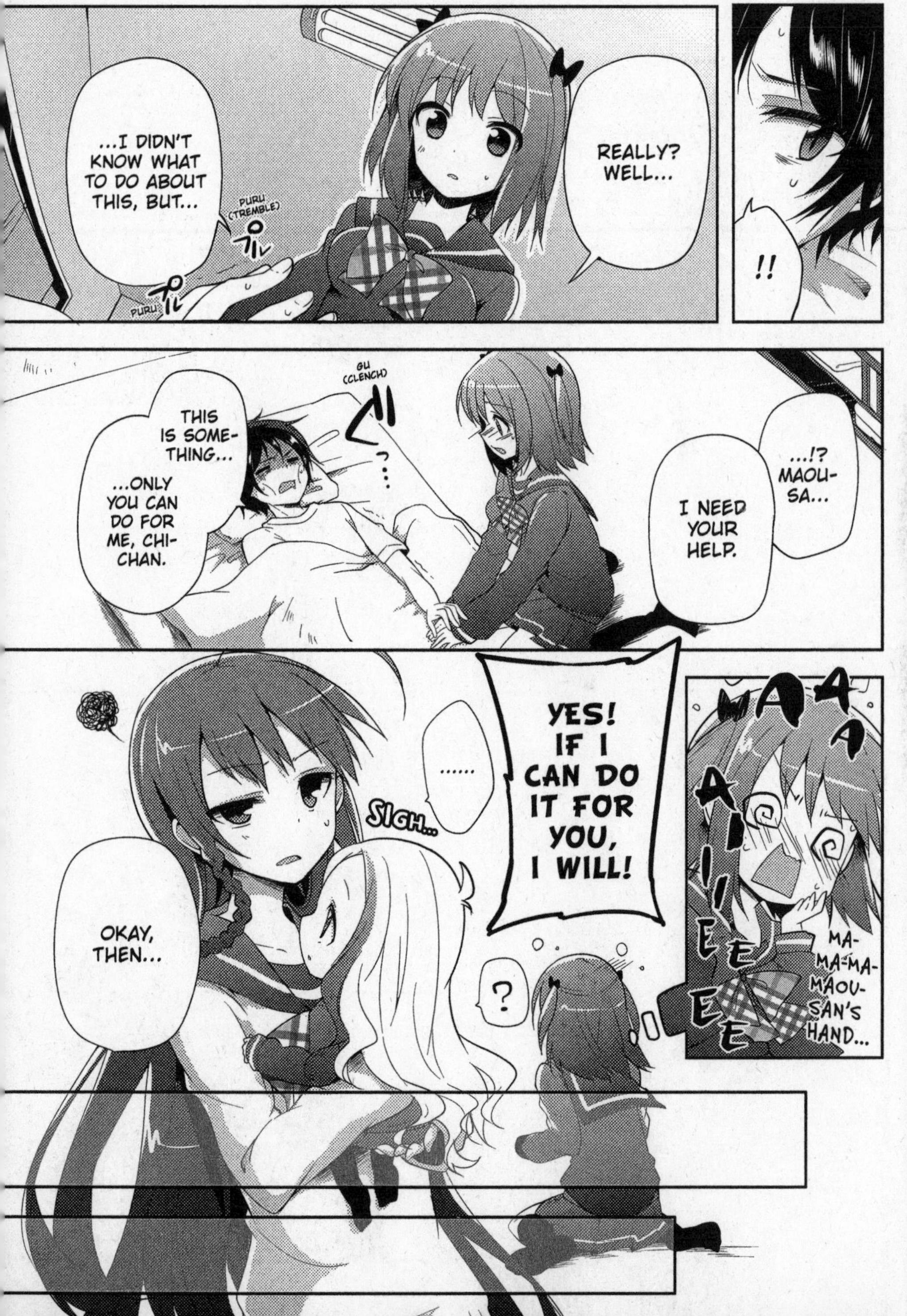
!!
REALLY? WELL...
...I DIDN'T KNOW WHAT TO DO ABOUT THIS, BUT...
PURU (TREMBLE)
プル
PURU
プル
...!? MAOU-SA...
I NEED YOUR HELP.
GU (CLENCH)
ぐっ
THIS IS SOME-THING...
...ONLY YOU CAN DO FOR ME, CHI-CHAN.
AAAA-IIEEEE
MA-MA-MA-MAOU-SAN'S HAND...
YES! IF I CAN DO IT FOR YOU, I WILL!
......
SIGH...
?
OKAY, THEN...

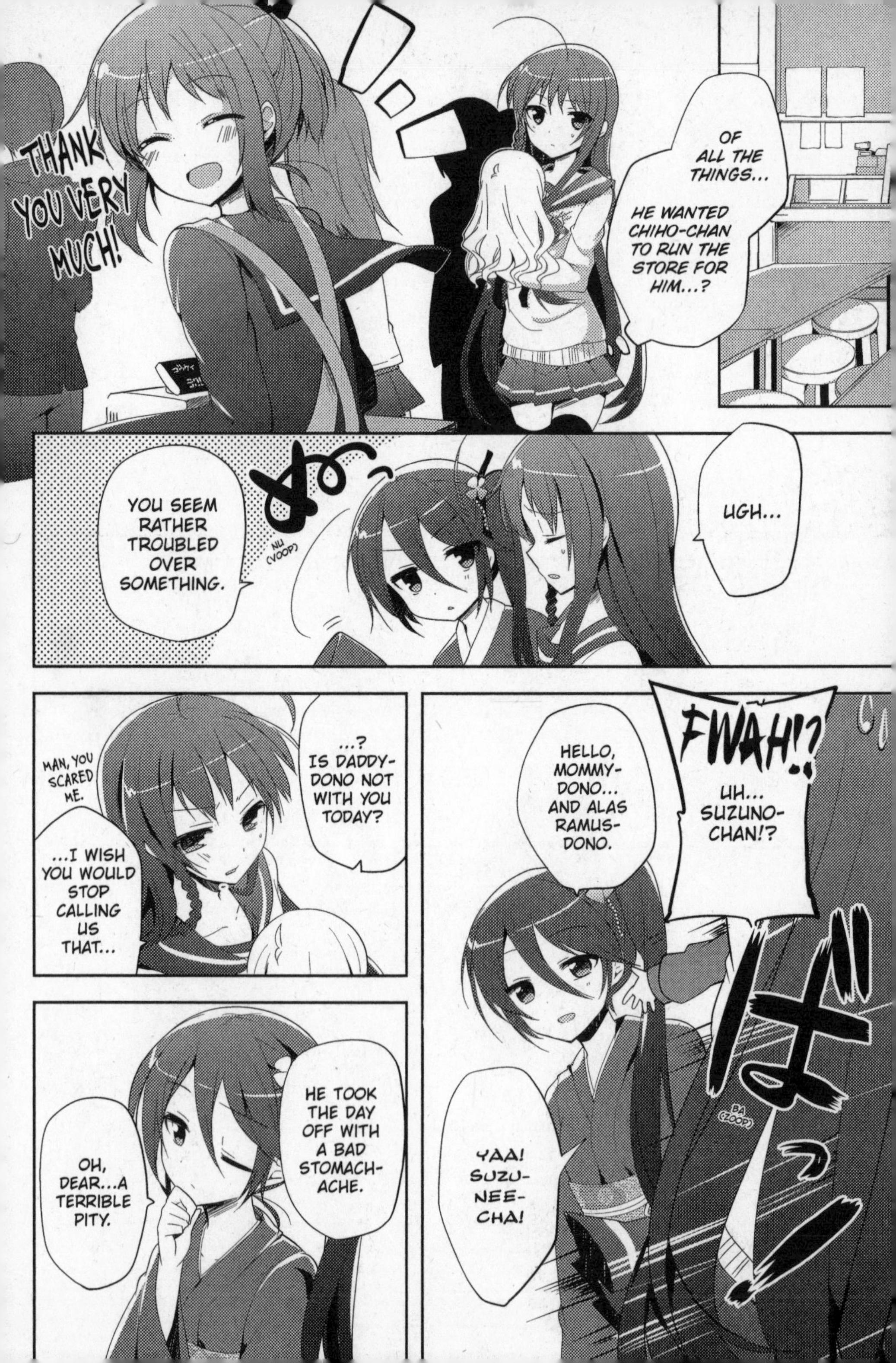
OF ALL THE THINGS...
HE WANTED CHIHO-CHAN TO RUN THE STORE FOR HIM...?
THANK YOU VERY MUCH!
UGH...
NU (VOOP)
YOU SEEM RATHER TROUBLED OVER SOMETHING.
FWAH!?
UH... SUZUNO-CHAN!?
HELLO, MOMMY-DONO... AND ALAS RAMUS-DONO.
BA (ZOOP)
YAA! SUZU-NEE-CHA!
...? IS DADDY-DONO NOT WITH YOU TODAY?
MAN, YOU SCARED ME.
...I WISH YOU WOULD STOP CALLING US THAT...
HE TOOK THE DAY OFF WITH A BAD STOMACH-ACHE.
OH, DEAR...A TERRIBLE PITY.

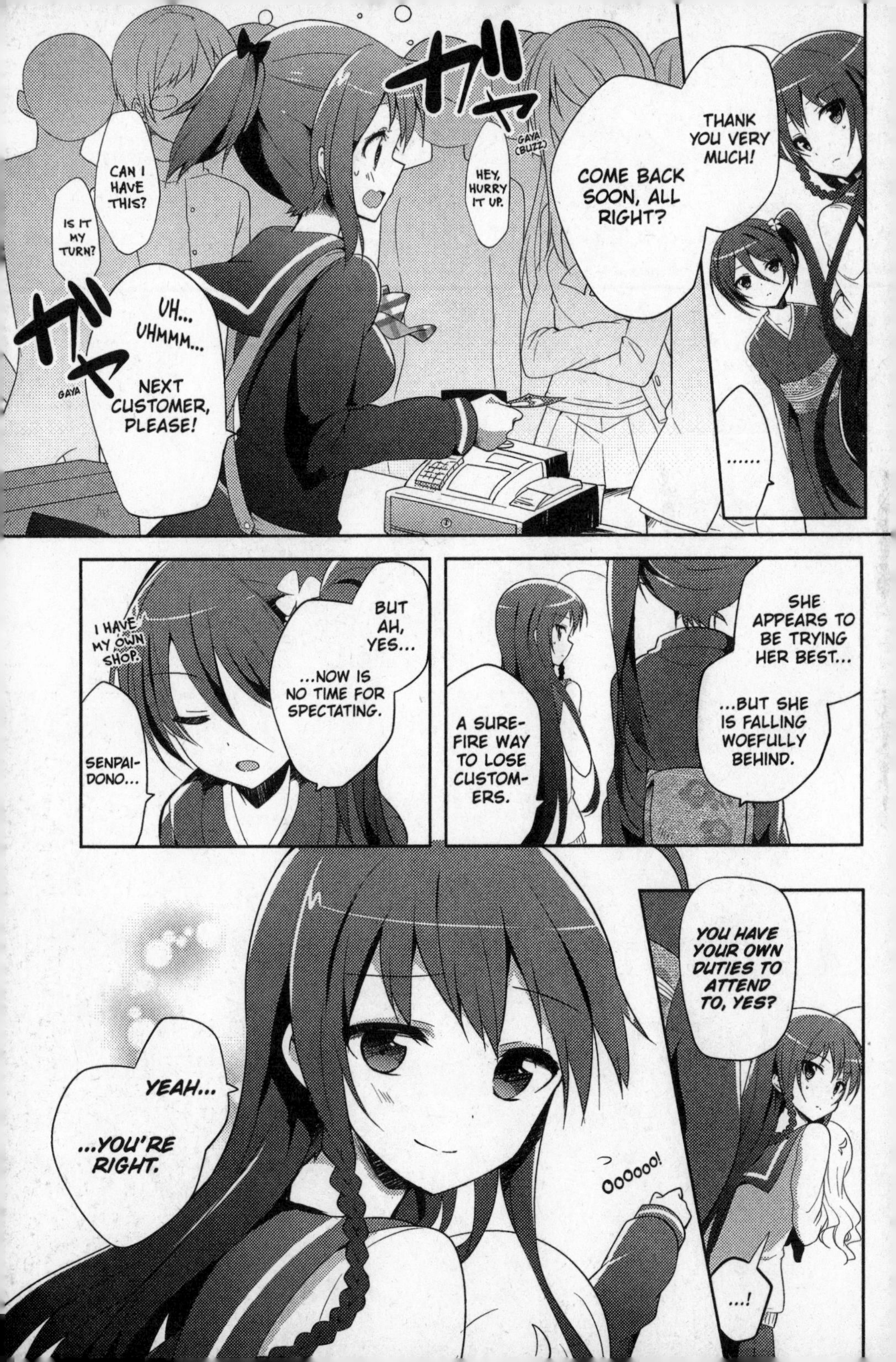
THANK YOU VERY MUCH!
COME BACK SOON, ALL RIGHT?
......
HEY, HURRY IT UP.
GAYA (BUZZ)
CAN I HAVE THIS?
IS IT MY TURN?
UH... UHMMM...
NEXT CUSTOMER, PLEASE!
GAYA
SHE APPEARS TO BE TRYING HER BEST...
...BUT SHE IS FALLING WOEFULLY BEHIND.
A SURE-FIRE WAY TO LOSE CUSTOMERS.
BUT AH, YES...
...NOW IS NO TIME FOR SPECTATING.
I HAVE MY OWN SHOP.
SENPAI-DONO...
YOU HAVE YOUR OWN DUTIES TO ATTEND TO, YES?
OOOOOO!
...!
YEAH...
...YOU'RE RIGHT.

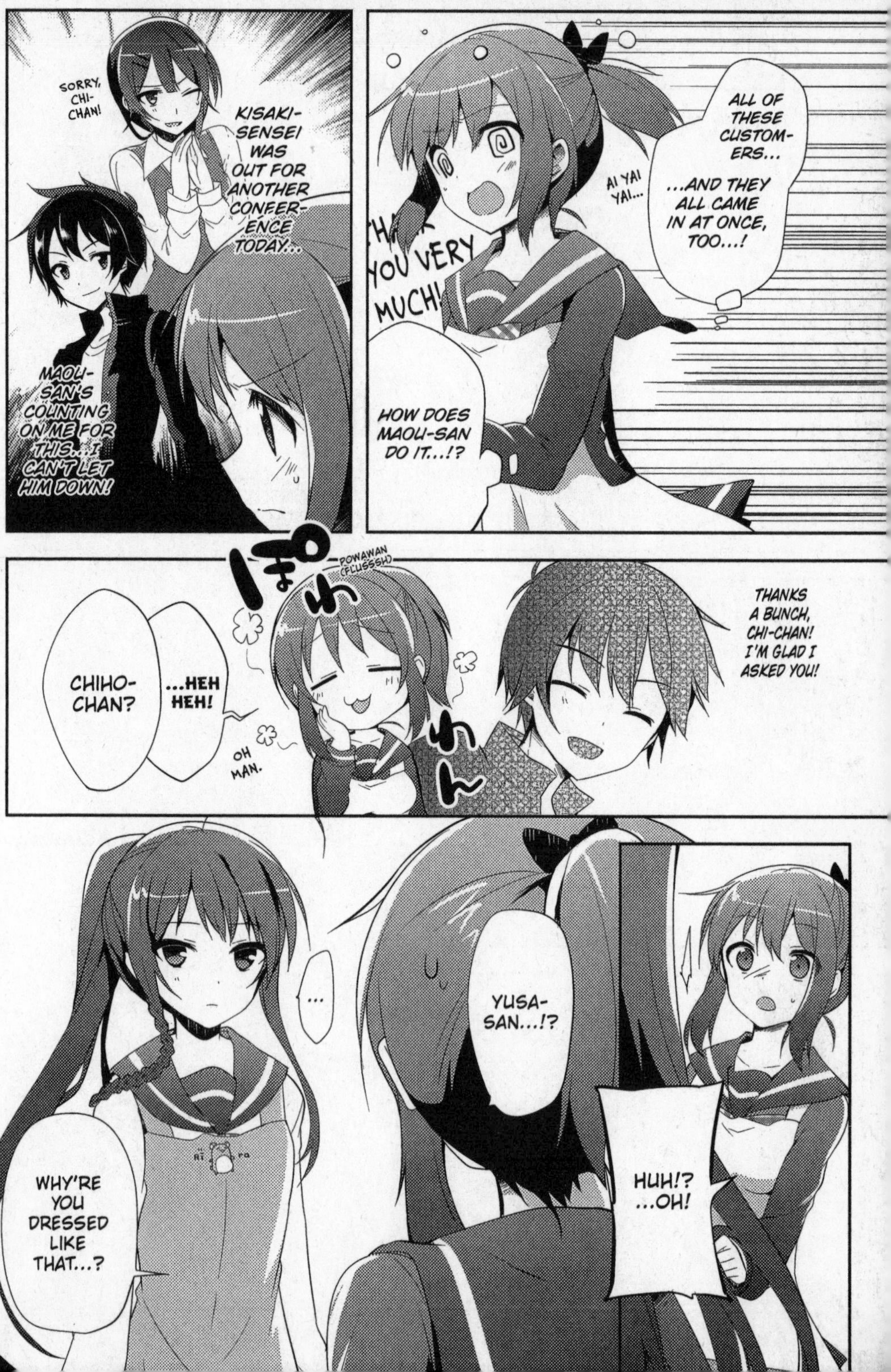
ALL OF THESE CUSTOMERS...
...AND THEY ALL CAME IN AT ONCE, TOO...!
AI YAI YAI...
YOU VERY MUCH!
HOW DOES MAOU-SAN DO IT...!?
KISAKI-SENSEI WAS OUT FOR ANOTHER CONFERENCE TODAY...
SORRY, CHI-CHAN!
MAOU-SAN'S COUNTING ON ME FOR THIS... I CAN'T LET HIM DOWN!
THANKS A BUNCH, CHI-CHAN! I'M GLAD I ASKED YOU!
POWAWAN (FLUSSSH)
...HEH HEH!
OH MAN.
CHIHO-CHAN?
YUSA-SAN...!?
...
WHY'RE YOU DRESSED LIKE THAT...?
HUH!? ...OH!

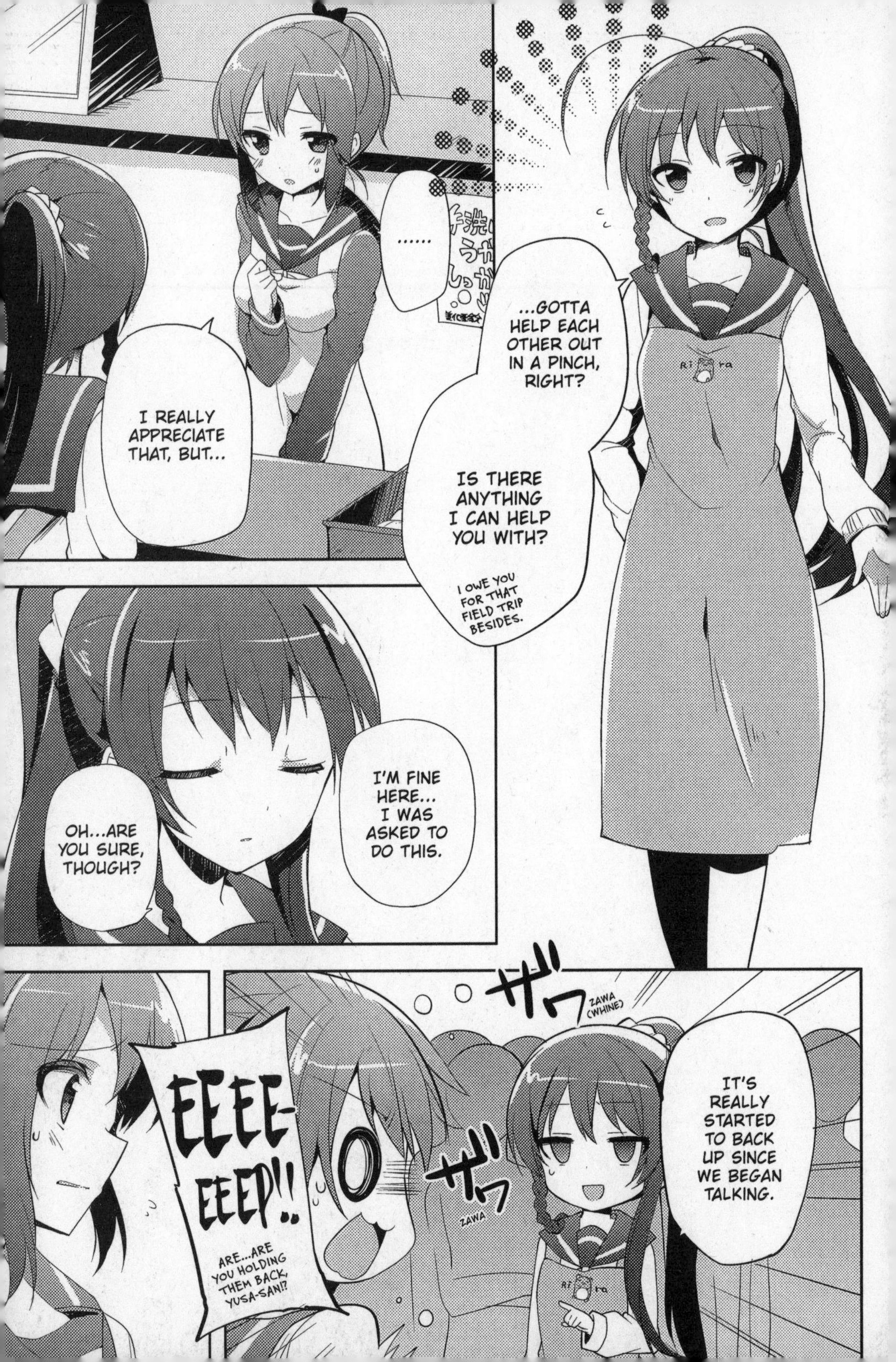

...GOTTA HELP EACH OTHER OUT IN A PINCH, RIGHT?
IS THERE ANYTHING I CAN HELP YOU WITH?
I OWE YOU FOR THAT FIELD TRIP BESIDES.
......
I REALLY APPRECIATE THAT, BUT...
I'M FINE HERE... I WAS ASKED TO DO THIS.
OH...ARE YOU SURE, THOUGH?
ザワ
ZAWA (WHINE)
IT'S REALLY STARTED TO BACK UP SINCE WE BEGAN TALKING.
ザワ
ZAWA
EEEE-EEEP!!
ARE...ARE YOU HOLDING THEM BACK, YUSA-SAN!?

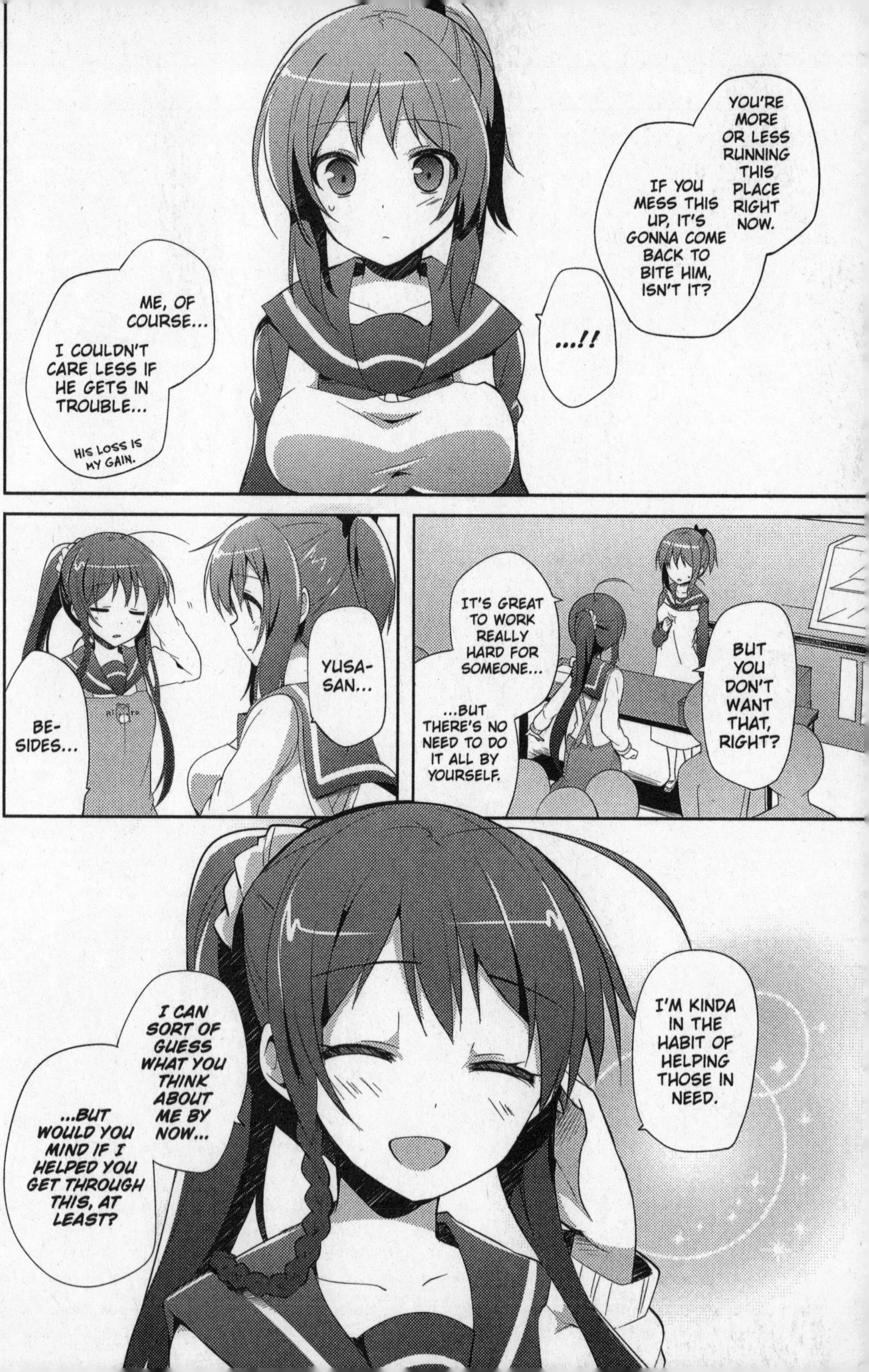
YOU'RE MORE OR LESS RUNNING THIS PLACE RIGHT NOW.
IF YOU MESS THIS UP, IT'S GONNA COME BACK TO BITE HIM, ISN'T IT?
...!!
ME, OF COURSE...
I COULDN'T CARE LESS IF HE GETS IN TROUBLE...
HIS LOSS IS MY GAIN.
IT'S GREAT TO WORK REALLY HARD FOR SOMEONE...
...BUT THERE'S NO NEED TO DO IT ALL BY YOURSELF.
BUT YOU DON'T WANT THAT, RIGHT?
YUSA-SAN...
BE-SIDES...
I'M KINDA IN THE HABIT OF HELPING THOSE IN NEED.
I CAN SORT OF GUESS WHAT YOU THINK ABOUT ME BY NOW...
...BUT WOULD YOU MIND IF I HELPED YOU GET THROUGH THIS, AT LEAST?

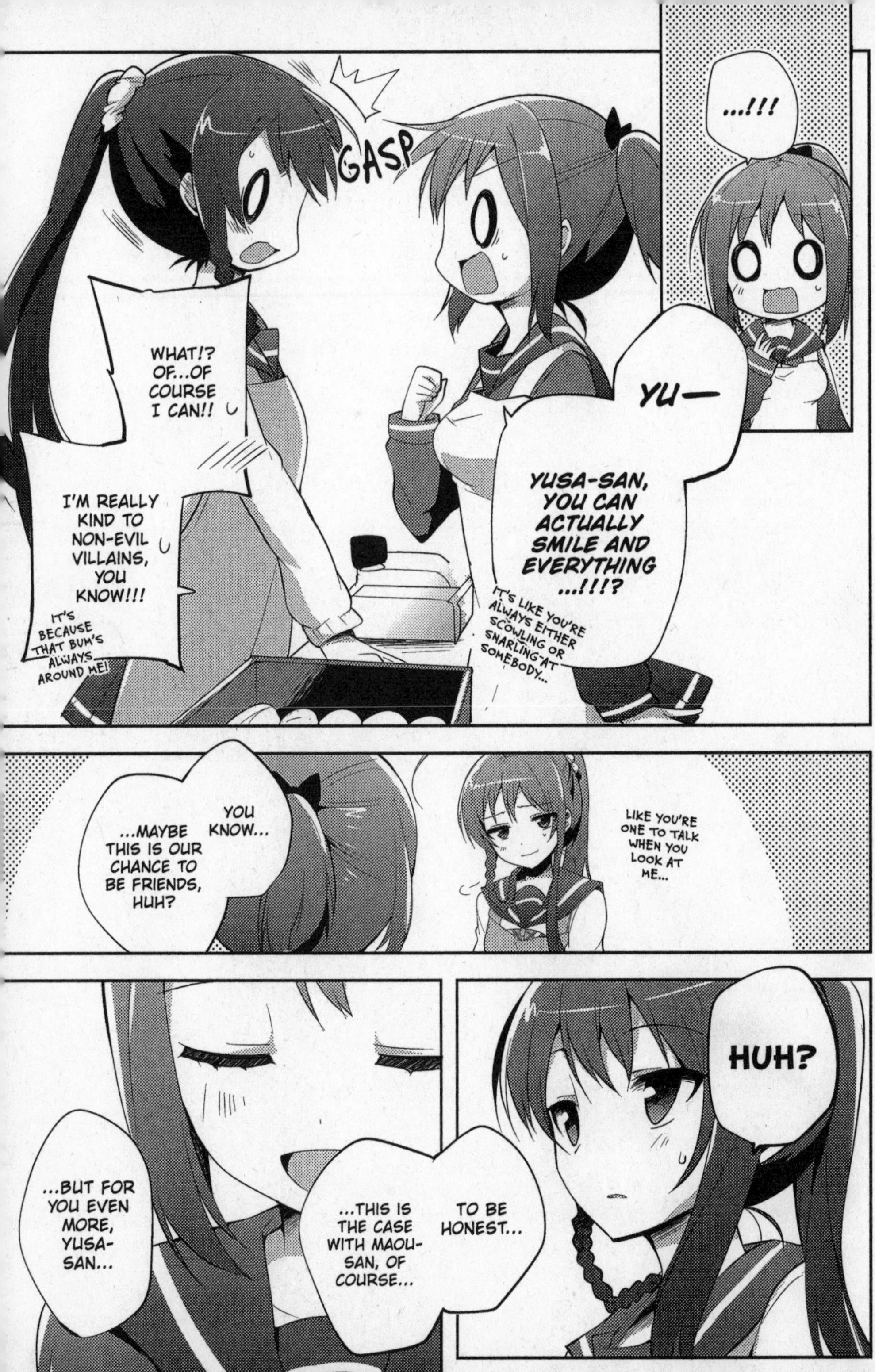
...!!!
YU—
GASP
YUSA-SAN, YOU CAN ACTUALLY SMILE AND EVERYTHING ...!!!?
IT'S LIKE YOU'RE ALWAYS EITHER SCOWLING OR SNARLING AT SOMEBODY...
WHAT!? OF...OF COURSE I CAN!!
I'M REALLY KIND TO NON-EVIL VILLAINS, YOU KNOW!!!
IT'S BECAUSE THAT BUM'S ALWAYS AROUND ME!
LIKE YOU'RE ONE TO TALK WHEN YOU LOOK AT ME...
YOU KNOW... ...MAYBE THIS IS OUR CHANCE TO BE FRIENDS, HUH?
HUH?
TO BE HONEST... ...THIS IS THE CASE WITH MAOU-SAN, OF COURSE...
...BUT FOR YOU EVEN MORE, YUSA-SAN...

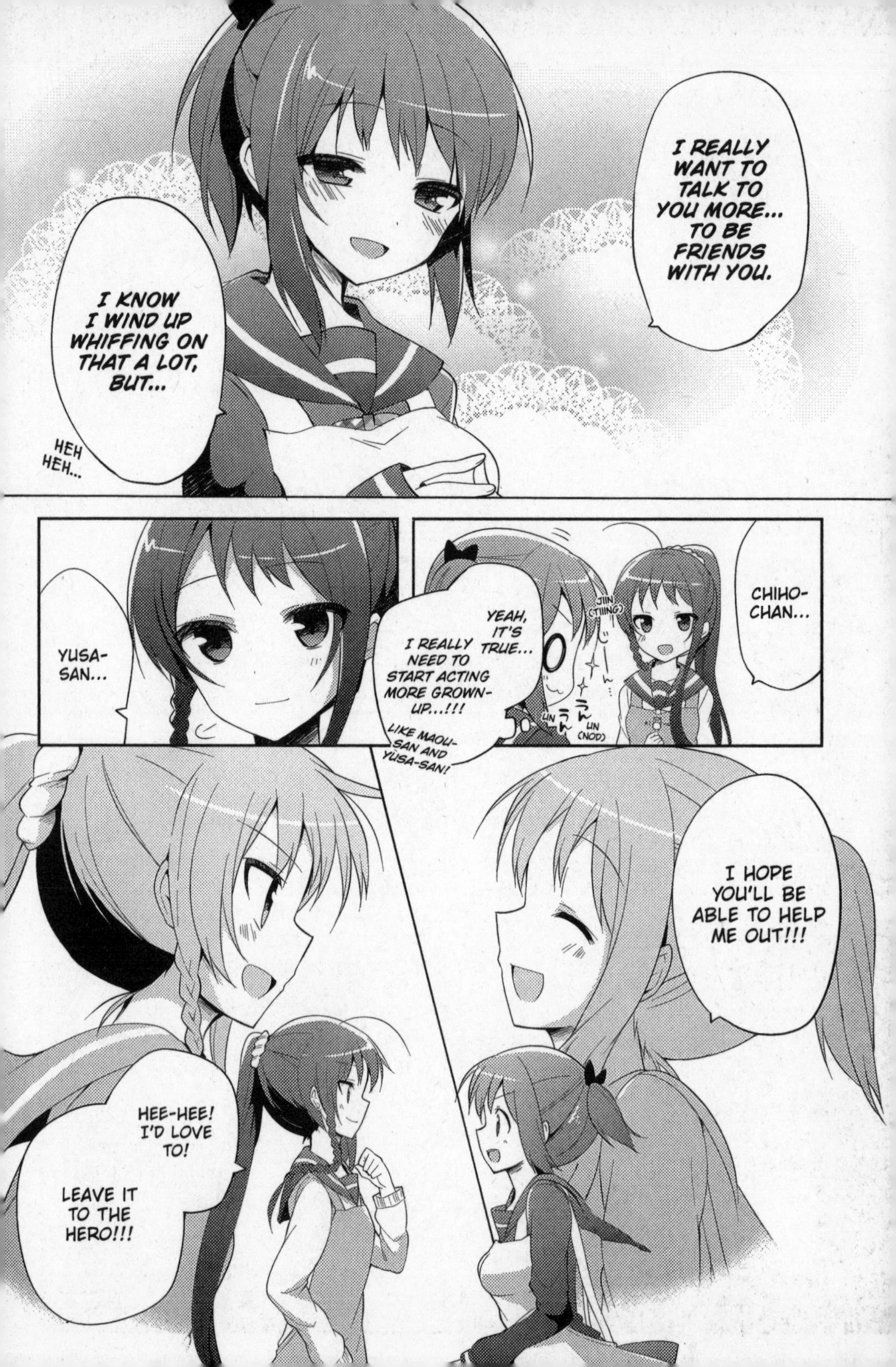
I REALLY WANT TO TALK TO YOU MORE... TO BE FRIENDS WITH YOU.
I KNOW I WIND UP WHIFFING ON THAT A LOT, BUT...
HEH HEH...
CHIHO-CHAN...
JIIN (TIIING)
YEAH, IT'S TRUE... I REALLY NEED TO START ACTING MORE GROWN-UP...!!!
LIKE MAOU-SAN AND YUSA-SAN!
UN UN (NOD)
YUSA-SAN...
I HOPE YOU'LL BE ABLE TO HELP ME OUT!!!
HEE-HEE! I'D LOVE TO!
LEAVE IT TO THE HERO!!!

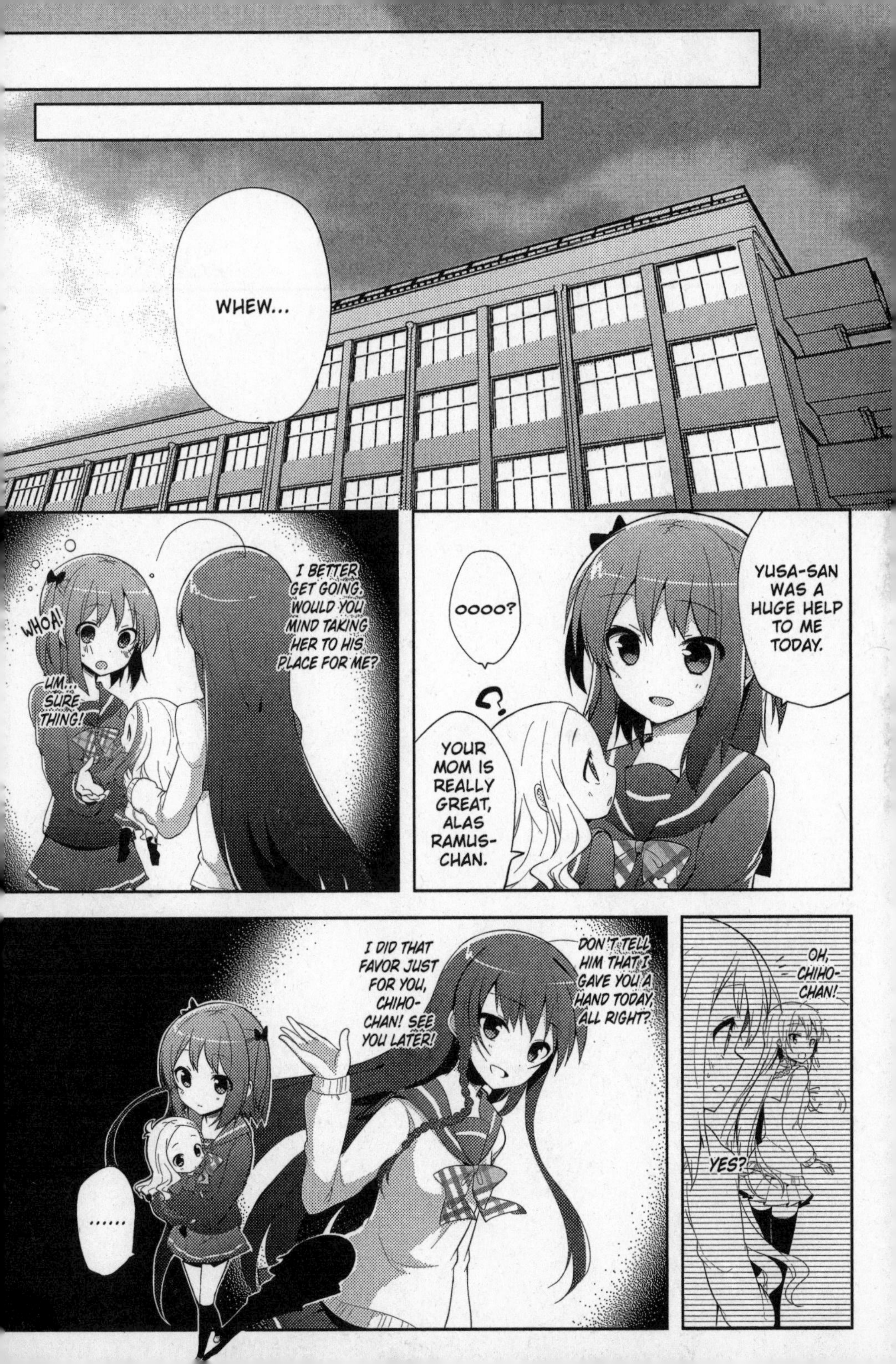
WHEW...
YUSA-SAN WAS A HUGE HELP TO ME TODAY.
OOOO?
YOUR MOM IS REALLY GREAT, ALAS RAMUS-CHAN.
I BETTER GET GOING. WOULD YOU MIND TAKING HER TO HIS PLACE FOR ME?
WHOA!
UM... SURE THING!
OH, CHIHO-CHAN!
YES?
DON'T TELL HIM THAT I GAVE YOU A HAND TODAY, ALL RIGHT?
I DID THAT FAVOR JUST FOR YOU, CHIHO-CHAN! SEE YOU LATER!
......

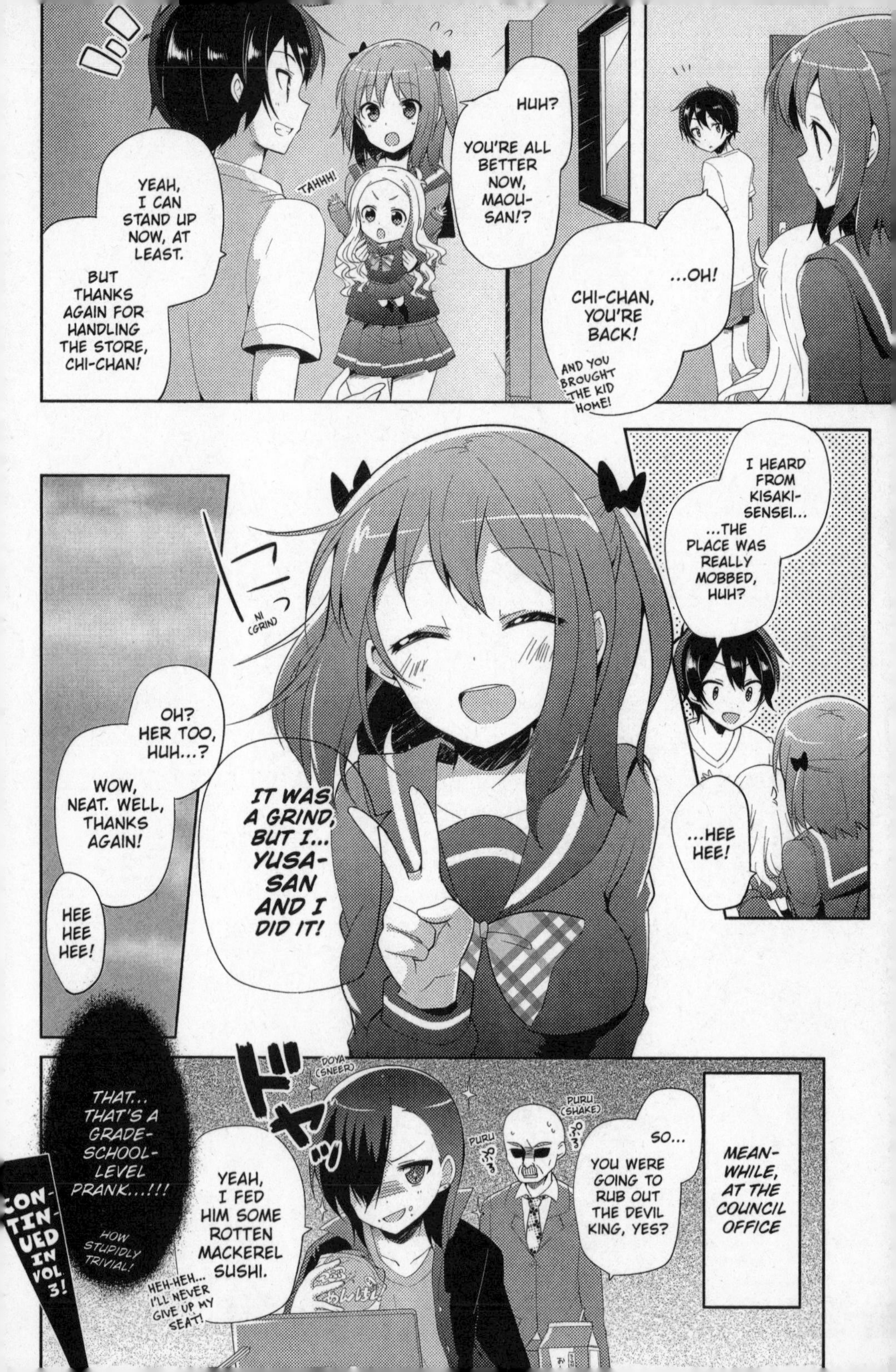
...OH!
CHI-CHAN, YOU'RE BACK!
AND YOU BROUGHT THE KID HOME!
HUH?
YOU'RE ALL BETTER NOW, MAOU-SAN!?
TAHHH!
YEAH, I CAN STAND UP NOW, AT LEAST.
BUT THANKS AGAIN FOR HANDLING THE STORE, CHI-CHAN!
I HEARD FROM KISAKI-SENSEI...
...THE PLACE WAS REALLY MOBBED, HUH?
...HEE HEE!
NI (GRIN)
IT WAS A GRIND, BUT I... YUSA-SAN AND I DID IT!
OH? HER TOO, HUH...?
WOW, NEAT. WELL, THANKS AGAIN!
HEE HEE HEE!
MEAN-WHILE, AT THE COUNCIL OFFICE
SO...
YOU WERE GOING TO RUB OUT THE DEVIL KING, YES?
PURU (SHAKE)
PURU
DOYA (SNEER)
YEAH, I FED HIM SOME ROTTEN MACKEREL SUSHI.
HEH-HEH... I'LL NEVER GIVE UP MY SEAT!
THAT... THAT'S A GRADE-SCHOOL-LEVEL PRANK...!!!
HOW STUPIDLY TRIVIAL!
CONTINUED IN VOL. 3!

THE DEVIL IS A PART-TIMER! HIGH SCHOOL!

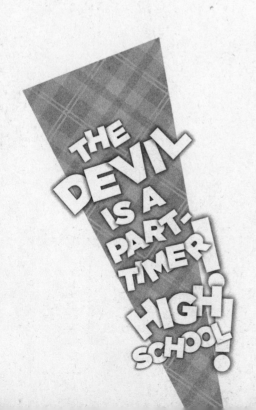

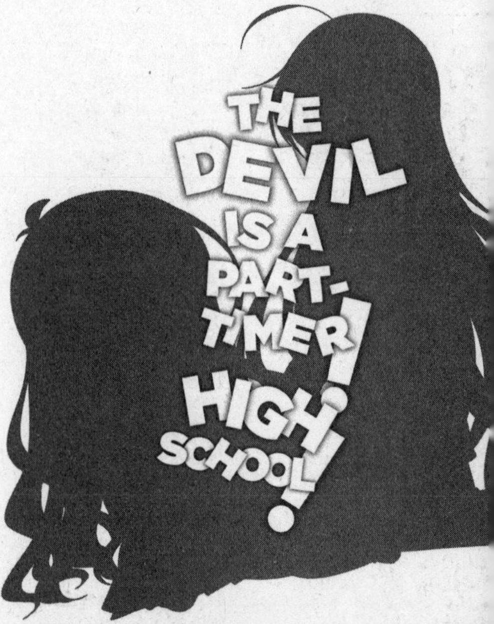
THE DEVIL IS A PART-TIMER! HIGH SCHOOL!

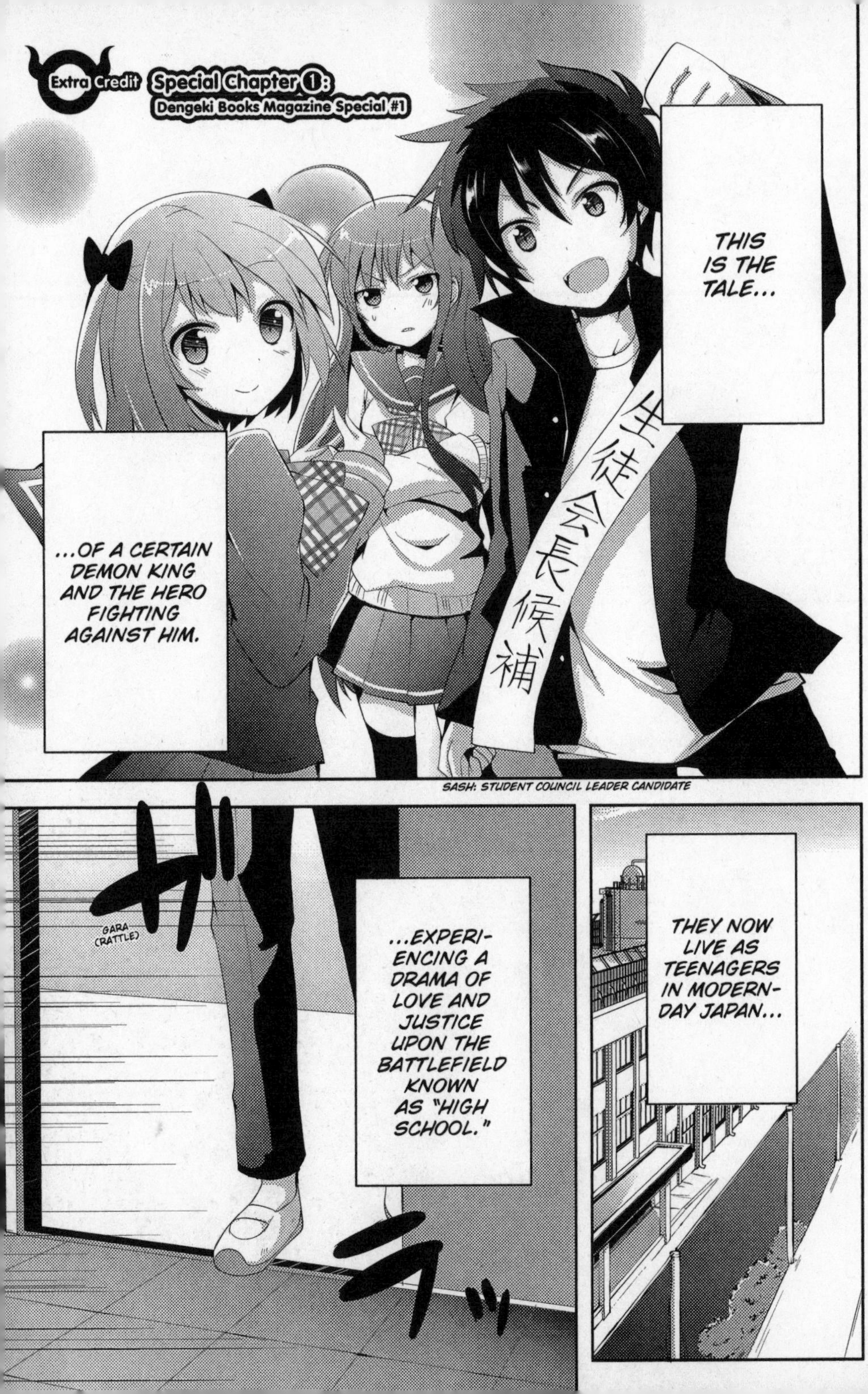

Extra Credit Special Chapter 1: Dengeki Books Magazine Special #1
THIS IS THE TALE...
...OF A CERTAIN DEMON KING AND THE HERO FIGHTING AGAINST HIM.
生徒会長候補
SASH: STUDENT COUNCIL LEADER CANDIDATE
THEY NOW LIVE AS TEENAGERS IN MODERN-DAY JAPAN...
...EXPERIENCING A DRAMA OF LOVE AND JUSTICE UPON THE BATTLEFIELD KNOWN AS "HIGH SCHOOL."
ガラ
GARA (RATTLE)
ラッ

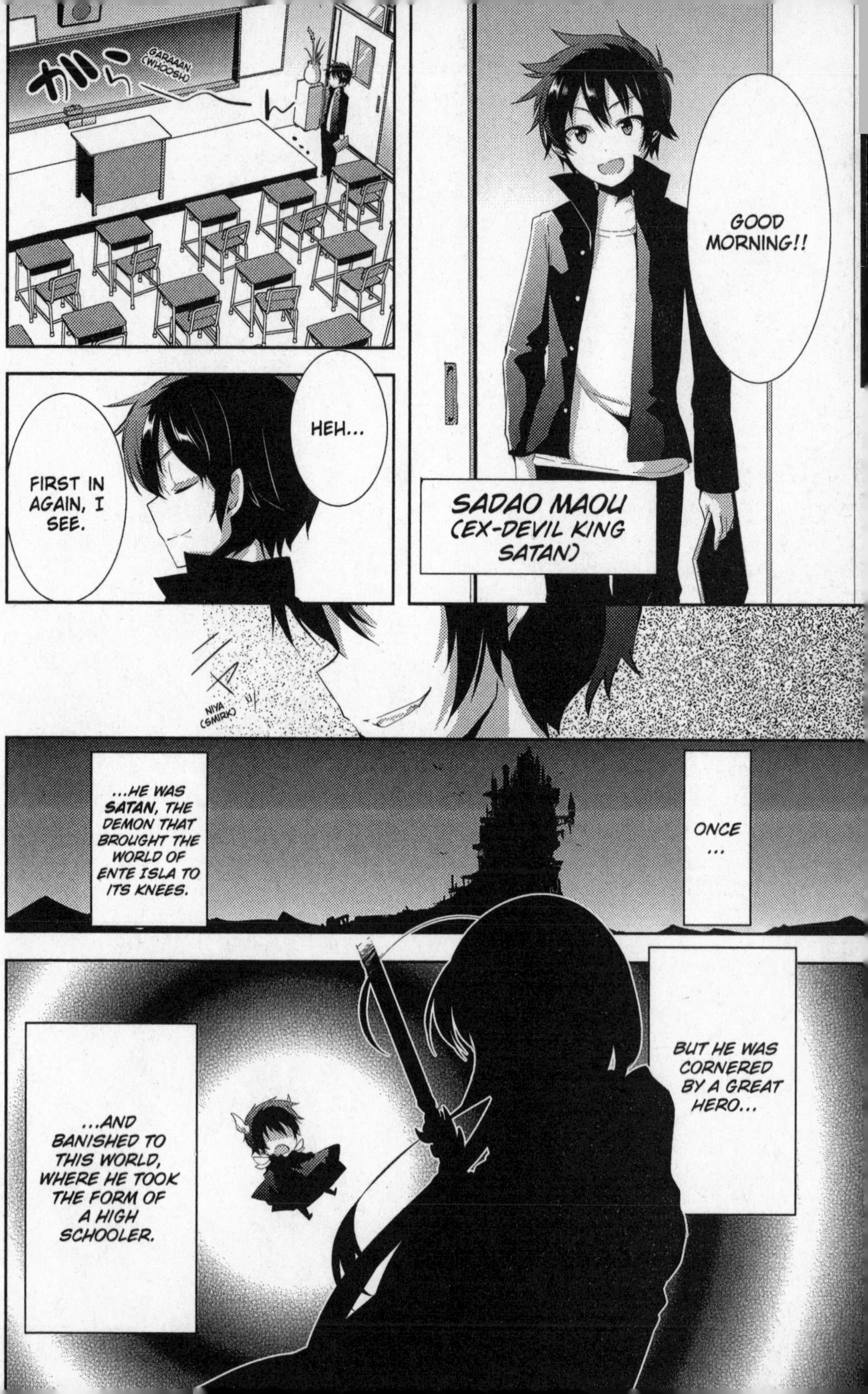
GOOD MORNING!!
SADAO MAOU (EX-DEVIL KING SATAN)
GARAAAN (WHOOSH)
HEH...
FIRST IN AGAIN, I SEE.
NIYA (SMIRK)
ONCE ...
...HE WAS SATAN, THE DEMON THAT BROUGHT THE WORLD OF ENTE ISLA TO ITS KNEES.
BUT HE WAS CORNERED BY A GREAT HERO...
...AND BANISHED TO THIS WORLD, WHERE HE TOOK THE FORM OF A HIGH SCHOOLER.

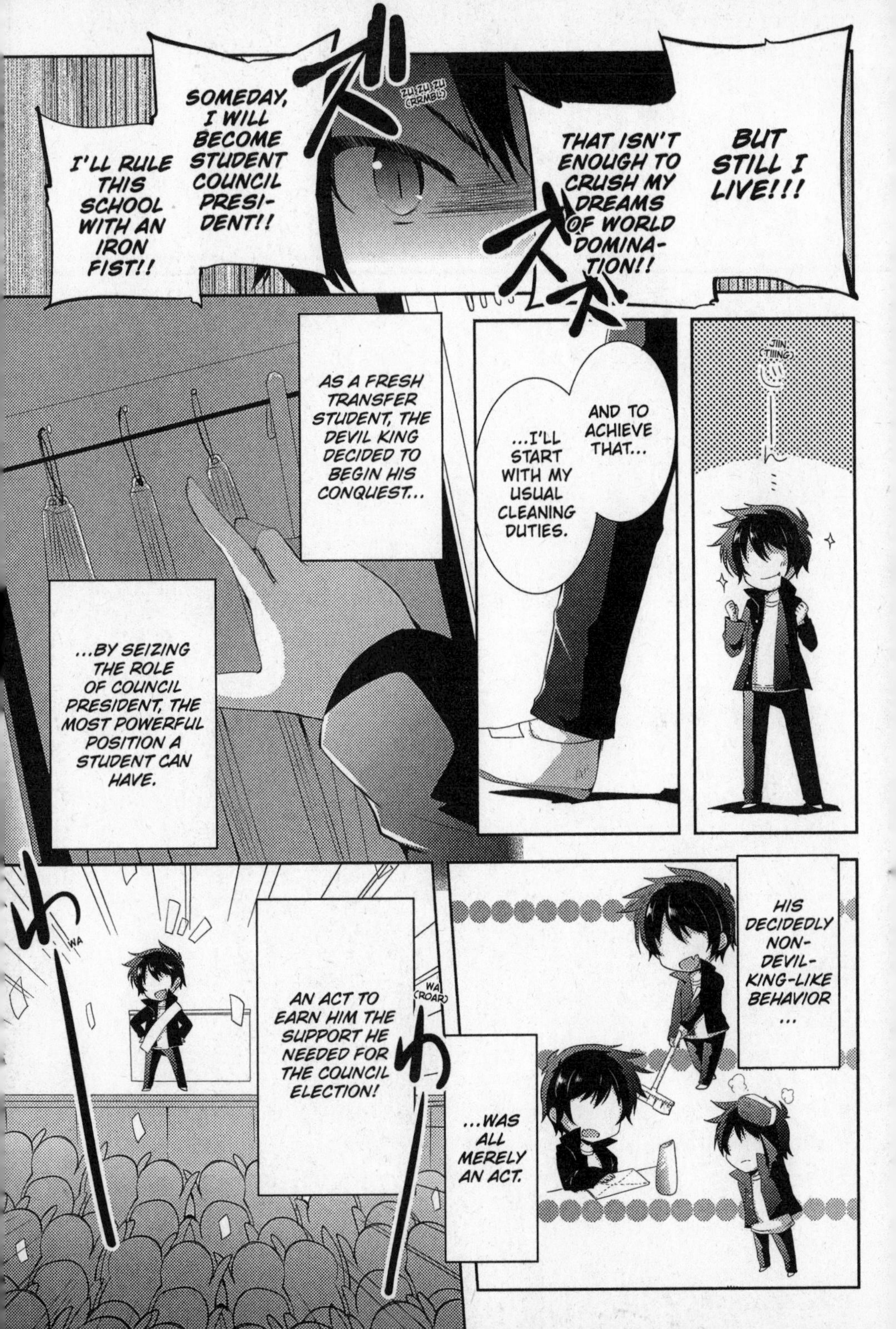
BUT STILL I LIVE!!!
THAT ISN'T ENOUGH TO CRUSH MY DREAMS OF WORLD DOMINATION!!
ZU ZU ZU (RRMBL)
SOMEDAY, I WILL BECOME STUDENT COUNCIL PRESIDENT!!
I'LL RULE THIS SCHOOL WITH AN IRON FIST!!
JIIN (TIIING)
AND TO ACHIEVE THAT...
...I'LL START WITH MY USUAL CLEANING DUTIES.
AS A FRESH TRANSFER STUDENT, THE DEVIL KING DECIDED TO BEGIN HIS CONQUEST...
...BY SEIZING THE ROLE OF COUNCIL PRESIDENT, THE MOST POWERFUL POSITION A STUDENT CAN HAVE.
HIS DECIDEDLY NON-DEVIL-KING-LIKE BEHAVIOR...
...WAS ALL MERELY AN ACT.
WA (ROAR)
AN ACT TO EARN HIM THE SUPPORT HE NEEDED FOR THE COUNCIL ELECTION!
WA

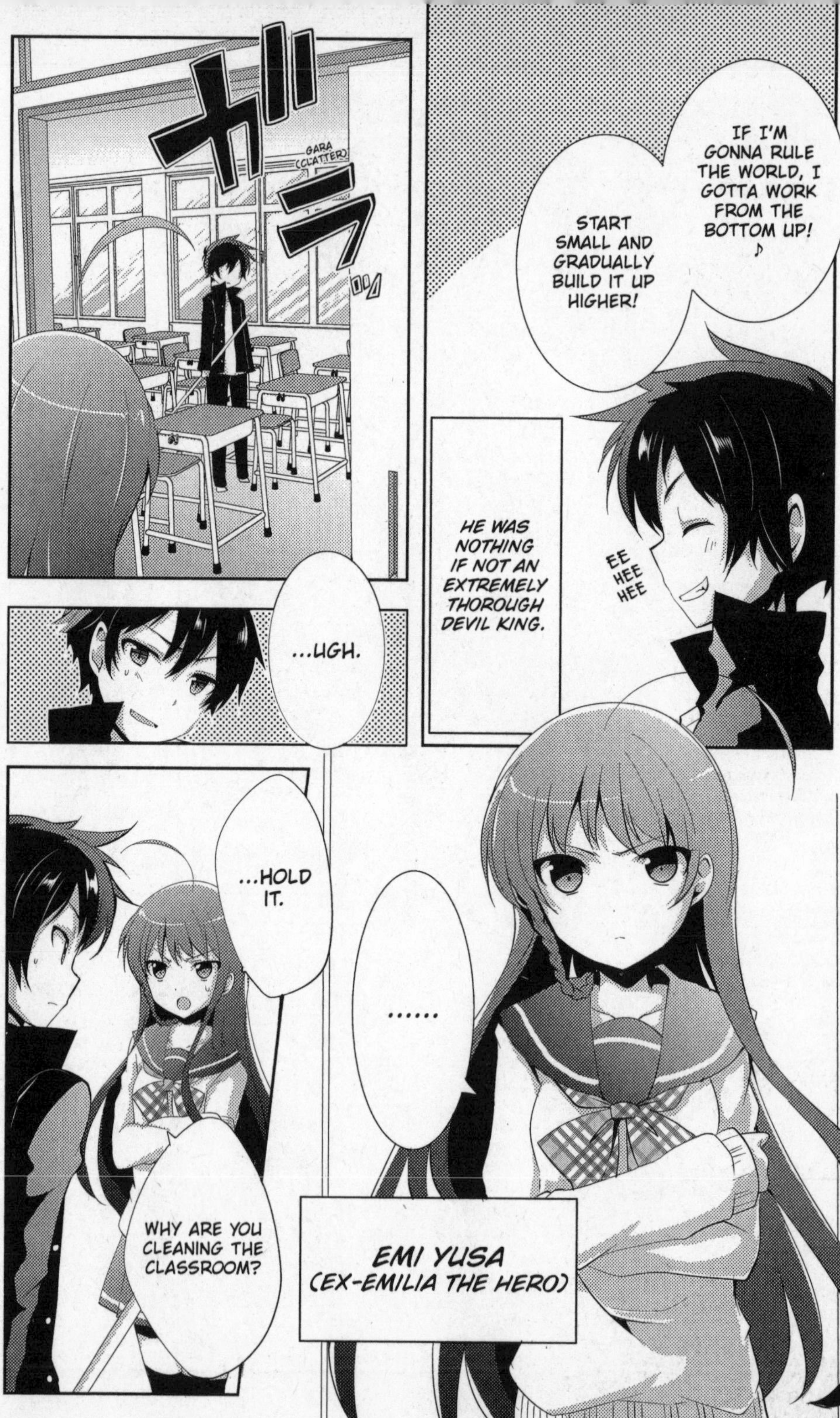
IF I'M GONNA RULE THE WORLD, I GOTTA WORK FROM THE BOTTOM UP! ♪
START SMALL AND GRADUALLY BUILD IT UP HIGHER!
EE HEE HEE
HE WAS NOTHING IF NOT AN EXTREMELY THOROUGH DEVIL KING.
GARA (CLATTER)
...UGH.
......
EMI YUSA (EX-EMILIA THE HERO)
...HOLD IT.
WHY ARE YOU CLEANING THE CLASSROOM?

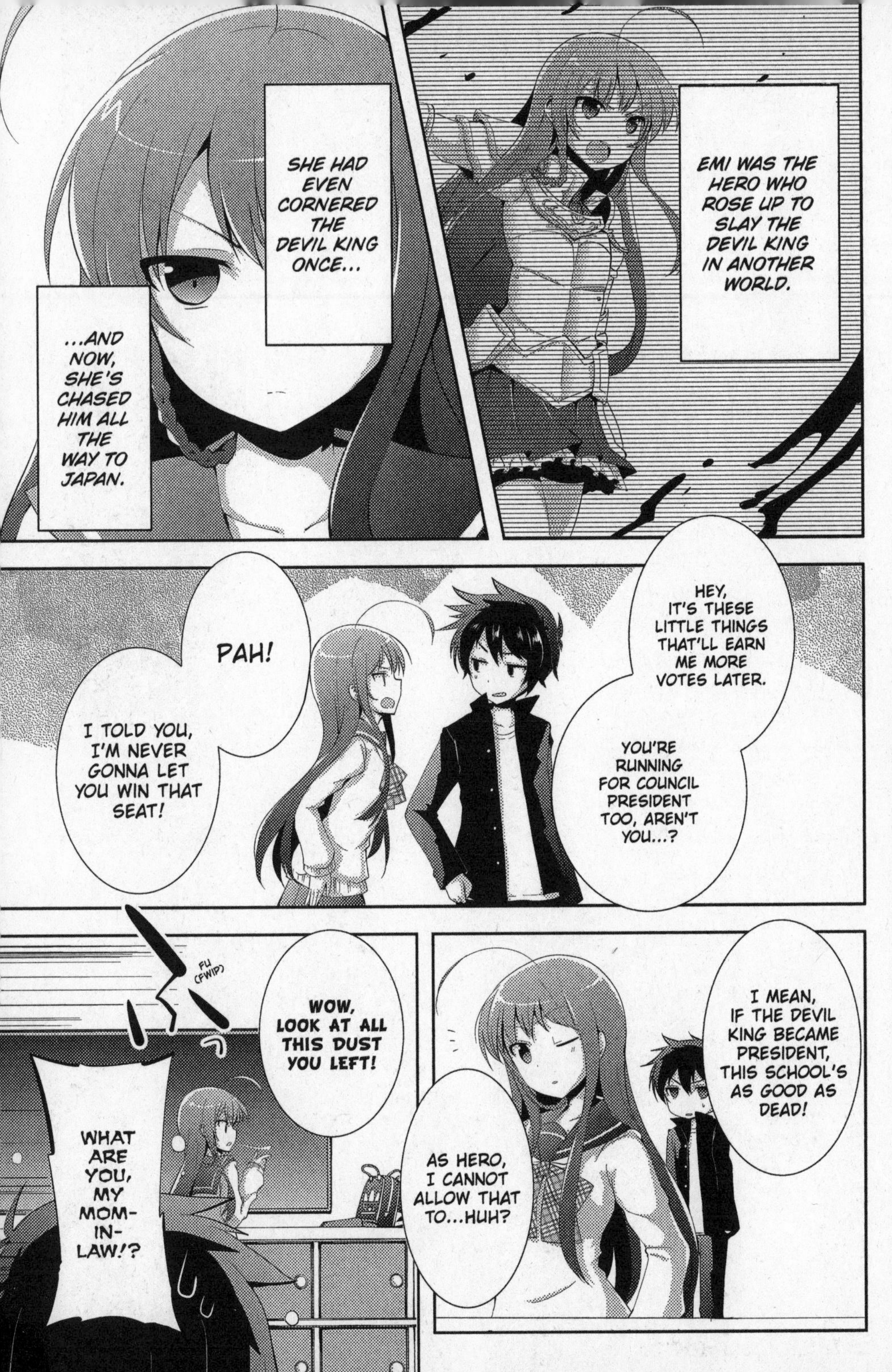
EMI WAS THE HERO WHO ROSE UP TO SLAY THE DEVIL KING IN ANOTHER WORLD.
SHE HAD EVEN CORNERED THE DEVIL KING ONCE...
...AND NOW, SHE'S CHASED HIM ALL THE WAY TO JAPAN.
HEY, IT'S THESE LITTLE THINGS THAT'LL EARN ME MORE VOTES LATER.
YOU'RE RUNNING FOR COUNCIL PRESIDENT TOO, AREN'T YOU...?
PAH!
I TOLD YOU, I'M NEVER GONNA LET YOU WIN THAT SEAT!
I MEAN, IF THE DEVIL KING BECAME PRESIDENT, THIS SCHOOL'S AS GOOD AS DEAD!
AS HERO, I CANNOT ALLOW THAT TO...HUH?
FU (FWIP)
WOW, LOOK AT ALL THIS DUST YOU LEFT!
WHAT ARE YOU, MY MOM-IN-LAW!?

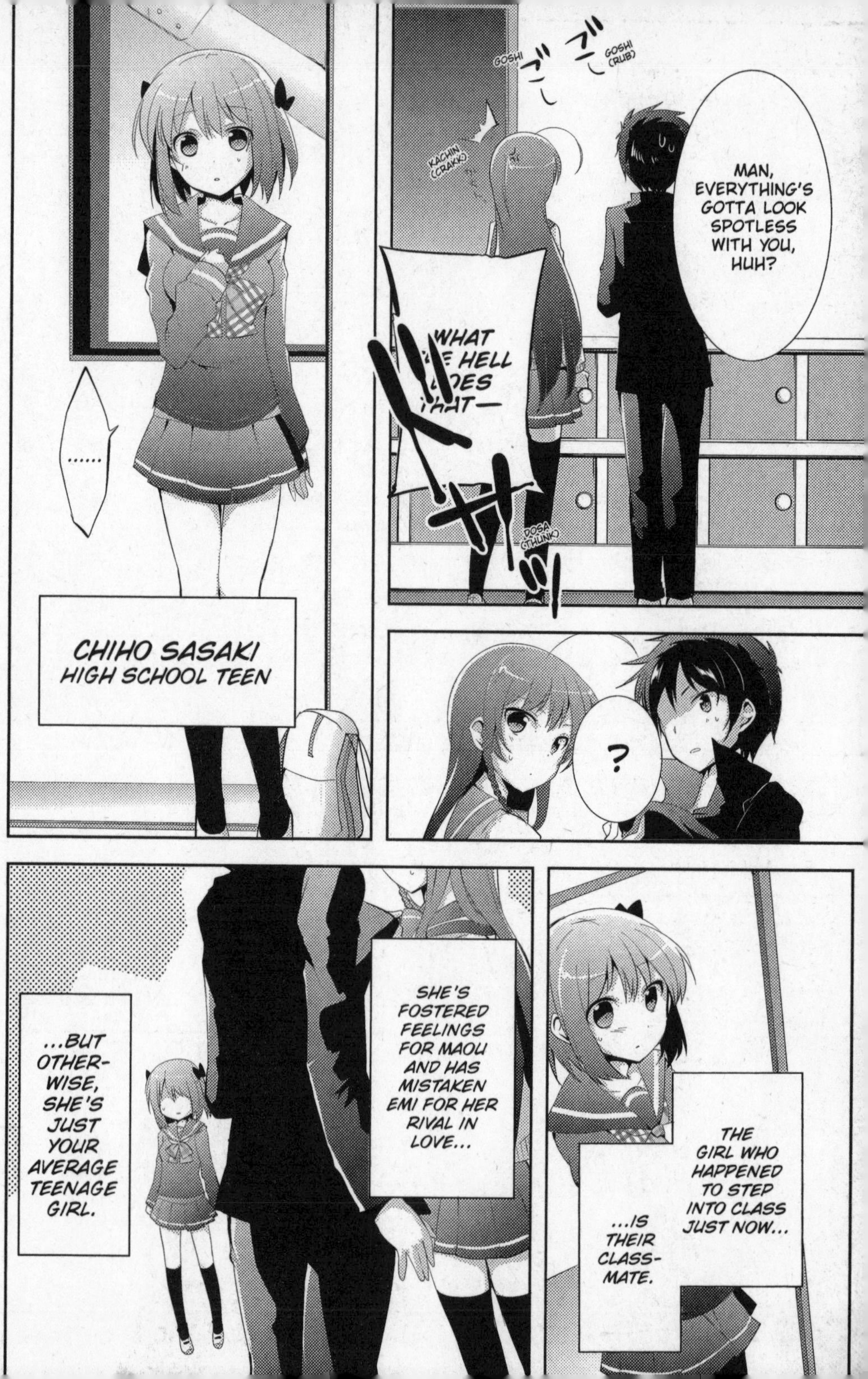
GOSHI (RUB)
GOSHI
MAN, EVERYTHING'S GOTTA LOOK SPOTLESS WITH YOU, HUH?
KACHIN (CRAKK)
WHAT THE HELL DOES THAT—
DOSA (THUNK)
?
......
CHIHO SASAKI HIGH SCHOOL TEEN
THE GIRL WHO HAPPENED TO STEP INTO CLASS JUST NOW...
...IS THEIR CLASS-MATE.
SHE'S FOSTERED FEELINGS FOR MAOU AND HAS MISTAKEN EMI FOR HER RIVAL IN LOVE...
...BUT OTHER-WISE, SHE'S JUST YOUR AVERAGE TEENAGE GIRL.

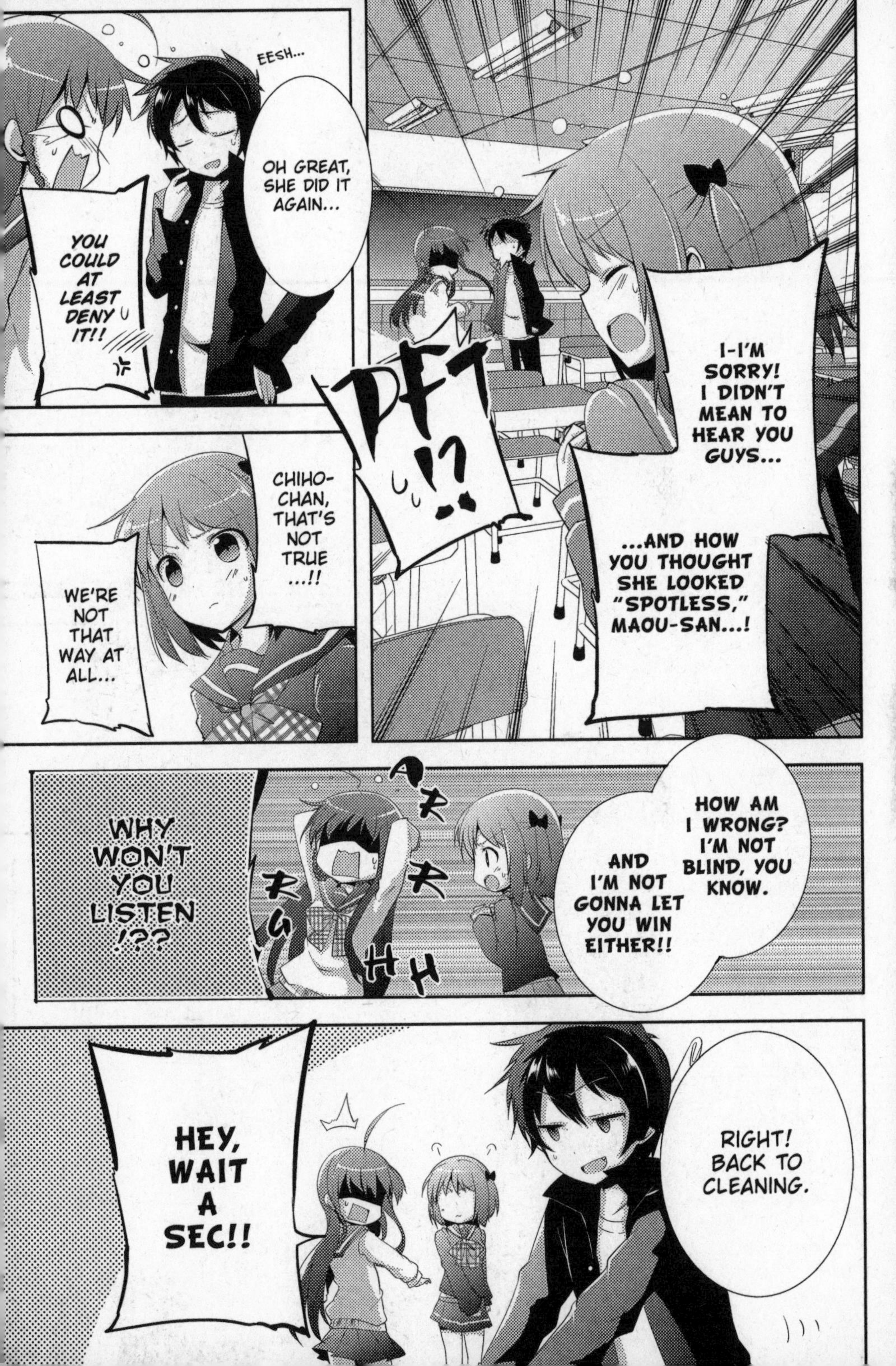
I-I'M SORRY! I DIDN'T MEAN TO HEAR YOU GUYS...
...AND HOW YOU THOUGHT SHE LOOKED "SPOTLESS," MAOU-SAN...!
PFT!?
EESH...
OH GREAT, SHE DID IT AGAIN...
YOU COULD AT LEAST DENY IT!!
CHIHO-CHAN, THAT'S NOT TRUE...!!
WE'RE NOT THAT WAY AT ALL...
HOW AM I WRONG? I'M NOT BLIND, YOU KNOW.
AND I'M NOT GONNA LET YOU WIN EITHER!!
WHY WON'T YOU LISTEN!??
RIGHT! BACK TO CLEANING.
HEY, WAIT A SEC!!

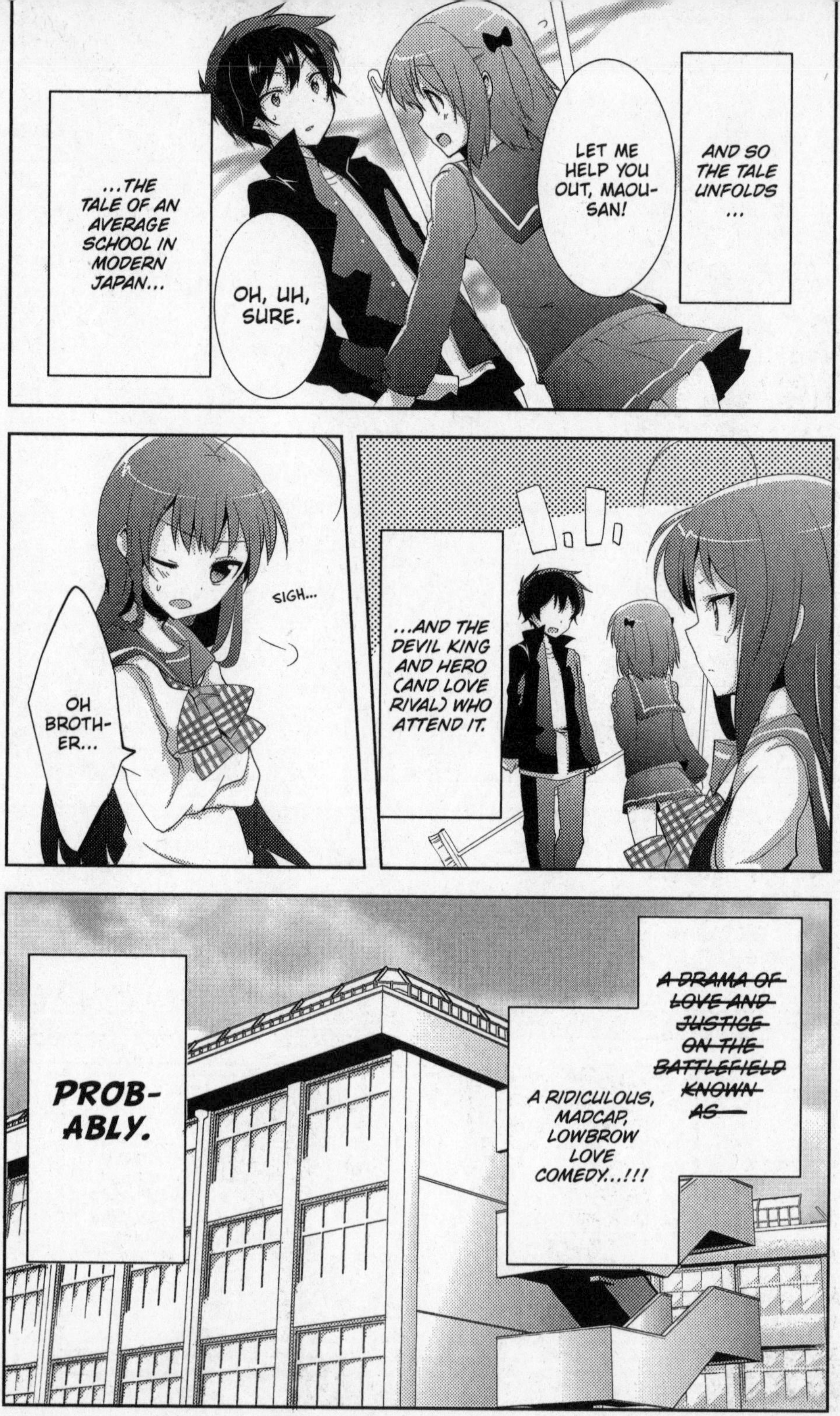
AND SO THE TALE UNFOLDS ...
LET ME HELP YOU OUT, MAOU-SAN!
OH, UH, SURE.
...THE TALE OF AN AVERAGE SCHOOL IN MODERN JAPAN...
...AND THE DEVIL KING AND HERO (AND LOVE RIVAL) WHO ATTEND IT.
SIGH...
OH BROTHER...
~~A DRAMA OF LOVE AND JUSTICE ON THE BATTLEFIELD KNOWN AS~~
A RIDICULOUS, MADCAP, LOWBROW LOVE COMEDY...!!!
PROB-ABLY.

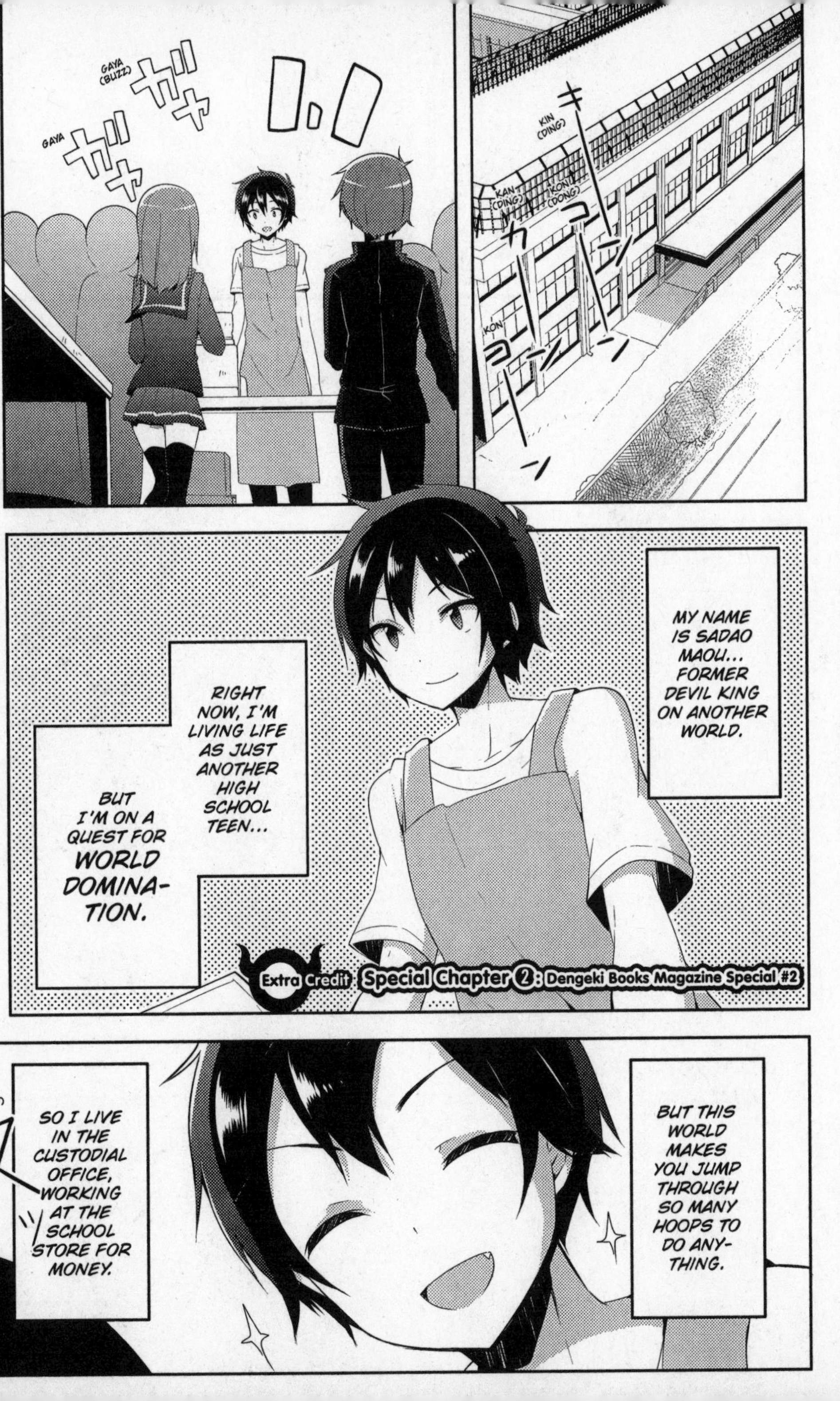
KIN (DING)
KAN (DING)
KON (DONG)
KON
GAYA (BUZZ)
GAYA
MY NAME IS SADAO MAOU... FORMER DEVIL KING ON ANOTHER WORLD.
RIGHT NOW, I'M LIVING LIFE AS JUST ANOTHER HIGH SCHOOL TEEN...
BUT I'M ON A QUEST FOR WORLD DOMINATION.
Extra Credit Special Chapter 2: Dengeki Books Magazine Special #2
BUT THIS WORLD MAKES YOU JUMP THROUGH SO MANY HOOPS TO DO ANYTHING.
SO I LIVE IN THE CUSTODIAL OFFICE, WORKING AT THE SCHOOL STORE FOR MONEY.
SU (FWOOP)

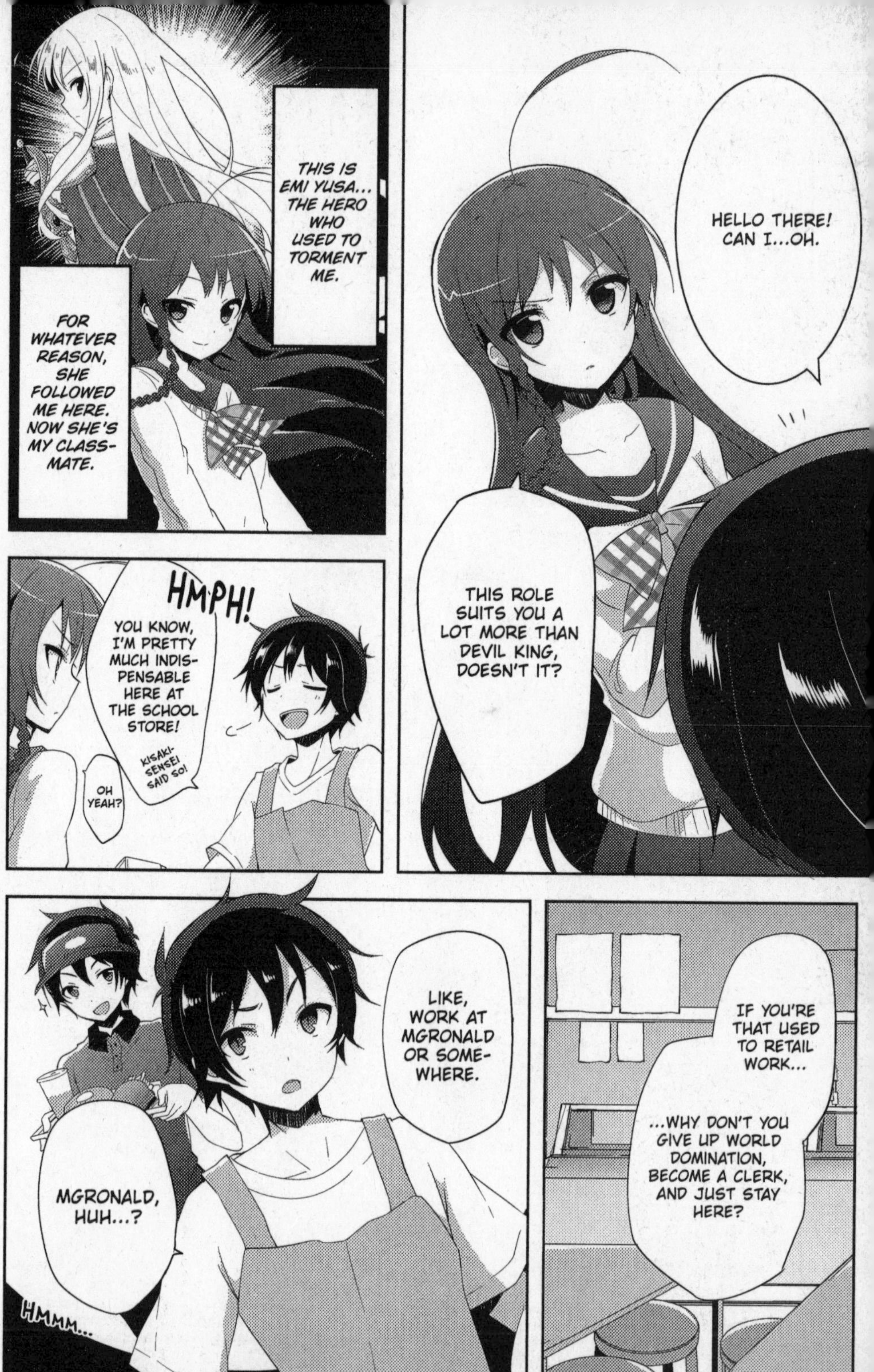
HELLO THERE! CAN I...OH.
THIS ROLE SUITS YOU A LOT MORE THAN DEVIL KING, DOESN'T IT?
THIS IS EMI YUSA... THE HERO WHO USED TO TORMENT ME.
FOR WHATEVER REASON, SHE FOLLOWED ME HERE. NOW SHE'S MY CLASSMATE.
HMPH!
YOU KNOW, I'M PRETTY MUCH INDISPENSABLE HERE AT THE SCHOOL STORE!
KISAKI-SENSEI SAID SO!
OH YEAH?
IF YOU'RE THAT USED TO RETAIL WORK...
...WHY DON'T YOU GIVE UP WORLD DOMINATION, BECOME A CLERK, AND JUST STAY HERE?
LIKE, WORK AT MGRONALD OR SOMEWHERE.
MGRONALD, HUH...?
HMMM...

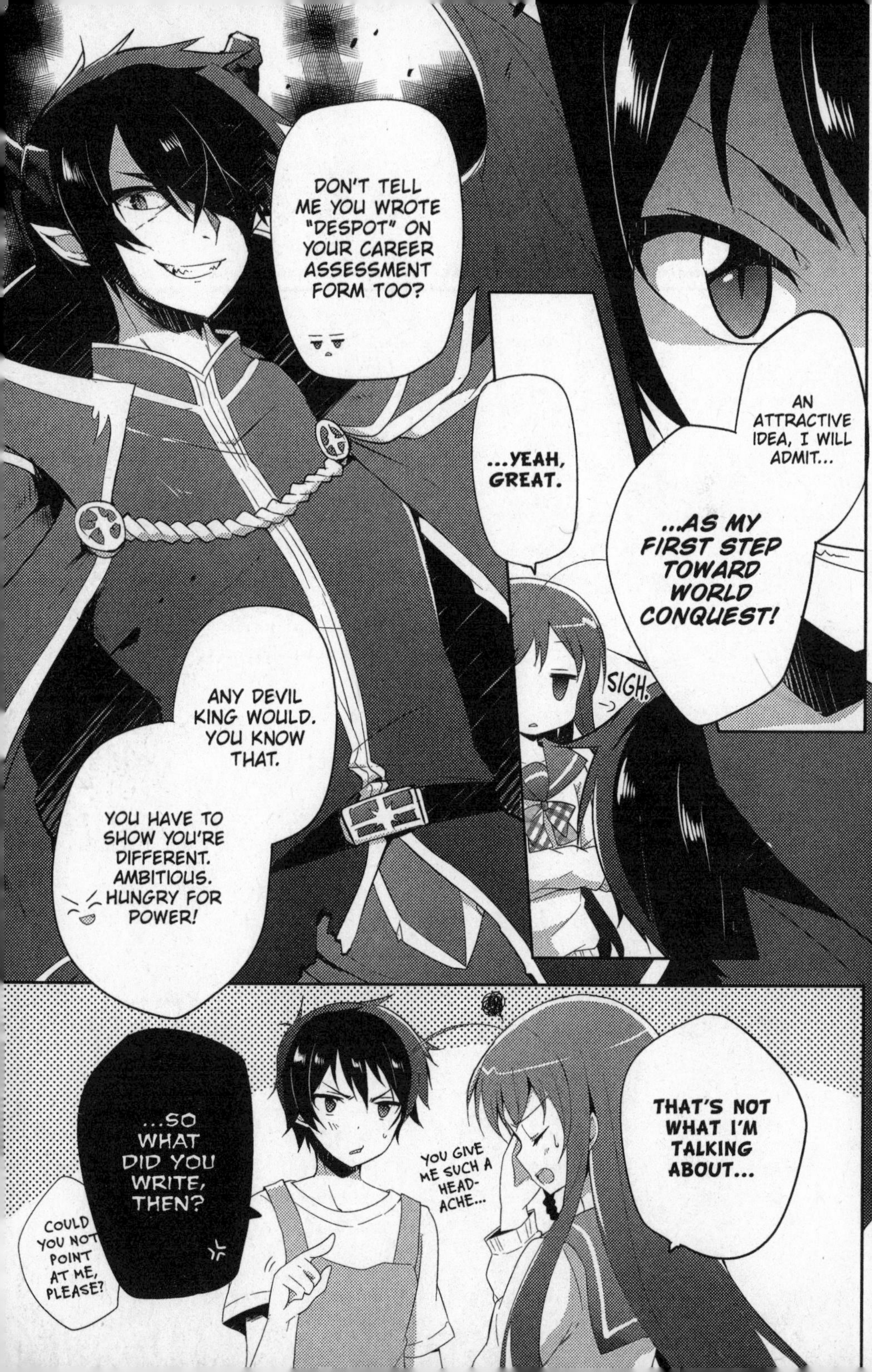
AN ATTRACTIVE IDEA, I WILL ADMIT...
...AS MY FIRST STEP TOWARD WORLD CONQUEST!
...YEAH, GREAT.
SIGH.
DON'T TELL ME YOU WROTE "DESPOT" ON YOUR CAREER ASSESSMENT FORM TOO?
ANY DEVIL KING WOULD. YOU KNOW THAT.
YOU HAVE TO SHOW YOU'RE DIFFERENT. AMBITIOUS. HUNGRY FOR POWER!
THAT'S NOT WHAT I'M TALKING ABOUT...
YOU GIVE ME SUCH A HEAD-ACHE...
...SO WHAT DID YOU WRITE, THEN?
COULD YOU NOT POINT AT ME, PLEASE?

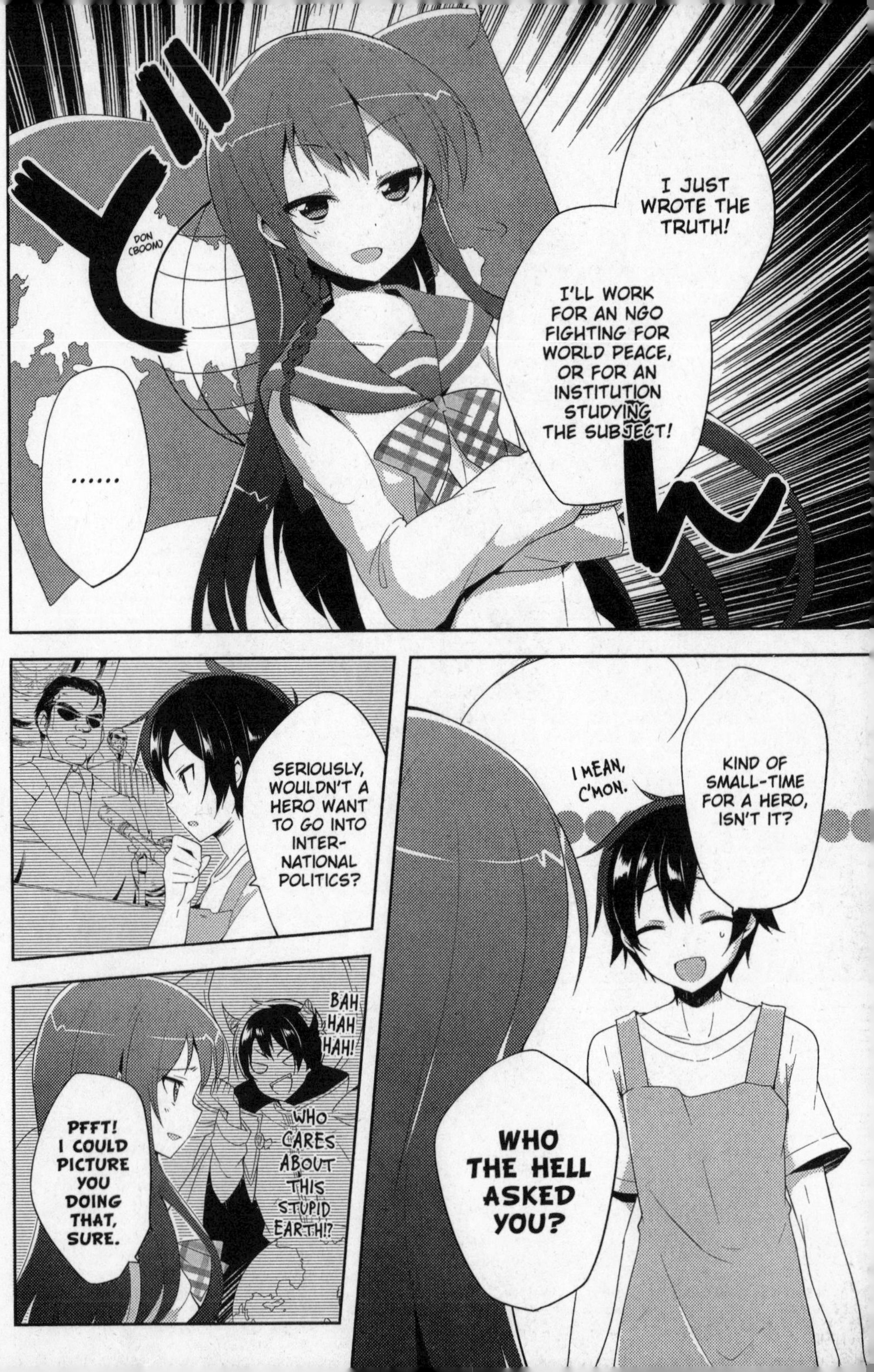
I JUST WROTE THE TRUTH!
I'LL WORK FOR AN NGO FIGHTING FOR WORLD PEACE, OR FOR AN INSTITUTION STUDYING THE SUBJECT!
DON (BOOM)
......
KIND OF SMALL-TIME FOR A HERO, ISN'T IT?
I MEAN, C'MON.
WHO THE HELL ASKED YOU?
SERIOUSLY, WOULDN'T A HERO WANT TO GO INTO INTER-NATIONAL POLITICS?
BAH HAH HAH!
WHO CARES ABOUT THIS STUPID EARTH!?
PFFT! I COULD PICTURE YOU DOING THAT, SURE.

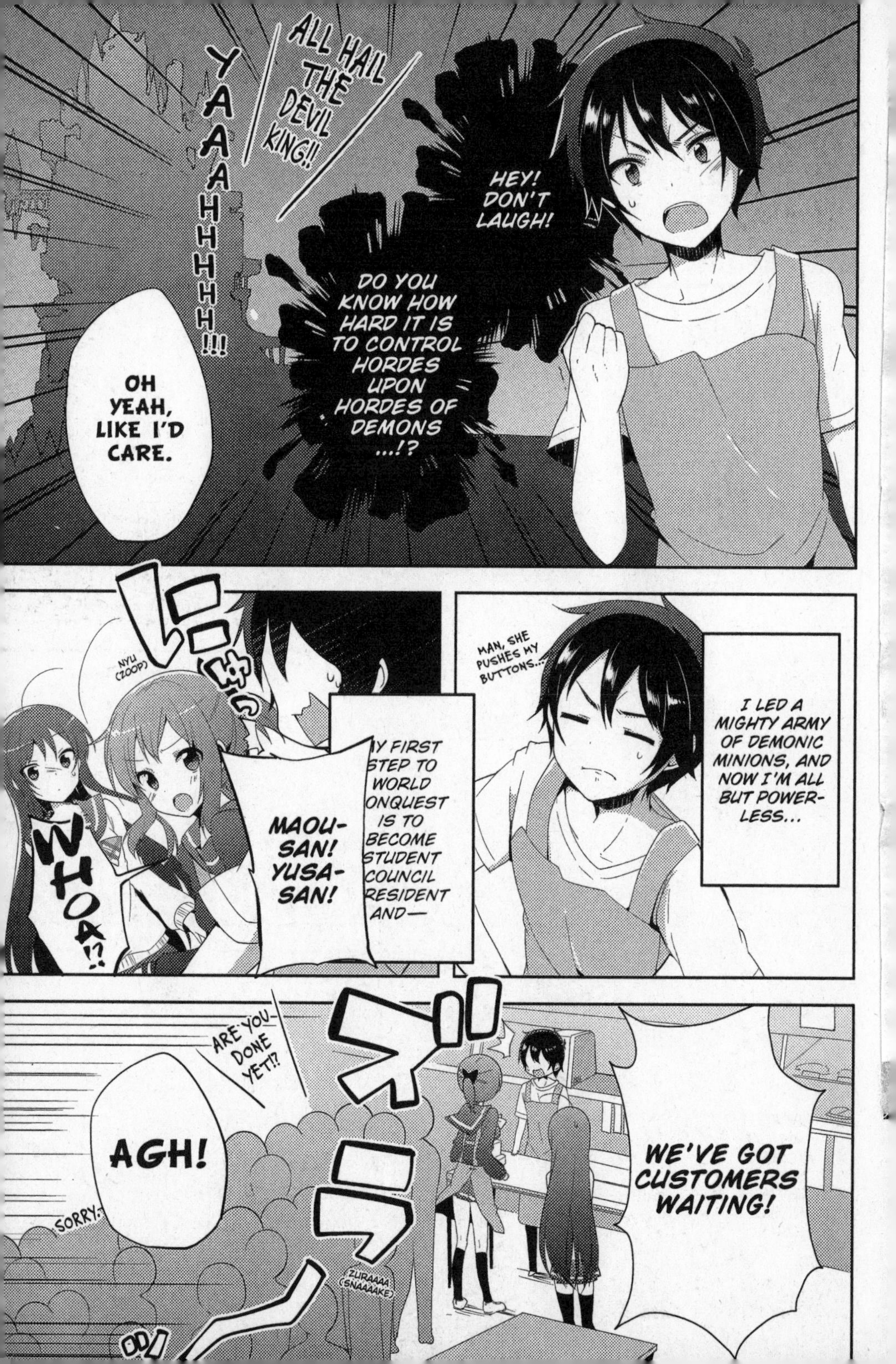
HEY! DON'T LAUGH!
DO YOU KNOW HOW HARD IT IS TO CONTROL HORDES UPON HORDES OF DEMONS ...!?
ALL HAIL THE DEVIL KING!!
YAAAAHHHHHH!!!
OH YEAH, LIKE I'D CARE.
I LED A MIGHTY ARMY OF DEMONIC MINIONS, AND NOW I'M ALL BUT POWER-LESS...
MAN, SHE PUSHES MY BUTTONS...
Y FIRST STEP TO WORLD ONQUEST IS TO BECOME STUDENT COUNCIL RESIDENT AND—
MAOU-SAN! YUSA-SAN!
NYU (ZOOP)
WHOA!?
WE'VE GOT CUSTOMERS WAITING!
ARE YOU DONE YET!?
AGH!
SORRY...
ZURAAAA (SNAAAAKE)

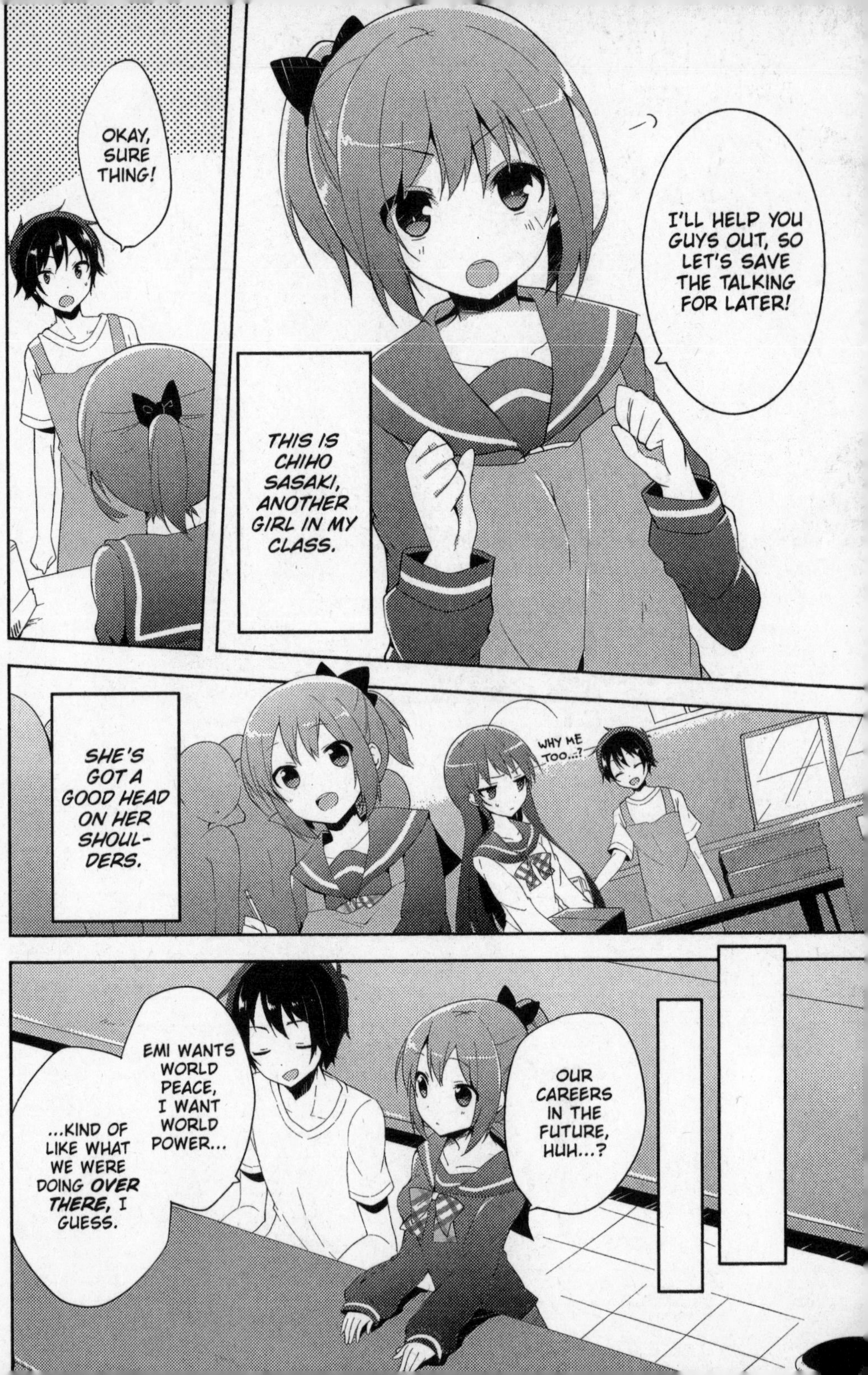
I'LL HELP YOU GUYS OUT, SO LET'S SAVE THE TALKING FOR LATER!
THIS IS CHIHO SASAKI, ANOTHER GIRL IN MY CLASS.
OKAY, SURE THING!
WHY ME TOO...?
SHE'S GOT A GOOD HEAD ON HER SHOUL-DERS.
OUR CAREERS IN THE FUTURE, HUH...?
EMI WANTS WORLD PEACE, I WANT WORLD POWER...
...KIND OF LIKE WHAT WE WERE DOING OVER THERE, I GUESS.

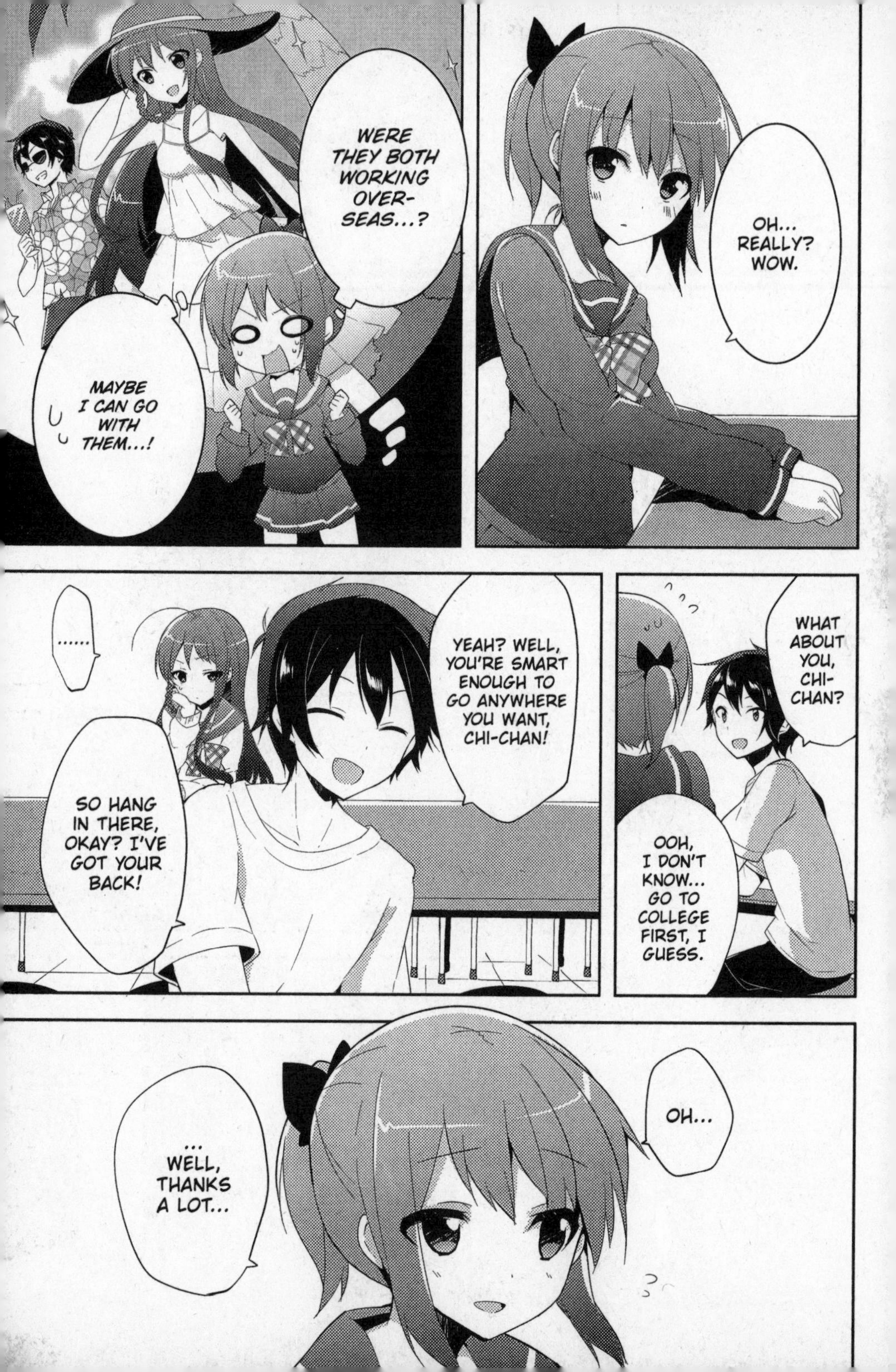
OH... REALLY? WOW.
WERE THEY BOTH WORKING OVERSEAS...?
MAYBE I CAN GO WITH THEM...!
WHAT ABOUT YOU, CHI-CHAN?
OOH, I DON'T KNOW... GO TO COLLEGE FIRST, I GUESS.
YEAH? WELL, YOU'RE SMART ENOUGH TO GO ANYWHERE YOU WANT, CHI-CHAN!
......
SO HANG IN THERE, OKAY? I'VE GOT YOUR BACK!
OH...
...WELL, THANKS A LOT...

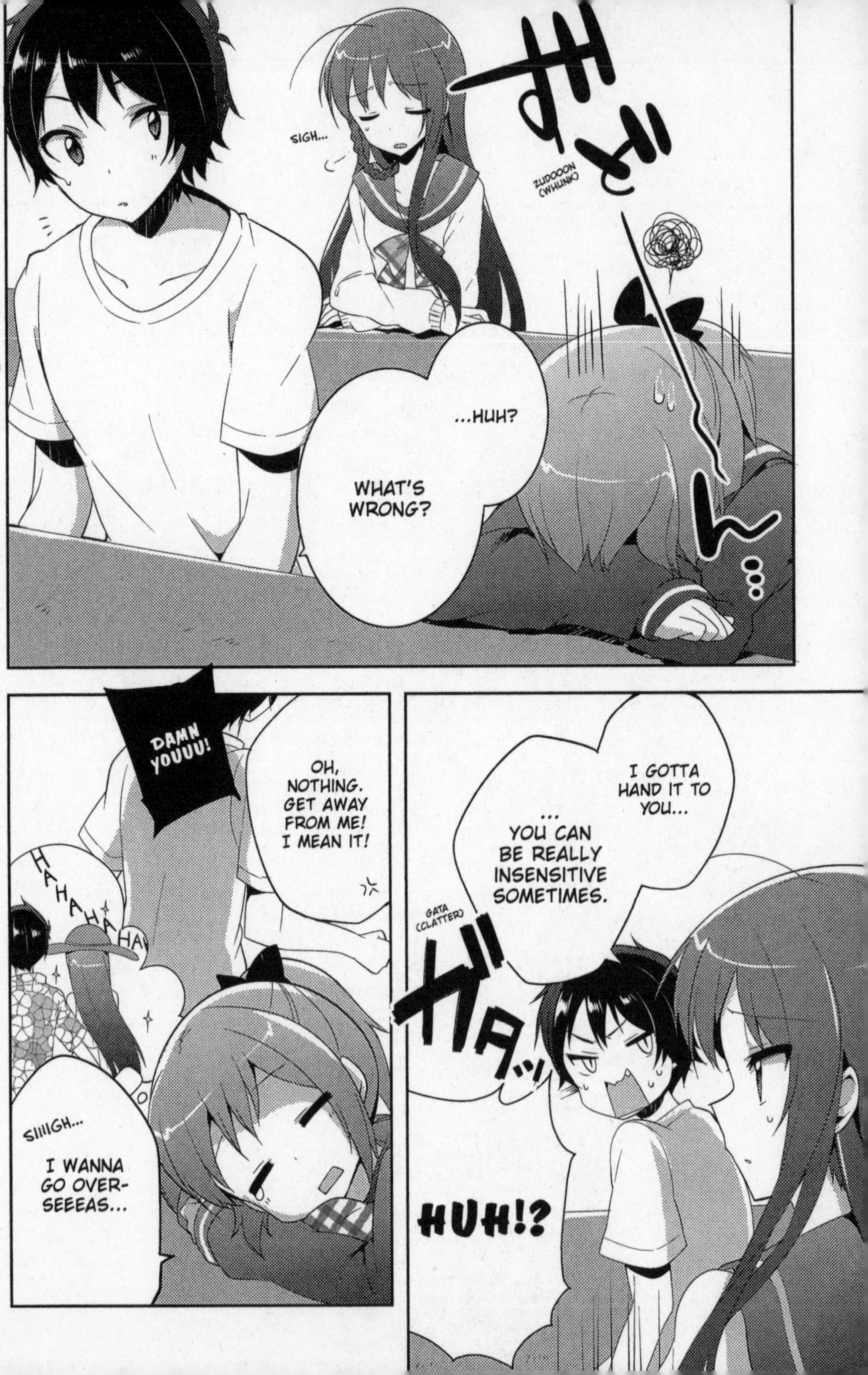
ZUDOOON (WHUNK)
SIGH...
...HUH?
WHAT'S WRONG?
I GOTTA HAND IT TO YOU...
...YOU CAN BE REALLY INSENSITIVE SOMETIMES.
GATA (CLATTER)
HUH!?
OH, NOTHING. GET AWAY FROM ME! I MEAN IT!
DAMN YOUUU!
HAHAHAHA
SIIIGH...
I WANNA GO OVER-SEEEAS...

THE DEVIL IS A PART-TIMER! HIGH SCHOOL!

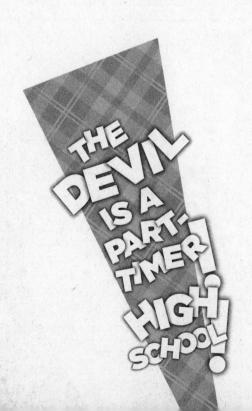

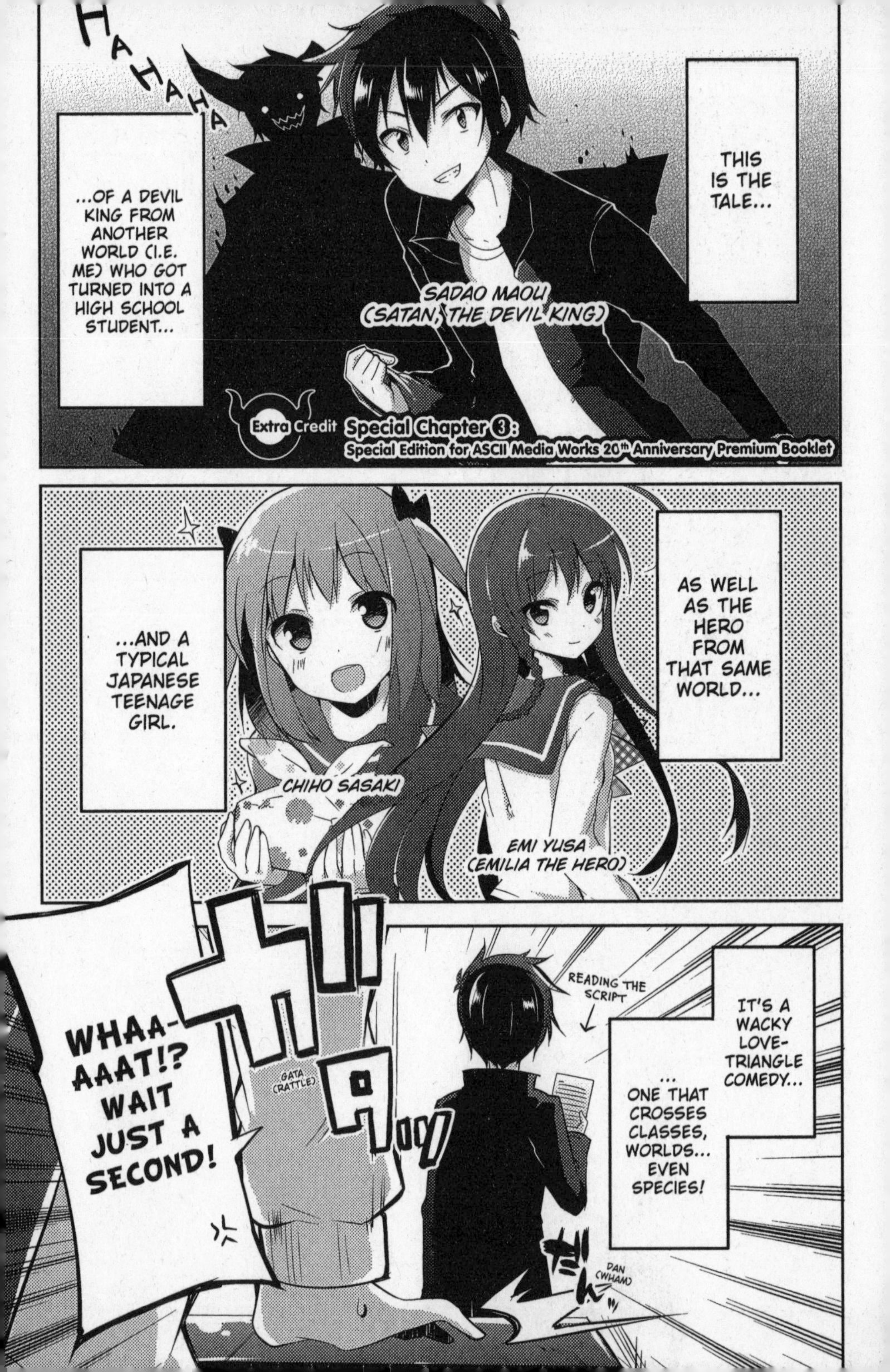
THIS IS THE TALE...
HAHAHAHA
...OF A DEVIL KING FROM ANOTHER WORLD (I.E. ME) WHO GOT TURNED INTO A HIGH SCHOOL STUDENT...
SADAO MAOU (SATAN, THE DEVIL KING)
Extra Credit Special Chapter 3:
Special Edition for ASCII Media Works 20th Anniversary Premium Booklet
AS WELL AS THE HERO FROM THAT SAME WORLD...
...AND A TYPICAL JAPANESE TEENAGE GIRL.
CHIHO SASAKI
EMI YUSA (EMILIA THE HERO)
IT'S A WACKY LOVE-TRIANGLE COMEDY...
... ONE THAT CROSSES CLASSES, WORLDS... EVEN SPECIES!
READING THE SCRIPT
DAN (WHAM)
GATA (RATTLE)
WHAA-AAAT!? WAIT JUST A SECOND!

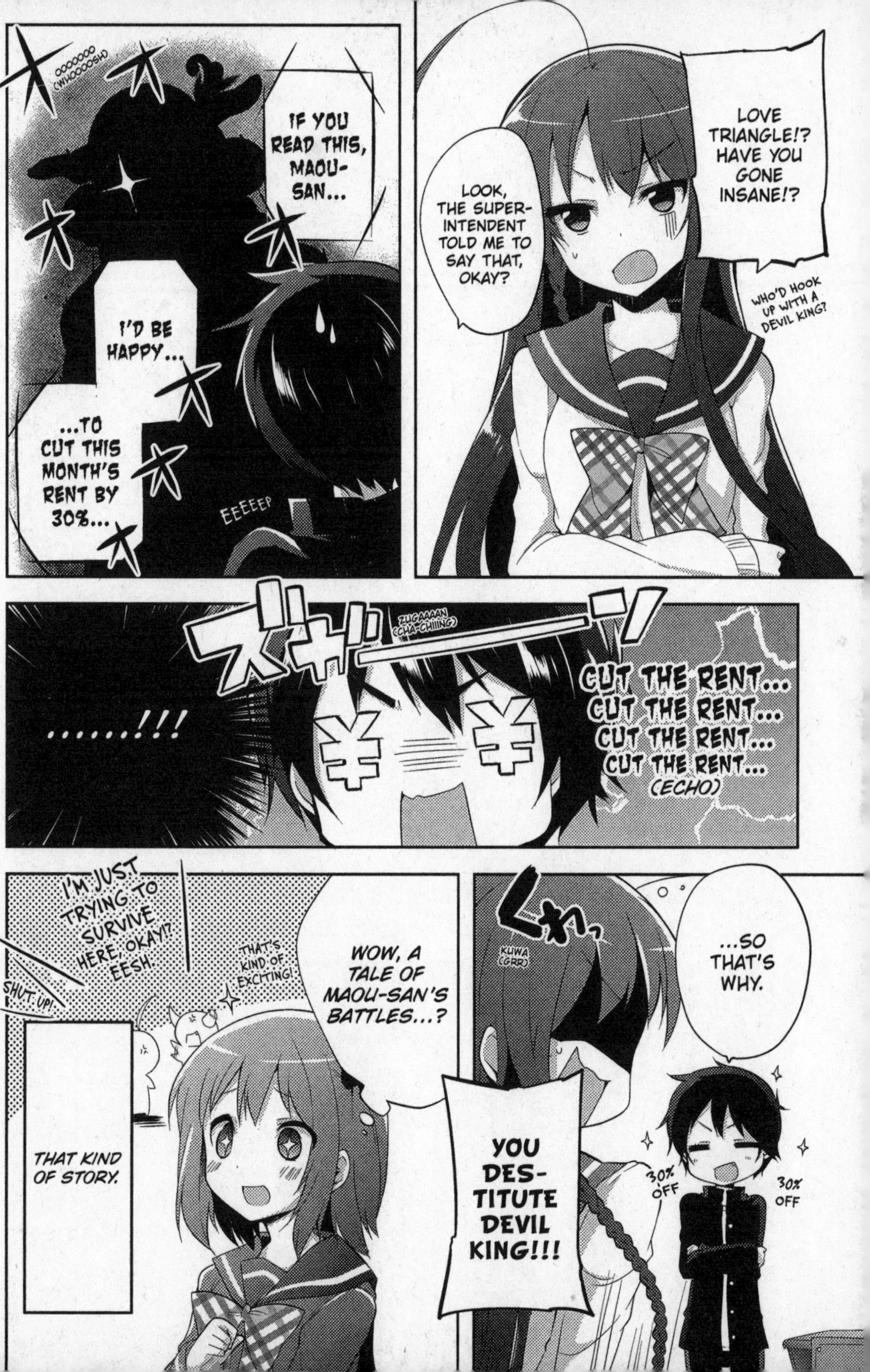
LOVE TRIANGLE!? HAVE YOU GONE INSANE!?
LOOK, THE SUPER-INTENDENT TOLD ME TO SAY THAT, OKAY?
WHO'D HOOK UP WITH A DEVIL KING?
OOOOOOO (WHOOOOSH)
IF YOU READ THIS, MAOU-SAN...
I'D BE HAPPY...
...TO CUT THIS MONTH'S RENT BY 30%...
EEEEEP
ZUGAAAAN (CHA-CHIIING)
CUT THE RENT... CUT THE RENT... CUT THE RENT... CUT THE RENT... (ECHO)
......!!!
KUWA (GRR)
...SO THAT'S WHY.
YOU DES-TITUTE DEVIL KING!!!
30% OFF
30% OFF
WOW, A TALE OF MAOU-SAN'S BATTLES...?
THAT'S KIND OF EXCITING!
I'M JUST TRYING TO SURVIVE HERE, OKAY!? EESH.
SHUT UP!
THAT KIND OF STORY.

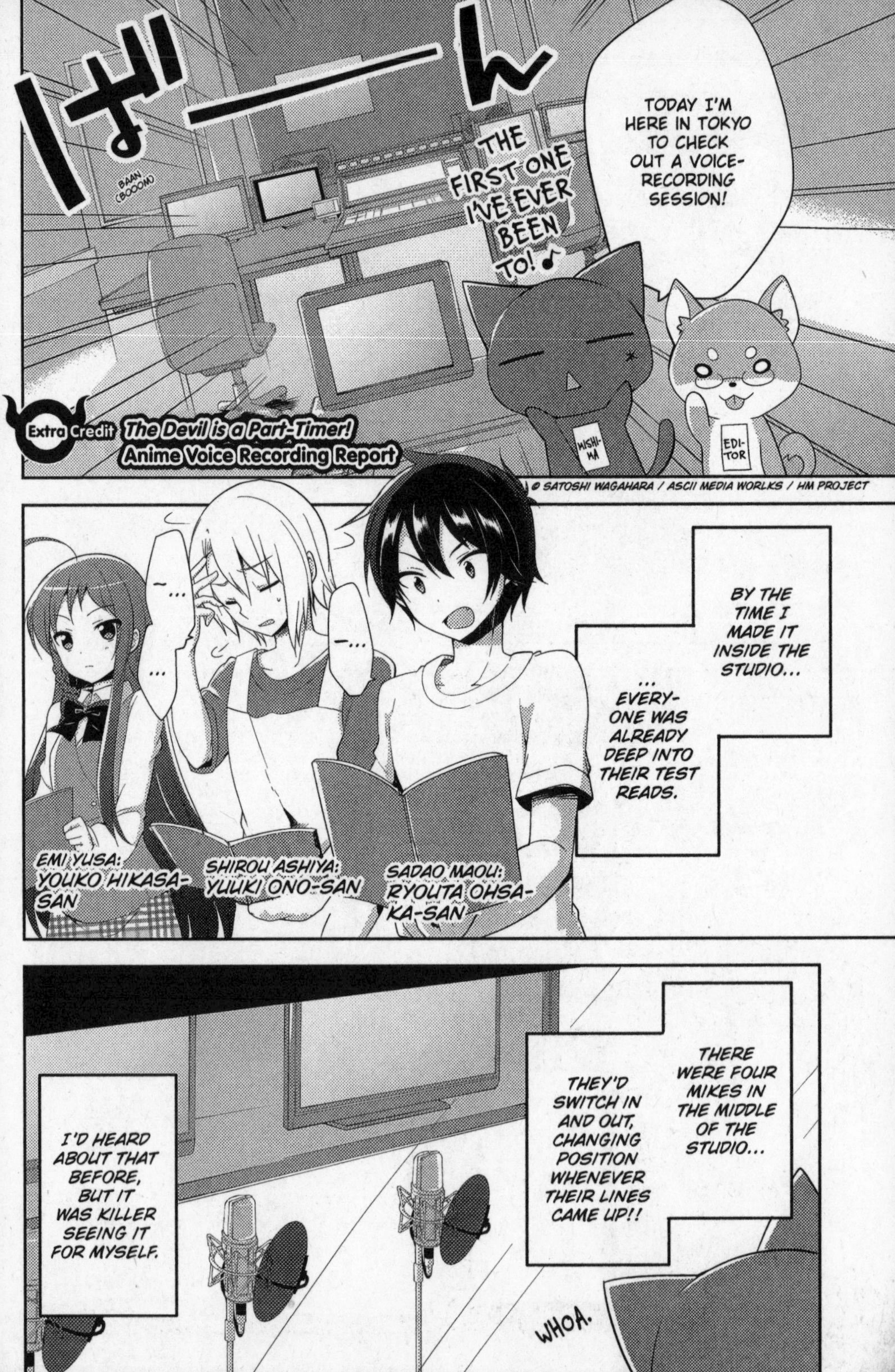
TODAY I'M HERE IN TOKYO TO CHECK OUT A VOICE-RECORDING SESSION!
THE FIRST ONE I'VE EVER BEEN TO! ♪
ばーーん
BAAN (BOOOM)
EDI-TOR
MISHI-MA
Extra Credit The Devil is a Part-Timer! Anime Voice Recording Report
© SATOSHI WAGAHARA / ASCII MEDIA WORLKS / HM PROJECT
BY THE TIME I MADE IT INSIDE THE STUDIO...
...EVERY-ONE WAS ALREADY DEEP INTO THEIR TEST READS.
—...
~...
...
SADAO MAOU: RYOUTA OHSA-KA-SAN
SHIROU ASHIYA: YUUKI ONO-SAN
EMI YUSA: YOUKO HIKASA-SAN
THERE WERE FOUR MIKES IN THE MIDDLE OF THE STUDIO...
THEY'D SWITCH IN AND OUT, CHANGING POSITION WHENEVER THEIR LINES CAME UP!!
I'D HEARD ABOUT THAT BEFORE, BUT IT WAS KILLER SEEING IT FOR MYSELF.
WHOA.

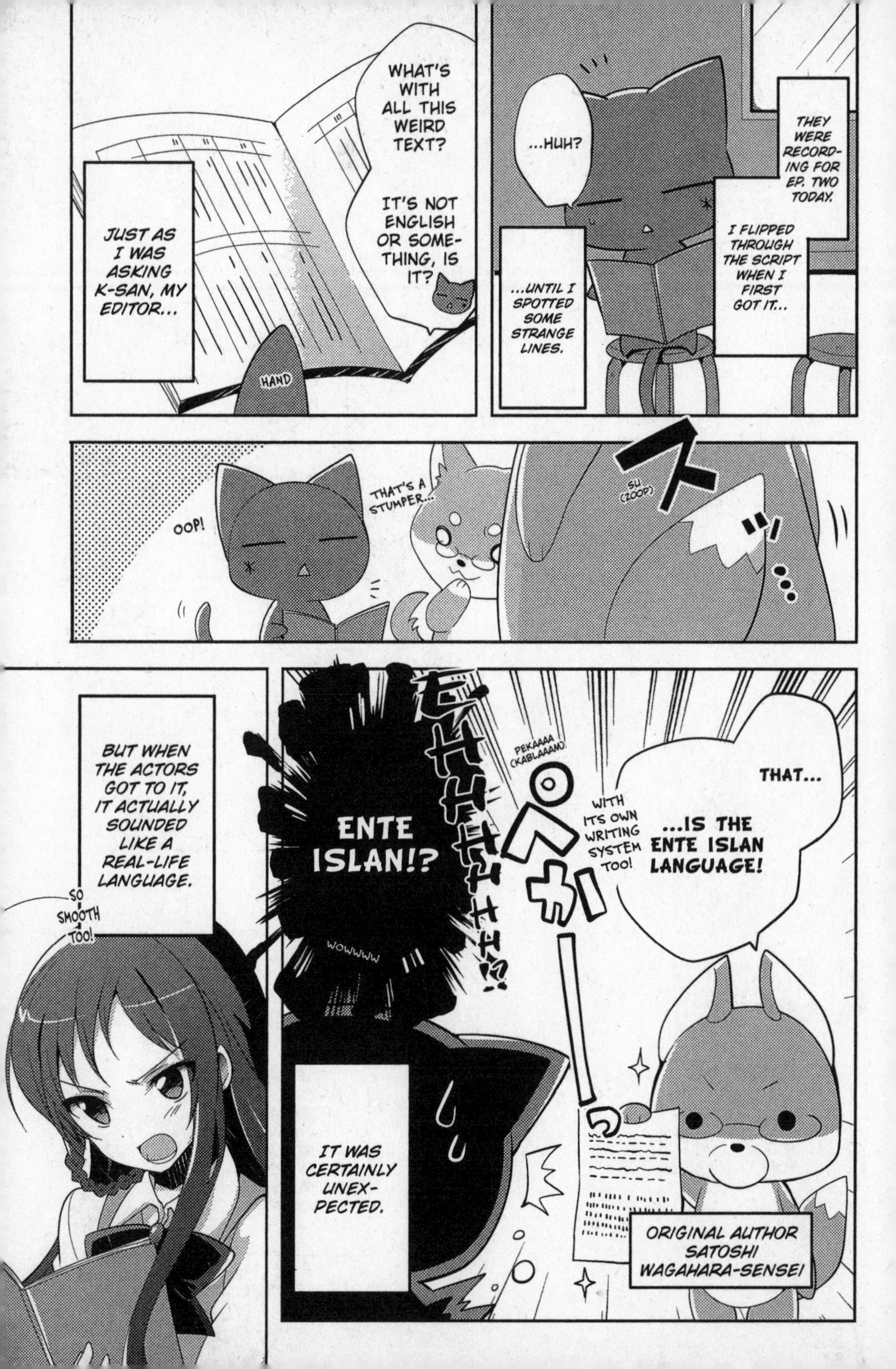
THEY WERE RECORDING FOR EP. TWO TODAY.
I FLIPPED THROUGH THE SCRIPT WHEN I FIRST GOT IT...
...HUH?
...UNTIL I SPOTTED SOME STRANGE LINES.
WHAT'S WITH ALL THIS WEIRD TEXT?
IT'S NOT ENGLISH OR SOMETHING, IS IT?
JUST AS I WAS ASKING K-SAN, MY EDITOR...
HAND
SU (ZOOP)
THAT'S A STUMPER...
OOP!
THAT...
...IS THE ENTE ISLAN LANGUAGE!
WITH ITS OWN WRITING SYSTEM TOO!
PEKAAAA (KABLAAAM)
ENTE ISLAN!?
WOWWWW
ORIGINAL AUTHOR SATOSHI WAGAHARA-SENSEI
IT WAS CERTAINLY UNEXPECTED.
BUT WHEN THE ACTORS GOT TO IT, IT ACTUALLY SOUNDED LIKE A REAL-LIFE LANGUAGE.
SO SMOOTH TOO!

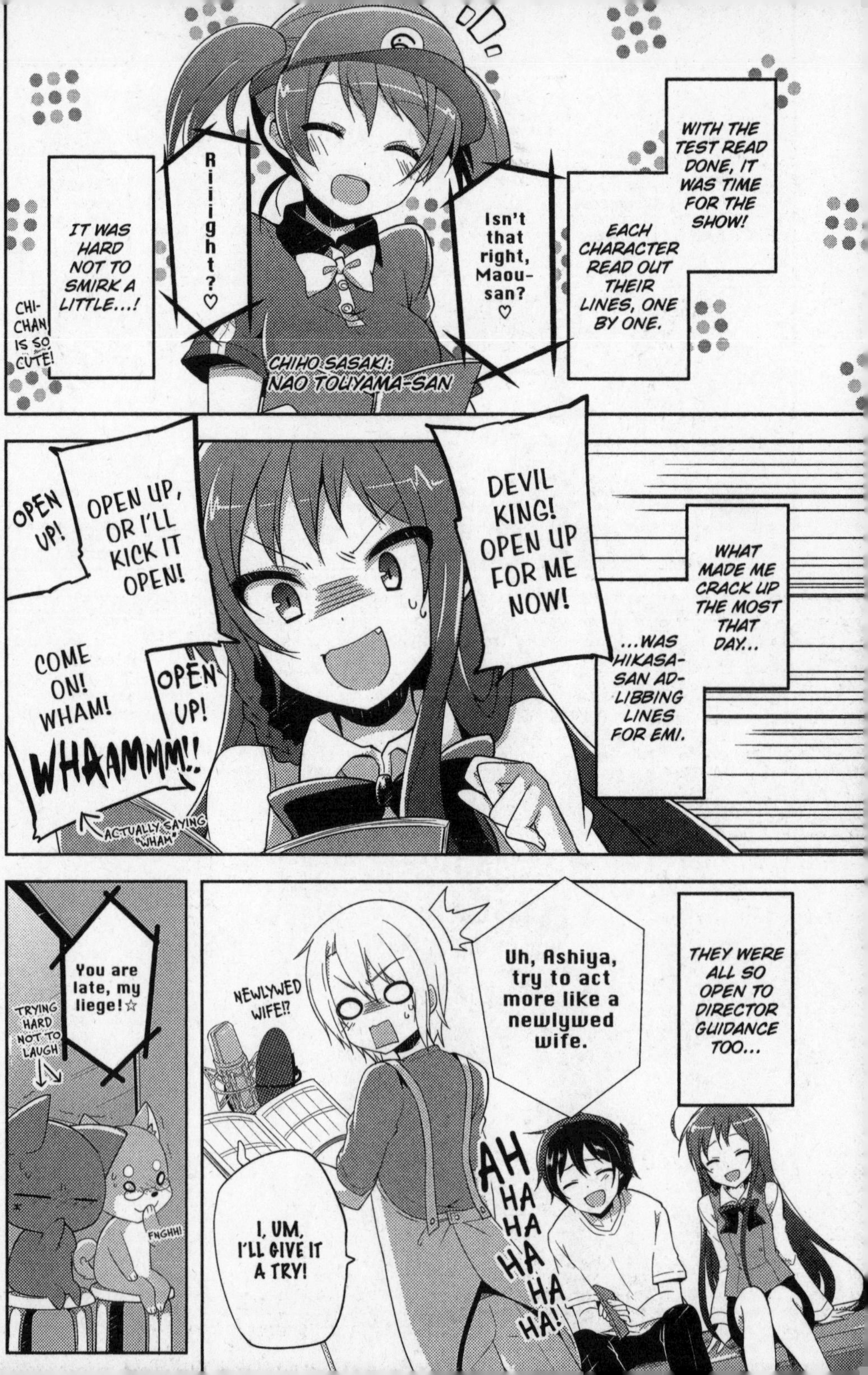
WITH THE TEST READ DONE, IT WAS TIME FOR THE SHOW!
EACH CHARACTER READ OUT THEIR LINES, ONE BY ONE.
Isn't that right, Maou-san? ♡
Riiight? ♡
CHIHO SASAKI: NAO TOUYAMA-SAN
IT WAS HARD NOT TO SMIRK A LITTLE...!
CHI-CHAN IS SO CUTE!
WHAT MADE ME CRACK UP THE MOST THAT DAY...
...WAS HIKASA-SAN AD-LIBBING LINES FOR EMI.
DEVIL KING! OPEN UP FOR ME NOW!
OPEN UP, OR I'LL KICK IT OPEN!
OPEN UP!
OPEN UP!
COME ON! WHAM!
WHAAMMM!!
ACTUALLY SAYING "WHAM"
THEY WERE ALL SO OPEN TO DIRECTOR GUIDANCE TOO...
Uh, Ashiya, try to act more like a newlywed wife.
NEWLYWED WIFE!?
AH HA HA HA HA HA HA HA!
I, UM, I'LL GIVE IT A TRY!
You are late, my liege!☆
TRYING HARD NOT TO LAUGH
FNGHH!

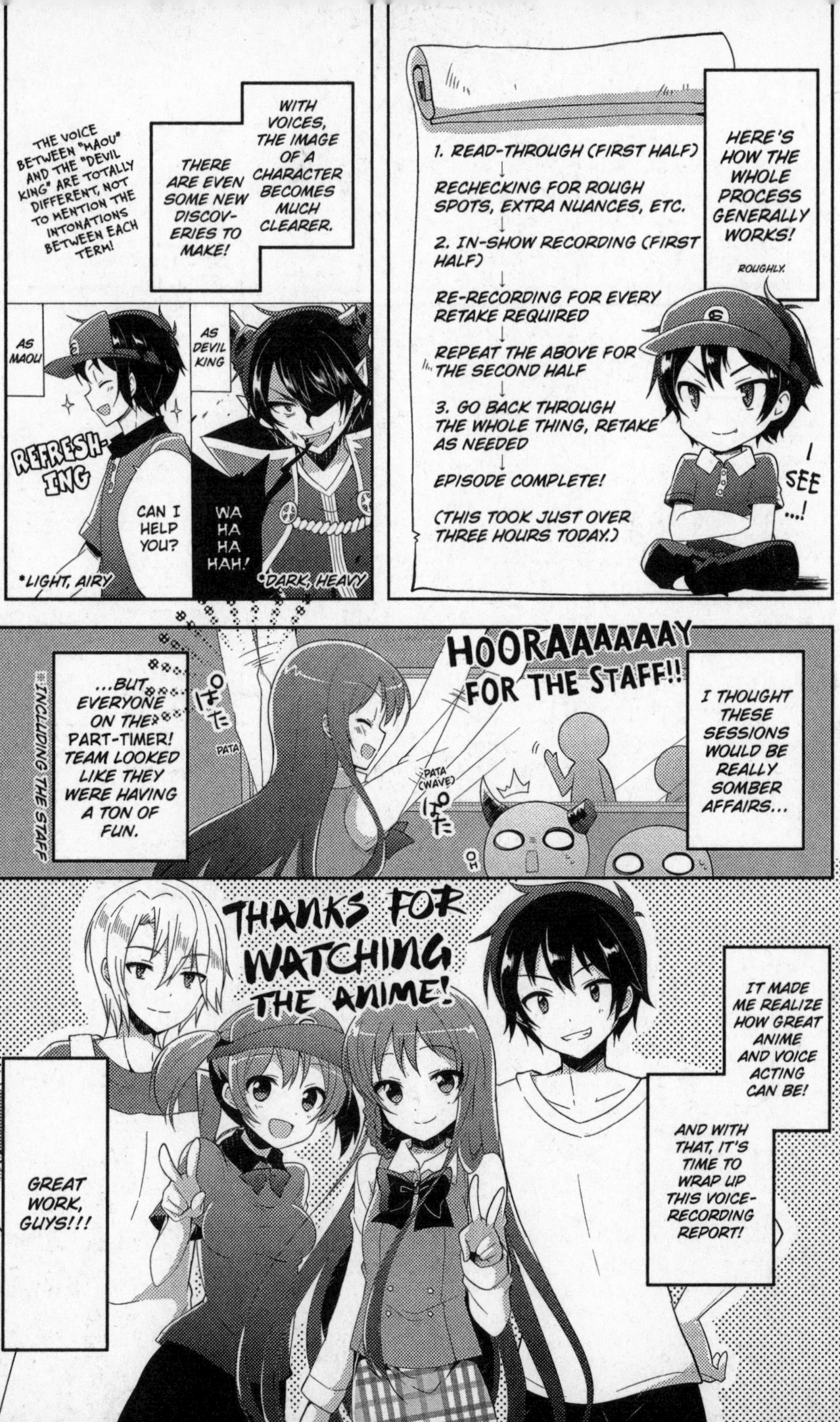
HERE'S HOW THE WHOLE PROCESS GENERALLY WORKS!
ROUGHLY.
1. READ-THROUGH (FIRST HALF)
↓
RECHECKING FOR ROUGH SPOTS, EXTRA NUANCES, ETC.
2. IN-SHOW RECORDING (FIRST HALF)
↓
RE-RECORDING FOR EVERY RETAKE REQUIRED
↓
REPEAT THE ABOVE FOR THE SECOND HALF
↓
3. GO BACK THROUGH THE WHOLE THING, RETAKE AS NEEDED
↓
EPISODE COMPLETE!
(THIS TOOK JUST OVER THREE HOURS TODAY.)
I SEE...!
WITH VOICES, THE IMAGE OF A CHARACTER BECOMES MUCH CLEARER.
THERE ARE EVEN SOME NEW DISCOVERIES TO MAKE!
THE VOICE BETWEEN "MAOU" AND THE "DEVIL KING" ARE TOTALLY DIFFERENT, NOT TO MENTION THE INTONATIONS BETWEEN EACH TERM!
AS DEVIL KING
WA HA HA HAH!
*DARK, HEAVY
AS MAOU
REFRESHING
CAN I HELP YOU?
*LIGHT, AIRY
I THOUGHT THESE SESSIONS WOULD BE REALLY SOMBER AFFAIRS...
HOORAAAAAAY FOR THE STAFF!!
ぱた
PATA (WAVE)
OI
ぱた
PATA
...BUT EVERYONE ON THE PART-TIMER! TEAM LOOKED LIKE THEY WERE HAVING A TON OF FUN.
※INCLUDING THE STAFF
IT MADE ME REALIZE HOW GREAT ANIME AND VOICE ACTING CAN BE!
AND WITH THAT, IT'S TIME TO WRAP UP THIS VOICE-RECORDING REPORT!
THANKS FOR WATCHING THE ANIME!
GREAT WORK, GUYS!!!

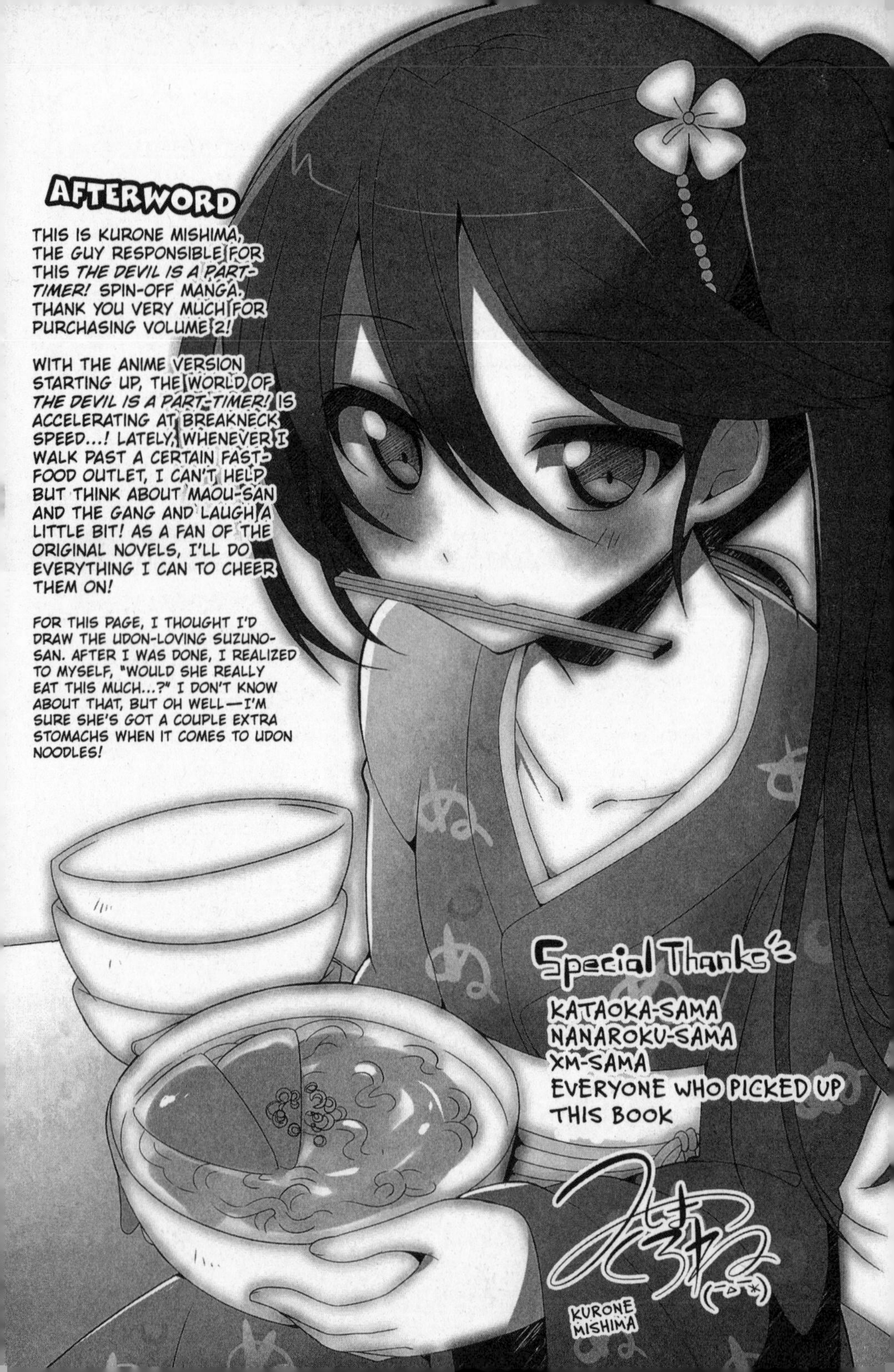

AFTERWORD

THIS IS KURONE MISHIMA, THE GUY RESPONSIBLE FOR THIS *THE DEVIL IS A PART-TIMER!* SPIN-OFF MANGA. THANK YOU VERY MUCH FOR PURCHASING VOLUME 2!

WITH THE ANIME VERSION STARTING UP, THE WORLD OF *THE DEVIL IS A PART-TIMER!* IS ACCELERATING AT BREAKNECK SPEED...! LATELY, WHENEVER I WALK PAST A CERTAIN FAST-FOOD OUTLET, I CAN'T HELP BUT THINK ABOUT MAOU-SAN AND THE GANG AND LAUGH A LITTLE BIT! AS A FAN OF THE ORIGINAL NOVELS, I'LL DO EVERYTHING I CAN TO CHEER THEM ON!

FOR THIS PAGE, I THOUGHT I'D DRAW THE UDON-LOVING SUZUNO-SAN. AFTER I WAS DONE, I REALIZED TO MYSELF, "WOULD SHE REALLY EAT THIS MUCH...?" I DON'T KNOW ABOUT THAT, BUT OH WELL—I'M SURE SHE'S GOT A COUPLE EXTRA STOMACHS WHEN IT COMES TO UDON NOODLES!

Special Thanks

KATAOKA-SAMA
NANAROKU-SAMA
XM-SAMA
EVERYONE WHO PICKED UP THIS BOOK

KURONE MISHIMA

FROM THE ORIGINAL CREATOR

SADAO MAOU AND EMI YUSA, WEARING THEIR BEST SCHOOL UNIFORMS. THERE WAS EVERY POSSIBILITY OF THIS SCENE APPEARING IN THE ORIGINAL *THE DEVIL IS A PART-TIMER!* NOVELS. BUT I CAN GUARANTEE THAT I NEVER, EVER, IMAGINED ALAS RAMUS PUTTING ON A SCHOOL OUTFIT. THAT, AND EVEN THOUGH ALAS OBSERVES THE SCHOOL DRESS CODE, SUZUNO-SAN STUBBORNLY REFUSES TO WEAR ANYTHING BESIDES HER BELOVED KIMONOS.

STILL, IF SHE'S GOING TO STAY A STUDENT FOR LONG, I'M SURE THE POISONED FANGS OF SCHOOL REGULATIONS WILL REACH EVEN SUZUNO SOONER OR LATER.

AND I'M SURE THAT, SOMEDAY, WE'LL SEE EMERALDA, GABRIEL, EVEN ALBERT (!?) MAKE APPEARANCES AS THE SECOND- AND THIRD-WAVE OF SCHOOL-UNIFORM CHARACTERS. (THERE ARE NO PLANS FOR THIS. –ED)

UNTIL THE ENTIRE WORLD IS CLAD IN SCHOOL UNIFORMS, THE BATTLE OF MAOU AND THE GANG SHALL NEVER END!

THE (SOMEWHAT OFF-KILTER) NOVEL WRITER, SATOSHI WAGAHARA

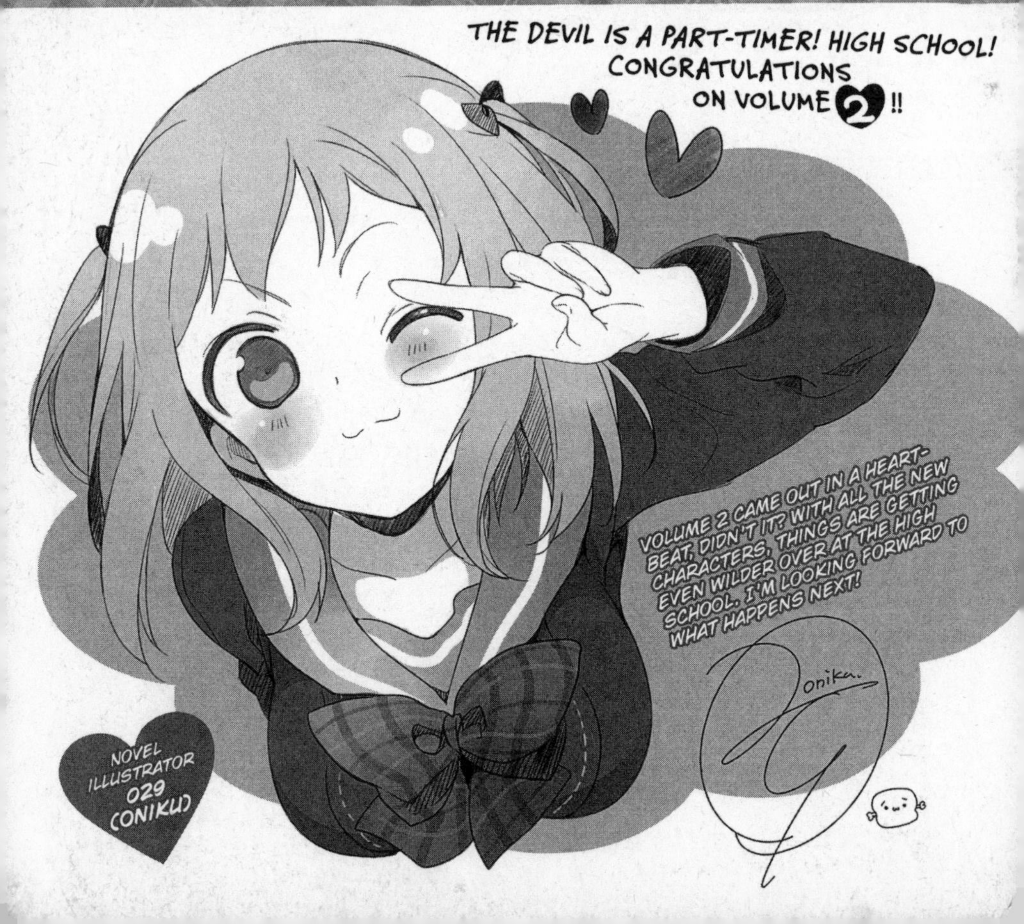
THE DEVIL IS A PART-TIMER! HIGH SCHOOL! CONGRATULATIONS ON VOLUME 2!!
VOLUME 2 CAME OUT IN A HEART-BEAT, DIDN'T IT? WITH ALL THE NEW CHARACTERS, THINGS ARE GETTING EVEN WILDER OVER AT THE HIGH SCHOOL. I'M LOOKING FORWARD TO WHAT HAPPENS NEXT!
NOVEL ILLUSTRATOR 029 (ONIKU)

THE DEVIL IS A PART-TIMER! HIGH SCHOOL! ②

ART: KURONE MISHIMA
ORIGINAL STORY: SATOSHI WAGAHARA
CHARACTER DESIGN: 029 (ONIKU)

Translation: Kevin Gifford

Lettering: Brndn Blakeslee & Lys Blakeslee

HATARAKU MAOUSAMA! HIGH SCHOOL! Vol. 2
© SATOSHI WAGAHARA / KURONE MISHIMA 2013
All rights reserved.
Edited by ASCII MEDIA WORKS
First published in Japan in 2013 by KADOKAWA CORPORATION, Tokyo.
English translation rights arranged with KADOKAWA CORPORATION, Tokyo, through Tuttle-Mori Agency, Inc., Tokyo.

Translation © 2015 by Hachette Book Group, Inc.

Yen Press
Hachette Book Group
1290 Avenue of the Americas
New York, NY 10104

www.HachetteBookGroup.com
www.YenPress.com

Yen Press is an imprint of Hachette Book Group, Inc. The Yen Press name and logo are trademarks of Hachette Book Group, Inc.

The publisher is not responsible for websites (or their content) that are not owned by the publisher.

First Yen Press Edition: November 2015

ISBN: 978-0-316-38512-1

10 9 8 7 6 5 4 3 2 1

BVG

Printed in the United States of America